THE GI BILL

PIVOTAL MOMENTS
IN AMERICAN HISTORY

Series Editors
David Hackett Fischer
James M. McPherson

THE GI BILL

A New Deal for Veterans

GLENN C. ALTSCHULER

STUART M. BLUMIN

OXFORD

UNIVERSITY PRESS

2009

OXFORD

UNIVERSITY PRESS

Oxford University Press, Inc., publishes works that further
Oxford University's objective of excellence
in research, scholarship, and education.

Oxford   New York
Auckland   Cape Town   Dar es Salaam   Hong Kong   Karachi
Kuala Lumpur   Madrid   Melbourne   Mexico City   Nairobi
New Delhi   Shanghai   Taipei   Toronto

With offices in
Argentina   Austria   Brazil   Chile   Czech Republic   France   Greece
Guatemala   Hungary   Italy   Japan   Poland   Portugal   Singapore
South Korea   Switzerland   Thailand   Turkey   Ukraine   Vietnam

Copyright © 2009 by Glenn C. Altschuler and Stuart M. Blumin

Published by Oxford University Press, Inc.
198 Madison Avenue, New York, New York 10016

www.oup.com

Oxford is a registered trademark of Oxford University Press

Library of Congress Cataloging-in-Publication Data
Altschuler, Glenn C.
The GI Bill : a new deal for veterans / Glenn C. Altschuler, Stuart M. Blumin.
      p.   cm.
Includes bibliographical references and index.
ISBN 978-0-19-518228-6
1. Veterans—Legal status, laws, etc.—United States.
2. Veterans—Education—Law and legislation—United States.
I. Blumin, Stuart M.   II. Title.
UB357.A65 2009
362.868097309045—dc22   2008052714

1 3 5 7 9 8 6 4 2

Printed in the United States of America
on acid-free paper

President Roosevelt signing the Servicemen's Readjustment Act of 1944 (the GI Bill). Immediately behind the president are representatives John Rankin and Edith Nourse Rogers. John Stelle, chair of the American Legion's committee charged with writing and promoting a comprehensive veterans' benefits bill, is second from the right. (Courtesy American Legion Library)

Contents

Editor's Note

Few acts of Congress have been as widely celebrated and sharply condemned as the Servicemen's Readjustment Act of 1944, better known as the GI Bill. This landmark law has acquired mythical status in the United States and is fondly remembered for its achievements. It has also been reviled by iconoclasts who believe that it did not achieve nearly enough, and they complain of bias by race, class, and gender. This book by Glenn C. Altschuler and Stuart M. Blumin is a balanced history of the GI Bill that exceeds even the myths and countermyths in its drama, sweep, and significance.

Consider the evidence of scale. Ten years after World War II, the Census Bureau found that 15.7 million veterans had returned to civilian life in the United States. Of that number, 12.4 million (78 percent) benefited directly from the GI Bill. Even more striking than the scope of this program is the evidence of its impact on individual lives. When surveys asked veterans what difference it made to them, three-quarters answered, "The GI Bill changed my life."

This book gives us our most comprehensive survey of the many provisions—not only for college education, but also for training outside of college, and the acquisition of skills, tools, and capital. It helped veterans to buy family homes, build farms, start businesses. In that broad design, the GI Bill was a new invention in social legislation.

Altschuler and Blumin survey many efforts by Legislatures and Congresses to aid veterans of earlier American wars with pensions, grants, bonuses, and mustering-out pay. The authors conclude that the law of 1944 was "unique" by comparison with what had gone before. It helped millions of young Americans to help themselves throughout their lives. It also stimulated economic growth, and economic development, on an unprecedented scale.

The GI Bill of 1944 became a model for other laws that followed. It inspired a Korean GI Bill that reached an even larger proportion of 5.7 million veterans who served during that conflict. A Vietnam-era GI Bill followed, and yet another GI Bill in 2008, and other legislation for young Americans who were not veterans. Altogether, the authors conclude that "the GI Bill was, without question, one of the largest and most comprehensive government initiatives ever enacted in the United States." It was, in addition, one of the most successful.

Altschuler and Blumin also study the process by which the GI Bill was created—which is as important as the bill itself. Since 1789 the American republic has been riven by party conflict in every generation, and often by partisanship so poisonous that it paralyzed the federal government in 1801, 1860, 1876, 1919, and 1995. But it has not always been so. In rare moments of crisis and opportunity, we have been able to act as one people, even when we are not of one mind.

That is what happened in Washington during the Spring of 1944, when the Second World War was approaching its bloody climax. President Roosevelt was a brilliant politician, but in the elections of 1942 he had lost control of Congress. In 1944, a conservative majority of northern Republicans and southern Democrats was strongly against him on many questions.

Even so, a liberal president and a conservative Congress united in support of the GI Bill, though they had deep differences on that issue. Senate liberals and conservatives passed a GI Bill on March 24, 1944, without a single dissenting vote, and the House of Representatives followed on May 18, 1944, with a version, also unanimously. A conference committee between the two houses deadlocked on their differences, but in the end agreed, again unanimously, on the final draft. A photograph on June 22, 1944, shows Roosevelt surrounded by his political enemies, beaming as he signs the GI Bill into law.

Republicans and Democrats, liberals and conservatives, overcame their differences and worked together to construct one of the most inventive and far-reaching pieces of social legislation in United States history—and also one of the most original. The GI Bill did not spring from any single model, or theory, or plan. Altschuler and Blumin conclude that "far from being the end product of a grand design, the GI Bill grew in fits and starts, a temporary expedient that had been hastily cobbled together." They also conclude that no one leader invented the GI Bill. Franklin Roosevelt played a major role, but many others had a guiding hand: legislators, lobbyists, bureaucrats, and more. Most shared a common fear that the country could sink into the abyss of another Great Depression if they did not act, and a common hope for a better world.

This important book tells the story of how they went about it. The enactment of the GI Bill in 1944 and its creative amendment in 1945 has an enduring importance as a model for other Americans who embark upon great enterprises. It is full of clues about creative leadership in a free republic.

David Hackett Fischer

THE GI BILL

Introduction

Handwritten draft of the American Legion's proposed "Bill of Rights for GI Joe and GI Jane," enclosed in a flag-surrounded display case in the American Legion Library in Indianapolis. The portrait is of Harry W. Colmery, who wrote the draft. (Courtesy American Legion Library)

I N July 1995 President Bill Clinton spoke at a commemorative
service in Warm Springs, Georgia, soon after the fiftieth anniver-
sary of the death of Franklin Delano Roosevelt. Looking back on
FDR's long and remarkable presidency, Clinton identified as its "most
enduring legacy" an achievement that came neither from the Hundred
Days of initial New Deal legislation nor from the structural reforms
of the Second New Deal, nor even from FDR's successful prosecution
of World War II. Rather, Clinton pointed to the Servicemen's Readjustment Act of 1944—the GI Bill—a law passed late in Roosevelt's
presidency, following his initiatives but shaped by many others besides
himself. The GI Bill, Clinton observed, "gave generations of veterans
a chance to get an education, to build strong families and good lives,
and to build the nation's strongest economy ever, to change the face
of America." This one piece of legislation, he continued, perhaps with
an eye to his own presidential legacy, "helped to unleash a prosperity
never before known."[1] It was a New Deal for veterans and, through
them, for the postwar nation as a whole.

Fifty years earlier this would have seemed a very strange choice
for an FDR encomium, but by the 1990s it was as reasonable as
choosing Social Security, the WPA, or victory over the Nazis. When
Clinton spoke, praise for the GI Bill was widespread and partook
of the increasing respect and nostalgia among the vast majority of
Americans for what the journalist Tom Brokaw would soon call "the
Greatest Generation"[2]—the young adults (many of them boys and
girls who quickly *became* adults) who, in foxholes and bombers, ship-
yards and munitions factories, helped rescue the world from fascism.
The very large numbers who had served in the military during the
war returned to help create a peacetime society of unprecedented
prosperity, and it came to be generally understood that the GI Bill
was the essential instrument of their successful reintegration into
civilian life. Clinton, himself a postwar "baby boomer," spoke for a
generation of Americans who saw the GI Bill as the key to a kingdom
of peace and plenty.

Praise for the GI Bill was and is by no means restricted to members of FDR's political party. Bob Michel, a former Republican congressman from Peoria, Illinois, who served as minority leader in the House of Representatives for fourteen years (the longest minority leadership in U.S. history), has described the GI Bill as "a great piece of legislation" that "cut across the economic strata" and made it possible for "many thousands of veterans, including tens of thousands who would not have thought of college," to get undergraduate degrees. Michel points to the almost universal approval of the bill. "I don't know of anyone," he reflects, "who has ever maligned it." Michel was himself a highly decorated World War II veteran and a beneficiary of the GI Bill. Nonetheless, it is clear that his admiration for this legislation is not just informed by his own good fortune but also reflects the experiences of an entire generation.[3]

Leaders from outside of politics have also expressed admiration for the GI Bill, and these include many who do not ordinarily favor forceful government solutions to pressing social issues. Two years before Clinton's Warm Springs address the widely respected management theorist Peter F. Drucker wrote that future historians might well come to regard the bill as "the most important event of the 20th century" in that its provisions for government-subsidized college education for World War II veterans "signaled the shift to the knowledge society."[4] Drucker's was a sophisticated appraisal of how one public initiative could, even as a largely unintended effect, unleash larger forces that would in turn transform an entire society. His analysis reinforces, too, the popular perception of the bill as a product of bipartisan consensus, when what seemed to matter at the moment of its passage was not Democratic or Republican political advantage but the interests of the veterans and the nation at large. It bears the stamp of neither party. It is an American document, a mid-twentieth-century Bill of Rights. The American Legion, pressing hard from late 1943 for its version of a comprehensive veterans' bill, originally called it the Bill of Rights for GI Joe and GI Jane.

As is suggested by this language of rights and of GI Joe and Jane, much popular praise for the bill has been more personal than that of public leaders asked or inclined to reflect on its general significance. It was what gave your father or grandmother or some elderly veteran who told you his story the opportunity to realize in his or her own lifetime what could have been only distant dreams while in a foxhole in the Ardennes, in a field hospital in Italy, or in a breadline during the Great Depression. Personal success stories that trace back to the GI

Bill abound within families and well beyond, some of them known to us, to be sure, because, like Bob Michel's, they involve famous people.

The GI Bill–assisted career of William Rehnquist, former chief justice of the Supreme Court, is one such story. Rehnquist had a brief taste of college life at Kenyon College before entering the U.S. Army Air Corps in 1942. When his military service was finished, he used the GI Bill to enroll at Stanford University (he was attracted by the California climate), where he earned bachelor's and master's degrees in political science and eventually a law degree. He became a clerk for Supreme Court Justice Robert Jackson, and the rest, as they say, is history. When asked years later how he had chosen his profession, Rehnquist answered, perhaps with tongue in cheek, "The GI Bill paid for an occupation test that told you what you ought to be. They told me to be a lawyer."[5]

Stories such as this are legion, and they strengthen the connection between the bill, the long-cherished image of America as a land of opportunity, and the special role and merits of the Greatest Generation, among which are vast numbers of men and women whose successes did not result in celebrity or great wealth. Recent popular books and articles on the GI Bill emphasize its continuing personal resonance with peoples' lives. In particular, Edward Humes's *Over Here: How the G.I. Bill Transformed the American Dream*, published in 2006, is based almost entirely on the kinds of personal stories that reinforce Americans' reverence for veterans of the Good War and of that one act of Congress that constituted the veterans' just reward.[6]

It is easy to enjoy these personal stories, and to join them to the chorus of praise for the GI Bill. Yet we must recognize the ways the stories and the praise have somewhat complicated attempts to gain a more dispassionate understanding of the bill's role in the shaping of postwar America. In Humes's book and in the somewhat earlier *When Dreams Came True: The GI Bill and the Making of America*, written by Michael J. Bennett, are discussions of the bill's more general consequences, but these remain largely within an adulatory mode and fail to consider whether particular claims may or may not have been exaggerated. It is fair to say that they both accept and help perpetuate the bill's iconic status in American culture. At the same time, there has been something of a backlash against the GI Bill as a popular icon, especially among several scholars—Lizabeth Cohen and Ira Katznelson are prominent examples—who see the bill largely in terms of provisions and modes of administration that perpetuated racial and gender discrimination in American life.[7] These are serious criticisms, but the works of these scholars contain at the least a hint of an iconoclasm that is itself an unsteady bridge to the past.

We argue that the GI Bill should not simply sit in a sealed and flag-draped display case to be admired in splendid isolation from either the circumstances of its passage—the institutions, the ideological and partisan conflicts, the hopes and fears of the late war years—or the critical criteria we normally bring to bear on other events in our nation's past. Nor should the display case be smashed in anger. Instead, the bill should be removed for close and careful analysis, as, for example, Suzanne Mettler has done in her excellent *Soldiers to Citizens: The G.I. Bill and the Making of the Greatest Generation,* a book that examines the bill's positive effects on the political and civic engagement of World War II veterans in the decades following their participation in various benefit programs.[8] Here we build on Mettler's valuable contribution by focusing on the crafting of this new veterans' policy, on the shape and utilization of the programs created by the bill in its original and amended forms, and on the significant effects of these programs on American society and culture during the postwar period.

We begin by placing the GI Bill, as enacted in 1944 and amended in 1945, within the long historical context of veterans' benefits in the United States and within the more immediate political, social, and institutional contexts that shaped the new proposals for a package of veterans' benefits near and shortly after the end of World War II. We give particular attention to the central question of how the GI Bill related to the issue of whether to preserve, to build upon, or to undo the New Deal.

The end of the war was a pivotal moment in U.S. history not merely because of the return to peace and the prospect of prosperity after fifteen years of economic depression and total war but also because of the opportunity it provided to question in fundamental terms the nation's political direction. Franklin Roosevelt was dead, the heyday of the New Deal lay a decade in the past, and the United States had a new role to play in world affairs. The new president, Harry Truman, was a man of largely unknown qualities, and the Congress was dominated by conservatives of both parties who had long been unfriendly to the New Deal. What course should America take as war gave way to peace? And what role would the GI Bill play in shaping that course? The latter question was almost as difficult to answer as the former. Like two blindfolded individuals feeling different parts of an elephant, conservatives and liberals interpreted the new veterans' program and its implications very differently.

Conservatives of the mid-1940s did not contemplate a simple "return to normalcy" that Warren G. Harding promised in the aftermath of World War I. Along with other Americans, they worried about the consequences of the transition from a wartime to a peacetime economy, especially in light of the dismal conditions that prevailed before the war, and about the demobilization of more than 15 million soldiers and sailors into an uncertain economy. But they did not want to find solutions that might perpetuate the New Deal they had so long opposed. From their point of view, a comprehensive package of postwar benefits that focused exclusively on veterans' readjustment during the few years immediately following their demobilization was just the kind of policy they could favor. The formal name of the GI Bill—the Servicemen's Readjustment Act—perfectly expresses this attitude. It would not create another New Deal program for the population at large, and it would end when the veterans, with the temporary help of Uncle Sam, had found their way back into civilian society.

Liberals, on the other hand, saw the GI Bill as a public-sector program that, if successful, could provide models for more general and long-lasting domestic policy. Their attitude was well expressed in 1947 by John Higham, a young historian who would later establish himself as one of America's most distinguished scholars. Addressing the bill's educational benefits, Higham asked: "Will the infantryman make a better teacher than a 4F? Will the airman make a better doctor than his younger brother who never got beyond the Boy Scouts? A democracy hungry for leadership," he continued, "will not find its hunger appeased once the last veteran has secured his college degree." When the GI Bill ran out, Higham observed, "we can let our deflated and exhausted schools seal up the crack and return to business as usual, or we can exploit the wedge to open new opportunities for social welfare. With will and vision, we can transform a temporary windfall into a permanent triumph."[9]

In one respect, the liberal point of view had already triumphed. Important amendments made to the original GI Bill within a year and a half of its signing changed the tenor of the new veterans' policy from the immediate readjustment of the former GI to the realization of his longer-term ambitions. The bill changed, in effect, from being a safety net into an engine of opportunity for millions of young veterans. But what of the broader transformation Higham and other liberals called for? Historian Harold Hyman observes that the GI Bill's benefit programs were much like those created by the New Deal and argues that they "vastly reinforced" what he calls "enduring New Deal 'civilian' legacies."[10] That is, the GI Bill carried the New Deal into the post-war period under the cover of a veterans' benefit package and gave new legitimacy to the kinds of domestic programs enacted during the 1930s.

However, these programs, in the immediate instance, were limited to veterans, and it was by no means clear in the mid-1940s that they would later be expanded to the nonveteran population. According to historian Geoffrey Perrett, a "handful of New Dealers," though with the notable absence of support from FDR himself, "fought against the principle of veterans' exclusiveness" even before the GI Bill was passed. When Congress passed a bill limited to veterans, "Liberals mourned it as a great opportunity lost."[11] Would changing political winds, fanned perhaps by the successful implementation of the bill itself, revive that opportunity? Whether liberals eventually succeeded in using the bill as a springboard for broader and more permanent policies or whether conservatives were able to maintain its exclusive and temporary character while resisting similar programs for the nonveteran population are central questions in this story.

These are by no means the only important issues that arise from the GI Bill's history. As we explore that history, we consider topics such as fairness and effectiveness in the operation of its various benefit programs and the larger effects these programs had on American society—on the supply of labor to the peacetime economy, on institutions of higher education and subcollege training, on home ownership and the pace and character of postwar suburbanization, and on the quest for equal rights by women and racial and ethnic minorities.

Nonetheless, the pages that follow are devoted mainly to revealing how the GI Bill represented a dramatic departure from the history of veterans' benefits in the United States and a response to a unique moment in the nation's history. It is a story as significant in its larger patterns as it is in its individual successes and failures. We draw upon the experiences of particular veterans and the efforts and ideas of specific political leaders to illustrate and give a human face to our narrative. Yet our focus is on the larger story of the GI Bill and its role in the shaping of postwar America.

Before telling that story, we must acknowledge the scale of what was involved, the sheer numbers of World War II veterans whose return to civilian life was affected in some way by the use of one or more benefit programs established by the Servicemen's Readjustment Act of 1944. The veteran cohort created by the war was huge, dwarfing in absolute numbers the demobilization of any other armed conflict in

U.S. history. According to surveys conducted by the Veterans Administration and the Bureau of the Census in late 1955, a little more than a decade after V-J Day, there were some 15,750,000 World War II veterans in civilian life. The same surveys estimated the numbers of former GIs who had received any of the three major GI Bill benefits (each is described in detail in the following chapters). More than 8.3 million, or some 52 percent, received unemployment payments provided by the bill as "readjustment allowances"; about 7.8 million, a little less than half of the cohort, received graduate, college, or subcollege-level education and training benefits; and 4 million, or 25 percent, were granted a VA-guaranteed loan to finance a home, farm, or business. The total number who participated in one or more of these benefit programs was, according to the surveys, no less than 12.4 million, or 78 percent of the veteran cohort.[12] At first, most GIs paid little attention to the bill. However, after a shaky start, it became a huge government program, larger than any other in U.S. history to that date.

Large numbers of World War II veterans took advantage of some portion of the GI Bill. A smaller but still significant number (more than 3.3 million) did not. Books, articles, and films about the GI Bill invariably include stories of individual veterans who attended college under the bill's tuition and subsistence plan, bought a home with a VA-backed mortgage, or used some other benefit created by an unusually farsighted Congress. The stories of veterans who used none of these benefits also need telling. Albert Bleich, who entered the army as an enlisted man in 1942 and was mustered out as a major four years later, offers the story of one veteran who used none of these GI Bill programs. Bleich had already completed college and sought no further formal education. Having married during the war, he had a position awaiting him in his new father-in-law's paint and hardware business. When he and his wife, Edith, left the base at which he had been stationed, they moved into an apartment near the business, after which they moved only once more, to a larger apartment, before Albert's death thirty-seven years later.[13] Bleich received no benefits from the GI Bill for the simple reason that he did not need them. He was older, better educated, and more easily reestablished than most veterans, but we must imagine the stories of many younger men and women who returned to family businesses or their old jobs or who quickly found new jobs without unemployment payments, schooling, or vocational training provided by the GI Bill. Some of them rented apartments and purchased houses with loans that were not guaranteed by the Veterans Administration. Sharing the political values of congressional conservatives wary of the paths to which the GI Bill might lead, some preferred not to accept help from the government. These were the more than 3 million World War II veterans who, like Albert Bleich, found their own way into the postwar world.

We should also recognize a number of veterans who benefited from the GI Bill without participating in any of its direct-benefit programs. Some 670,000 soldiers and sailors received nonfatal wounds during the war, and many more ex-GIs returned with physical and emotional illnesses that needed medical attention. The VA hospital system preceded the GI Bill, which itself created no new programs of care for veterans with disabilities.[14] The bill did, however, provide funds for the construction of medical facilities that served veterans and stipulated that such facilities would have access to scarce building materials equal to that of the military services. Some World War II veterans who had sustained disabilities drew upon the bill in direct and visible ways; others benefited only indirectly as recipients of medical care they might not have so readily had if the bill had not been enacted.

The vast majority of ex-GIs, though, were direct beneficiaries of the bill, and the help they received was substantial. If more than 3 million did not avail themselves of any of the bill's direct benefits, more than twice that number used two or three of them during the first postwar decade. This is reason enough once again to take the bill outside of its shrine and to place the full story of veterans' benefits both before and after World War II in the broader flow of events and conditions as war gave way to peace.

ONE

Before the GI Bill

Veterans and Politics from the Revolution through World War I

Civil War veterans at the eastern branch of the National Home for Disabled
Volunteer Soldiers. (*Harper's Monthly Magazine*, October 1886)

THE ICONIC STATUS of the GI Bill derives mostly from the profound effects that have been ascribed to it—to its role in shaping both the lives of individual World War II veterans and the collective life of postwar America. In no small measure the bill's legendary status depends as well on its uniqueness. Here was an act like no other in the long legislative history of the United States—not merely a stunning instance of congressional wisdom and goodwill but also a substantive departure from the veterans' benefit laws that had followed all previous American wars. Many Americans seem to know that the bill was unique. However, it is fair to say that very few understand *how*. Setting the bill in the political and institutional contexts surrounding its enactment in 1944 is crucial to appreciating its significance. Yet to understand the uniqueness of the GI Bill we must also look back much further, to the longer evolution of American policy toward returning veterans.

The benefits of this longer narrative flow in two directions, not merely from historical contexts toward the GI Bill but also from it and its predecessors to those contexts. By looking closely at the bill in the stream of attempts to deal with the specific question of what to do about veterans—the able bodied, as well as the ill and wounded—we learn much about what the U.S. government could and would do at various stages of our past. The government, like any institution that endures through time, has been anything but static. Indeed, it has evolved in response to new challenges and in concert with structural changes in the larger society. Veterans who are returning from war might not appear at first glance to offer new challenges to political institutions or to impel structural change; rather, they seem to present essentially the same problem of peacetime reintegration and reward, a constantly recurring rather than a new or variable force in our political past. However, the issue of veterans' benefits has in fact been as mutable as history itself and in each instance has been resolved through processes and events that reflect the institutions, resources, values, and particular conflicts of its time. To trace the history of policies toward veterans—up to and including the GI Bill—is to trace the more general history of American political development.

Veterans' benefits laws stretch back at least as far as the measure adopted by the settlers of Plymouth in 1636 to maintain for life any soldier maimed in the colony's service.[1] Virtually every military conflict from skirmishes with nearby Indian tribes to global wars has produced at least one veterans' benefits law, and in the aftermath of major wars invariably a long series of laws sprang up, each adding to, subtracting from, or in other ways modifying the benefits created by its predecessors. In response to the American Revolution, for example, several dozen veterans' laws were enacted on the federal level alone, the first in 1776, with the war in its earliest stages, and the last in 1878 (for the adjustment of the pensions of a few remaining soldiers' widows), nearly a century after its conclusion.[2] Between these dates, two new foreign wars and a massive civil war added new laws and programs, including a post–Civil War pension plan that eventually became, as we will see, one of the costliest and most significant social measures in U.S. history, one that—in the aftermath of America's most traumatic domestic crisis—reflected and contributed mightily to the expansion of the role and size of the federal government.

Until the twentieth century nearly all veterans' programs took the form of pensions, and through at least the colonial period of British-American history these were restricted to soldiers and sailors disabled by illness or injury during their military service and to the widows and orphans of men who never returned. This fit well with traditions of public initiative and expenditure that stretched back to the poor laws of the Elizabethan era and beyond, as well as with definitions of the "deserving poor," which guided the outlays of local Guardians or Overseers of the Poor on both sides of the Atlantic. The soldier with a disability, unable to support his family, was much like the sober and honest bricklayer who fell from the scaffold or the good blacksmith burned at his forge. The war widow had the same need for support as a woman whose husband died of smallpox or under the wheels of a cart.

War, in short, created dependencies that were familiar to all communities, and it was no great stretch of any community's political culture to extend material relief to those whose livelihood was wrecked by military service. There were differences that could (and later would) press upon the edges of traditional poor relief. The pensions granted to veterans with disabilities and to war widows and orphans were defined and controlled by public bodies beyond the local community, by provincial and even national legislatures. Local Guardians or Over-seers of the Poor were not the source of these pensions, nor could they alter the flow of support—and thereby exert a powerful form of social control within the community—according to how they judged a person's moral behavior. Public largesse could be terminated if the injured bricklayer took to drink, but the tippling war pensioner was secure in the funds that supported his habits.

The war pension of this era should not, however, be understood solely as the disabled veteran's inalienable right, earned through sacrifice to his nation and his community. Legislators could think in quite different and more practical terms. When mobilization for war was a significant issue, as it was during even the early stages of the American Revolution, the promise of a pension could be made an inducement to serve. The first national pension law of the fledgling United States, enacted in August of 1776, was essentially an effort to recruit soldiers into the Continental Army and in this sense resembled the cash and land bounties that were also offered by the national government and by most of the new states to help spur enlistments. Land bounties were granted by all of those states that possessed significant tracts of frontier land within their borders or in western reserves,[3] and this points to yet another motive for the enactment of benefits to men who were to become veterans. States that offered bounties saw in this system a means of promoting postwar frontier development, as did the federal government after several states ceded some of their western claims to it. Veterans would move to the undeveloped lands set aside as military tracts, and so would other settlers, who would feel protected by the presence of so many men practiced in the use of arms.

The land bounty system is generally regarded as a failure as both an inducement to enlist and a spur to frontier migration by veterans, many of whom sold their bounty warrants to land speculators at deep discounts.[4] Failure or no, it underscores the connection between the specific forms of veterans' benefits and the political institutions, cultures, and issues of the eras in which they were enacted. It points as well to the shaping force of available resources. Twentieth-century lawmakers could provide veterans with college scholarships and guarantees for home mortgages; those of the earliest years of the republic could give them land.

Land bounties, which were offered at the beginning of one's military service, were not designed for those who were disabled by war. Other early measures loosened the tie between disability and the state's responsibility to its war veterans. Again for very practical reasons,

Congress passed a resolution in 1778 granting half pay for seven years to officers who served until the end of the war and two years later extended this to a lifetime pension. The driving force this time was retention rather than recruitment, more specifically, General Washington's fear, urgently and frequently communicated to Congress, of large-scale resignations of disgruntled officers. Without establishing the principle, Congress created in these resolutions the first federal military pensions unrelated to death or disability. As it happened, this limited pension program was no more successful than the land bounties. At the war's end, facing a real threat from officers to resist demobilization until their claims were satisfied but lacking money to fund the pensions it had promised, Congress commuted the half-pay pension into five years of full pay. In the end it rewarded the officers with unfunded, interest-bearing certificates that most sold to speculators at a fraction of their face value.[5]

A more substantial step toward the creation of a general military pension was taken some years later, as many of the Revolutionary War veterans were reaching the end of their productive lives. In the immediate aftermath of the war, very little fuss was made over these veterans, especially those who had fought in the Continental Army. As historian John Resch has argued, many Americans were reluctant to credit the efforts of Washington's men "because they conceived the Revolution to be a people's war, not a conflict won by regular troops."[6] Widespread fears of a national standing army—fears incorporated a few years later into the much-misunderstood Second Amendment to the new Constitution—further inclined post-Revolutionary Americans to self-congratulation rather than gratitude and to limit most of the gratitude they did express to the veterans of state militias rather than to those of the Continental Army.

By the early years of the nineteenth century, however, these feelings began to change. Apprehensions of a professional army receded somewhat, and from the distance of a generation the differences between Revolutionary militiamen and regular soldiers seemed less important. As Revolutionary veterans of all sorts began to age and as a dawning Romanticism encouraged an impulse toward sentimentality within the larger culture, Americans found themselves more inclined to celebrate the veterans of the Revolution as self-sacrificing heroes of the nation's founding. Moreover, as this sentiment deepened, so, too, did the federal pocketbook. During most of the years since the mid-1790s, the federal government had experienced modest budget surpluses. The War of 1812 generated deficits, as wars invariably do, but with the return of peace and a revived Atlantic economy, federal government surpluses, fed mainly by rapidly growing customs revenues, reached unprecedented levels. Those of 1816 and 1817 far exceeded the entirety of federal expenditure of any year before the war began and provided ample means for indulging the sentiment of gratitude toward the heroes of '76.[7]

In December of 1817 President James Monroe, flush with both good feelings and funds, proposed that Congress award pensions to Revolutionary War veterans, including those who had never qualified under earlier laws that restricted awards to officers and to enlisted men disabled by their military service. This was a significant departure from long-established policy, but after much wrangling between the House and the Senate a compromise was reached granting an annual pension ($240 for officers, $96 for common soldiers and sailors) to every veteran who had served in the Continental Forces for at least nine months or to the end of the war and who was now "in need of assistance from his country for support." Each applicant had to provide proof of his military service but, significantly, not his need.[8]

President Monroe and most members of the Fifteenth Congress assumed that the numbers of new applicants from the aging cohort of Revolutionary War veterans would not be very large and that the cost of the new program would not be great. They were much mistaken. Applications flowed in from all corners and at a rate that exceeded everyone's expectations. Before the 1818 Pension Act about 2,200 Revolutionary War pensioners were still living, and payments to them and to war widows (and now to the disabled veterans, widows, and orphans of the War of 1812) generally did not exceed 1 percent of annual federal expenditures. The new pension program generated 15,000 new applicants within four months of the bill's passage, five times the number that had been predicted, and by the end of 1819 the number had climbed to 25,000. What had been a minor national expense now accounted for at least 16 percent of all federal outlays. Second only to a rapid decay of customs revenues leading up to and especially after the economic crisis of 1819, the pension was responsible for the evaporation of the annual surplus.[9]

Ignoring the possible effects of the economic turndown, Congress concluded that many veterans were falsely claiming economic need, and it quickly took steps to eliminate fraud. New rules did reduce the numbers of claims and the cost, but, significantly, calls to repeal the new pension were resisted, and the United States retained its first pension program for veterans who had left military service without injury and in good health. In fact, in that it flowed only to those in economic need and only to veterans of the Revolution, it was not a general service pension. Able-bodied veterans of the War of 1812 were not included, and it was clearly not the intent of either President Monroe or the Congress to establish a model for the aftermath of America's future wars. With the special needs of a unique group of Americans now addressed, it could be assumed that this issue of veterans' benefits would now simply go away.

But it did not. By the early 1830s veterans' benefits became entangled in the central issues that animated the emerging political parties and developing regions of the Jacksonian era. This time it was almost entirely a matter of money. Starting in 1825, the federal treasury again enjoyed large annual surpluses, dramatically reducing the national debt. Democratic Republicans (or Democrats, as they would soon be called), especially those tied to the growing, export-dependent cotton industry of the southern states, pointed to these surpluses as a justification for reducing tariffs that their National Republican (a bit later, Whig) opponents wanted to retain in order to protect fledgling northern industries from overseas competition. Expanding the Revolutionary War veterans' pension was one way of finding a use for excess federal revenues produced by the tariff, and a new pension bill managed to work its way through Congress in 1832 over objections that came mostly from southern Democrats.[10] Revolutionary War veterans with a total of two years of service would now receive full-pay pensions irrespective of their current economic circumstances. Those who had served lesser terms (but not less than six months) were also eligible but would receive proportionately less than the two-year veterans.

There were fewer Revolutionary War veterans in 1832 than there had been in 1818, but the new bill's sponsors need not have feared the effects of mortality's toll. Once again, the numbers of applications astonished lawmakers and other officials. By January of 1833 Secretary of War Lewis Cass reported 24,260 applications, and in that year the cost of veterans' benefits increased fourfold, rising to nearly 20 percent of federal spending. Even proponents of the pension recoiled at this unexpected success. Early in 1834 the strait-laced John Quincy Adams wrote, "Uriah Tracy, thirty years ago, used to say that the soldiers of the Revolution claimants never died—that they were immortal. Had he lived to this time, he would have seen that they multiply with the lapse of time."[11]

Death did soon reverse the curious multiplication of this now aged cohort, and the cost of the pension program declined after 1833, although it was buoyed for some time by the claims of veterans' widows. Perhaps the most far-reaching effects of the 1832 law were not the immediate costs but the establishment of precedent for both a general service pension and the use of veterans' benefits as an element of more general political conflict. These precedents were mitigated for a time by the circumstances of war and peace. New veterans were being created by various Indian wars and in the mid-1840s by the war with Mexico. However, except for the veterans of the War of 1812 there was not yet a large cohort of aging veterans of post-Revolutionary military service, and in any case the sentiments that had become attached to the heroes of '76 were never extended to those who fought in these later conflicts. The War of 1812 was far from a great national triumph, perhaps better forgotten than commemorated, as were some of the Indian wars. The Mexican War had been opposed by most Northern Whigs, the very people who had been most inclined to support pensions for Revolutionary veterans. Unpopular wars, alas, produce unpopular veterans. The precedents established in 1818 and 1832 were eventually followed to the benefit of surviving veterans of these post-Revolutionary wars, but not until most of their comrades were in their graves.[12]

The Civil War, the most devouring conflict of them all, remains the greatest benchmark in U.S. history. Nonetheless, with respect to veterans' benefits, the transformations it wrought were primarily matters of scale and eventually of reaction and deliberate reversal. The precedent established by the various laws that pertained to Revolutionary War veterans allowed the military disability pension program to be expanded into a general-service pension for veterans of later wars, although for post-Revolutionary servicemen this would occur too late to benefit more than a few. Fortunately for many Civil War veterans and their families, the sentiments that had grown up around the heroes of '76 were quickly and easily attached to those who eventually saved the Union. Thus, the post-Revolution pattern of national pension legislation was repeated during and after the Civil War and on a far larger scale. No federal pension was to be contemplated for those who had rebelled against the Union, and former soldiers and sailors of the Confederacy had to rely on the limited resources of their home states. Union veterans, on the other hand, benefited from national pension laws that were increasingly broad in scope and generous in their provisions.

As in all earlier conflicts, the first Civil War pensions were restricted to veterans with disabilities and to the dependents of the fallen, although the many pension laws that followed the war expanded eligibility among both veterans and families. This same pattern describes the only other significant veterans' aid program initiated during this era, the National Asylum for Disabled Volunteer Soldiers, established by Congress near the end of the war to give medical care and shelter to thousands of wounded and sick Union veterans who could not be cared for in other ways. A small United States Soldiers' Home had been established in Washington during the 1850s for regular army veterans and Mexican War volunteers, and from this precedent now grew the larger system of four (and eventually twelve) branch residential institutions, soon to be renamed the National Home for Disabled Volunteer Soldiers. By the end of the century the National Home consisted of eight branches that stretched from Maine to California and over the years provided care and shelter for nearly one hundred thousand Union veterans. Not all of these men had, in fact, been disabled by the war. In 1884 Congress opened the residences to those now incapacitated "by age, disease, or otherwise," referring to military service only to exclude those debilitated by fighting against the United States.[13]

Similarly, in 1890 Congress extended the much larger pension program to all honorably discharged Union veterans of at least ninety days' service who suffered from any incapacitating physical or mental disability, whether or not it was traceable to military service, and excluded only those whose disabilities arose from "their own vicious habits."[14] As there were still large numbers of active breadwinners among the able-bodied Civil War veterans twenty-five years after Appomattox (the 1818 law for Revolutionary War veterans was enacted thirty-five years after the Treaty of Paris), this was something less than the general-service pension for which the largest veterans' group, the Grand Army of the Republic (GAR), was then lobbying. However, it soon evolved into an old-age pension for all Union veterans, and in the first decade of the twentieth century, first in 1904 by executive order of President Theodore Roosevelt, then by act of Congress in 1907, age was made an explicit qualification irrespective of either disability or need.[15]

Even more critical than this relatively rapid and decisive evolution toward a post–Civil War general-service pension was the unprecedented scale of the pension system as a whole. This is, of course, reflective of the scale of the war itself, which sent huge numbers of the nation's young men into battle and into the health-threatening environment of the military encampment. More than 2.2 million men served in Union forces during the Civil War; of these, more than 360,000 died of wounds and disease, while some 280,000 returned home with some

Pension certificate of Franziska Sternberger, widow of Jakob Sternberger, a Bohemian immigrant and Civil War veteran of the Wisconsin Volunteer Infantry. (Courtesy Max Kade Institute for German-American Studies, University of Wisconsin–Madison)

kind of injury.[16] (Uncounted in this grim official survey were those who returned significantly weakened by camp disease.) Pension claims did not immediately escalate after the war began, in part because of the removal from the roles of qualifying veterans of earlier wars who had sworn allegiance to the Confederacy, but after Congress clarified the eligibility of Union men in July of 1862 the cost of pension claims rose dramatically—increasing sixteenfold by the war's end, doubling again during the first few years after the war, and then stabilizing during most of the 1870s at approximately 10 percent of total federal expenditures.[17] According to Theda Skocpol's close analysis of the Civil War pension system, this impressive expansion occurred despite the failure of large majorities of wounded veterans (57 percent) and pension-eligible dependents (75 percent) to file claims by 1875.[18]

In this failure lay the seeds of further expansion. Perceiving an opportunity, pension attorneys and other agents worked hard to stimulate new claims and lobbied in Washington for a law that would allow claimants to collect for the years they had neglected to apply. The latter bore fruit with the Arrears of Pension Act of 1879, which drove pension costs upward again—first to more than 20 percent and within a decade to 30 percent of total federal outlays. The 1890 law later pushed them still higher. In that year the federal government for the first time spent more than $100 million on veterans' benefits, and it would never again spend less. For nearly a decade, more than a third of all federal expenditures were made to and on behalf of military veterans, and in 1893 the proportion exceeded 40 percent, far exceeding the amounts spent on the active military or any other aspect of the nation's public affairs. Its gradual decline thereafter would reflect the growth of other public outlays, not the decline of veterans' benefits, despite the dying off of Civil War veterans and their dependents. The wounded and the dead from western battlegrounds, from Cuba and the Philippines, and finally from Europe would allow no retreat in that part of the national budget.[19]

The Civil War pension system enlarged the role of the state in American life and helped shape the battles of the maturing political parties, as did the GAR and other organized lobbies. During the war Republican lawmakers, emboldened by the absence of southern Democrats from Congress, had undertaken a number of new initiatives and passed, for example, the Homestead Act, the Morrill Land Grant Act, and the National Bank Act. These laws and others like them expanded the federal government's reach into various aspects of American life and helped change expectations regarding the size and activities of the public sector despite the return to Congress of the southern Democrats, widespread fears of patronage and public corruption, and what the political scientist Stephen Skowronek calls the "patchwork" character of post–Civil War government expansion.[20] To some extent these changes can be measured by the size of the public bureaucracy, which expanded markedly in response to legislative initiatives. When the Civil War began, the federal government employed a little more than 36,000 people, of whom fully 30,000 worked for the post office. During the 1860s the nonpostal federal civilian workforce of 6,000 expanded to more than 14,000, grew further to 44,000 during the next ten years, and reached 62,000 in the 1880s. By the end of the century it approached 100,000.[21] Most of this growth occurred in the multiplying departments and agencies within the executive branch, and no small amount of it was located within the Pension Bureau and the National Home for Disabled Volunteer Soldiers.

Into this new political and administrative environment came the issues of veterans' benefits, most notably that of the role of military pensions in the politics of tariff legislation. Once again, it was argued that pensions safeguarded the protective tariff during periods of annual budget surplus, even while the new breed of organized lobbyists exerted their own pressure for the expansion of the pension system.[22] There was now quite a significant difference, however, in the balance of motives. During the 1830s the pension was distinctly secondary to the larger issue of the tariff, but by the 1870s it was itself a powerful political force, so much so that the relation might in some degree have been reversed. Skocpol doubts that the tariff influenced pension expansion and observes that, in 1879, the year of the Arrears of Pension Act, the federal budget surplus was quite small.[23] Clearly, other forces were at work, perhaps none more important than the pension itself as an element of renewed partisan competition in national politics.

Democrats, even while opposing the tariff, saw in pension expansion a chance to reestablish their credentials outside the South. It was, in fact, a Democratic-controlled House of Representatives that passed the Arrears of Pension Act, and when the bill went to the Senate, it was backed by nearly every Northern Democrat.[24] When the Democrats regained the White House, President Cleveland placed himself and his party in firm opposition to the profligacy of the pension program; as a result, from that time forward there would be a clearer Republican (and pro-tariff) imprint on expansive pension legislation. Nonetheless, the pension had outgrown its earlier role as a facilitator of other legislative objectives. The Civil War had been huge; accordingly, the rewards that flowed to its veterans, as well as to its widows and orphans, became a dominant political fact and by far the most expansive public program of the postwar decades.

Even so, in the period that followed, the story of veterans' pensions is one of sharp reversal. Skocpol astutely observes that an opportunity existed for expanding the Civil War pension system into a national old-age pension available to all citizens and that the decision to do so would have brought the United States into line with other Western nations that had recently introduced pensions or insurance programs for elderly citizens as part of a more general turn toward the welfare state.[25] However, this is exactly what the United States did not do. Political leaders during the decades before and after the turn of the century enacted a wide range of social programs on the local, state, and federal levels of government. Nonetheless, the springboard toward Progressive Era domestic policies was not the Civil War pension program. Quite to the contrary, rather than building upon this large social benefit (as some in fact proposed to do), American decision makers, echoing the sentiments of apparently large numbers among the general public, turned against it as a prime example of waste and political corruption.

By the turn of the century, criticism of the veterans' pension program was widespread. Its sheer cost was hard for many to swallow, while many others condemned it as a political boondoggle and a travesty of the program's original purpose. Still others, including many Progressives, considered it an archaic means for achieving a useful end. Historian William H. Glasson's two pioneering studies of military pensions and pension laws in the United States evolve from detailed, scholarly histories into polemics against the ever-expanding post–Civil War pension. In his *History of Military Pension Legislation*, published in 1900, Glasson characterizes the Dependent Pension Act of 1890 as a "bad law" that "lays an extravagant and unjust burden upon taxpayers to insure a privileged class against serious accident or disability. It stimulates dishonesty and dependence, fails to discriminate between the deserving and the undeserving, and prevents the pension list from being, as it should be, a roll of honor."[26]

The continuing force of older values reveals itself in statements of this sort, including the need to distinguish between the "deserving" and the "undeserving," the fear of widespread dependence on public benefit programs, and the legitimization of the military pension in terms of honor rather than personal need or social utility. Glasson was no political Progressive. Nonetheless, as Skocpol points out, even the most forward-looking were inclined to turn to other models—primarily those that originated in the roles, sensibilities, and needs of women and children—for the shaping of new social legislation.[27] The military pension, left unprotected by those who might have turned it to new uses, suffered the outrage of those who thought it corrupting and extravagant. Existing pension programs were never in danger of elimination, but the prospects of repeating the evolution toward a general service pension for veterans of future wars appeared

THE INSATIABLE GLUTTON.

"The Insatiable Glutton," a satirical cartoon of a Civil War pensioner feeding from the U.S. Treasury with many arms labeled, among other things, "Agent," "Fraudulent Attorney," "Bogus Widow," and even "Bogus Grandma." (*Puck*, December 20, 1882)

dim. Indeed, they seem to have been foreclosed by an alternative plan crafted in 1917 in anticipation of another huge cohort of freshly made veterans, returning this time from America's first European military adventure.

More than 4.7 million Americans served in the military during World War I. Only a little more than half were sent abroad, where they remained for an average stay of fewer than six months; still, the participation by U.S. troops in this devastating conflict was sufficient to claim more than 116,000 American lives and send more than 200,000 men home with nonmortal wounds.[28] The Spanish-American War had involved a much smaller force of only 300,000, of whom only 4,000 had been killed or wounded, and had not raised the pension issue to any significant extent. The disabled veterans of this war were, without much discussion or dissent, made beneficiaries of existing pension laws, and there was not yet any pressing need to consider whether able-bodied veterans might later qualify.[29] Still, the size of the World War I corps of veterans (more than twice that of the Union men of 1865) brought the unwanted effects of these laws into sharper focus. Before debate could even begin, a very different plan, one that drew on Progressive Era concepts of social insurance, was proposed, passed unanimously by both the Senate and the House, and signed into law by President Woodrow Wilson.

The War Risk Insurance Act of 1917 was the project of Secretary of the Treasury William McAdoo. It did a good deal more than transfer the management of new veterans' benefits from the Pension Bureau of the Department of the Interior to McAdoo's Treasury. The law established three distinct programs, two of which were quite new. The first was a system of compulsory monthly allotments from the salaries of enlisted men to their families, with an additional allowance to be provided to each family by the federal government. The second offered voluntary life and disability insurance to servicemen at rates much lower than these high-risk soldiers and sailors might have obtained on their own. This term insurance could be converted into standard civilian policies after the war. The third was not so new; indeed, it was very much like older pension laws for veterans with disabilities and for dependents of those killed in service, although the framers substituted the word "compensation" for "pension" and placed much emphasis on compensation-ending rehabilitation of veterans who were sick and wounded.[30] There was, of course, no opposition to the government's provision of financial assistance to those who were disabled, widowed, or orphaned by the war. The real question was whether assistance would later be extended to those disabled or killed by injuries or sickness not related to their military service and still later to those veterans—healthy or not and needy or not—who survived to old age. Wilson, McAdoo, and the congressmen who enacted the War Risk Insurance Act of 1917 seemed determined that this well-established postwar pattern would not recur.

The two new components of the law were more obviously self-liquidating. The allotment and allowance program was designed to end with each serviceman's mustering out, and the program itself was terminated in 1921. The insurance program would continue but on a contributory basis that reduced the government's cost to little more than administration. Although continuing policies were more expensive than expected, the cost of the program was greatly reduced by the failure of nine out of ten veterans to carry their policies into civilian life. The $40 billion of insurance in force during the war was reduced to $4 billion by the middle of 1920. The government seemed to be making a cleaner break with its new veterans than it had accomplished after any previous war.

Other programs and proposals either reflected or did little to counteract the desire to avoid the escalating costs of ever-expanding veterans' programs. One was the $60 one-time payment to every serviceman as he was mustered out. Another was the advantage given to World War I veterans on federal civil service exams (ten points for veterans with a disability, five points for the able bodied), a ruling that increased the number of veterans on the federal payroll but did not boost the cost of veterans' benefits.

There were more ambitious proposals, some of which reflected the increased ambitions of the Progressive Era state even while they kept sight of the bottom line. Chief among them was a veterans' rural resettlement plan proposed by Interior Secretary Franklin K. Lane and introduced in Congress by Wyoming Republican Frank Mondell. Reflecting concerns about rural population loss and the prospects of widespread postwar unemployment in the cities, the Lane-Mondell plan, or National Soldier Settlement Act, would have provided veterans with government loans secured by long-term, low-interest mortgages for the purchase of family-sized farms within planned rural settlements. The bill called for a $500 million appropriation, but much of the cost was to have been recaptured through the repayment of loans. This was a new way of thinking about the problem of mass military demobilization, and debate over the bill generated still more novel proposals, such as loans to veterans for the purchase of businesses and homes. Realization of such unusual ideas would, however, be postponed until the next war. Lane-Mondell was passed by the House in 1919 but was never brought to a vote in the Senate.[31]

These post–World War I programs and proposals were at once conceptually more expansive and practically more frugal than the military pensions that had followed every previous American conflict. If they reflect in some ways the new policy sciences of the Progressive Era, they more boldly proclaim an end to the expensive entitlement claims of able-bodied veterans. President Wilson insisted that those who had gone to war had merely performed a duty incumbent upon their citizenship, that they formed no special class of citizens, and that they earned no special rights once they left military service. (In this he was echoed at the time and for many years afterward by his assistant secretary of the navy, Franklin Delano Roosevelt.) The doughboys themselves might have accepted this principle, but some among them offered a practical observation that resulted in the most famous—and politically consequential—of the post–World War I veterans' programs. Unlike earlier veterans, the vast majority of World War I soldiers and sailors were conscripts, compelled by law to accept the meager pay of an enlisted man ($30 per month during stateside service, $33 while overseas), while the jobs many of them left behind had suddenly become more lucrative because of the very war the conscripts had been sent to fight. Here was an inequity obvious even to those determined to hold down the cost of veterans' benefits, and it led to a wide range of proposals for a bonus or, more formally, "adjusted service compensation" for World War I veterans above and generally well beyond the $60 mustering-out payment.

The origins of the idea of a monetary bonus are obscure; indeed, it may well have sprung simultaneously from many sources. It is most closely associated with the new and rapidly ascending veterans' organization, the American Legion, although the Legion was at first reluctant to embrace the concept. When it did, it linked the bonus with some of the loan and settlement plans that had already been debated in Congress, along with another new idea, the subsidization of veterans' attendance at approved programs of vocational training.[32] Again, however, these ideas fell by the wayside, and the bonus became the focus of a long political battle with the Harding and Coolidge administrations (Treasury Secretary Andrew Mellon was a particularly vocal opponent), the U.S. Chamber of Commerce, and others worried about the cost of the program. The first attempts at a bonus bill failed in the Senate, which also sustained President Harding's veto of the first bill to clear both houses of Congress in 1922.

The political tide turned when unexpected budget surpluses undermined Mellon's fiscal arguments against the bonus. In 1924 Congress overrode President Coolidge's veto of a bill modified somewhat to ease the immediate burden on the Treasury. As enacted, the 1924 bonus bill provided that each World War I veteran who had served for more than sixty days between April 5, 1917, and July 1, 1919, would receive $1 for each day of stateside service and $1.25 for each day overseas, up to a maximum of $625 for veterans who had gone abroad and $500 for those who had not. Only those who were entitled to $50 or less, however, would receive immediate cash payment. The rest would receive a bonus certificate, payable in 1945 or upon the recipient's death. Unlike the other programs that benefited able-bodied veterans, this one was large—its estimated cost to the government was approximately $4 billion—but the deferral of most payments meant that each year's federal contribution to the Adjusted Service Certificate Trust Fund created by the bill would be relatively small, especially in the early years.

The doughboys had won, but most of them found that they had little they could take to the bank.[33]

The majority of veterans appear to have been content with this outcome and remained so during the relatively prosperous years that immediately followed. With the onset of hard times at the end of the decade, however, attitudes changed. Veterans who lost their jobs or feared unemployment began to press for immediate payment on their bonus certificates, a fiscally unpalatable idea to President Hoover, Secretary Mellon, and other political leaders who believed that the deepening depression required a tightening of federal expenditure. Even before the stock market crash in the autumn of 1929, there had been a few calls for immediate cash disbursement, but now the idea took hold in Congress and among the rank and file of the American Legion. Various bills were introduced. The one that prevailed was a compromise measure based on the loan feature of the original bonus plan. The bill raised the loan limit on each certificate from 22.5 to 50 percent and lowered the interest rate from 6 to 4.5 percent. This measure was passed by large majorities in both houses early in 1931 and became law when Congress overrode Hoover's veto.

It was not enough, however, to stop the call for full cash payment among rank-and-file Legionnaires, members of the smaller Veterans of Foreign Wars, and even some members of Congress, most notably Wright Patman, a young Texas Democrat who would make veterans' benefits his signature issue. During the early 1930s the bonus issue was actually growing in significance despite the determined opposition of fiscal conservatives and of liberals who wanted the money to go toward more general depression-countering measures rather than to so specific a group. It would grow larger still when groups of veterans, beginning with a few hundred men from Oregon but eventually amounting to a "bonus expeditionary force" of some twenty thousand men from many parts of the country, marched on Washington in the spring and early summer of 1932, thereby establishing a confrontation with Congress and the Hoover administration that would end only with the July 28 "Battle of Washington"—the clearing of the bonus marchers' billets in Washington and on the flats just across the Anacostia River by U.S. troops under the command of Army Chief of Staff Douglas MacArthur.

The army used a good deal of tear gas during this operation. No bullets appear to have been fired, however, and there were no further deaths to add to the two bonus marchers who had been killed earlier in the day in a fracas with local police. However, the temporary shacks that formed the large encampment on the Anacostia Flats were, by order or accident, burned to the ground, and this, along with the mere fact of an attack by U.S. troops on American war veterans helped turn the bonus march into a major election-year embarrassment for the struggling Hoover administration. Still, neither Wright Patman nor anyone else could force a cash payment bill through Congress either before or immediately after the Battle of Washington. All that was offered the marchers was a loan authorized by Congress in June at Hoover's behest to help those who would take it to return to their homes.[34]

When World War I veterans returned to Washington in 1933 in much smaller numbers, they found a new president, more genial and politically astute but no less opposed to cash payment of the bonus. The administration of Franklin D. Roosevelt treated the marchers as respectable citizens, housed them in a military fort, fed them well, and paid their expenses. In a masterful stroke, Roosevelt signed an executive order that reserved twenty-five thousand places for unemployed veterans in the new Civilian Conservation Corps and gave priority within that number to those who had come to Washington. Moreover, he sent the First Lady to visit with the men. It hardly needs saying that this bonus march adjourned without tear gas or fire. The next year's march was no less tame. Still, the former doughboys did not get their cash bonus.[35]

They would get it in 1936 over Roosevelt's veto. A year earlier Patman had steered a cash redemption bill through Congress, and Roosevelt had taken the unusual step of delivering his veto message in person, arguing that veterans should be treated no differently from other citizens and that the new social security bill then before Congress was a far better means for providing protection against unemployment and old age than legislation aimed at any specific group. "The veteran who suffers from this depression," Roosevelt pointed out, "can best be aided by the rehabilitation of the country as a whole. His country with honor and gratitude returned him at the end of the war to the citizenry from which he came." Veterans with disabilities are a special group, FDR acknowledged, and deserve the utmost in special attention from the government, but the able bodied "are American citizens who should be accorded equal privileges and equal rights to enjoy life, liberty, and the pursuit of happiness—no less and no more." The president concluded by folding the veterans' needs into an eloquent reinforcement of the New Deal relief program:

I am thinking of those who served their country in the Army and in the Navy during the period which convulsed the entire civilized world. I am thinking of those millions of men and women who increased crops, who made munitions, who ran our railroads, who worked in the mines, who loaded our ships during the war period....I am thinking of five millions of Americans who, with their families, are today in dire need, supported in whole or in part by Federal, State, and local governments who have decreed that they shall not starve.[36]

The speech was very effective, and the Senate sustained the veto. In 1936, however, with substantial backing from the American Legion, a new bill called for the voluntary redemption of bonus certificates mainly by exchanging them for U.S. savings bonds, and this time a less eloquently defended veto was overridden. Most veterans promptly made the exchange, and about three-fourths of them immediately cashed in the bonds—to the extent of more than $1.4 billion. This made 1936 the record year by far in the history of federal expenditure on veterans' benefits. Only some thirty thousand bonus certificates remained in force when the redemption date finally arrived in 1945.[37]

The fight over the bonus and its cash redemption, enlivened by the 1932 bonus march and its fiery conclusion, has overshadowed the equally significant battle over post–World War I pensions. The Wilson administration, as well as those that followed, had hoped that the War Risk Insurance Act of 1917 would foreclose the possibility of an expanded postwar pension program, and the other proposals we have noted were offered as less costly and less open-ended forms of veterans' compensation. Nevertheless, the various loan programs had not been adopted, only one in ten war-risk insurance policies were continued into civilian life, and until 1936 the bonus certificate was to most veterans a promise on a piece of paper.

It is perhaps not so surprising, therefore, that the old pattern of expanding veterans' pensions asserted itself once again, at first by liberalizing the criteria for assessing the service-connected character of various disabilities and then, in part because such assessments were difficult to make, by allowing disability payments to needy veterans who could not prove that their physical or mental problems resulted from military service. After an initial veto, President Hoover in 1930 signed into law a compensation program expanded to include World War I veterans with non-service-related disabilities and with incomes insufficient to be subject to federal income tax.[38] The word "pension" was still not used, but a pension it was, and, for all the efforts to avoid such a plan, it appeared with unprecedented speed. Revolutionary War veterans had waited thirty-five years and Civil War veterans twenty-five for the enactment of a non-service-related disability or need-based pension. World War I veterans waited only twelve.

Would the World War I "compensation" plan evolve toward a general-service pension? Further expansion—indeed, the future of the 1930 plan itself—was soon complicated by President Roosevelt's determination to cut federal expenditures and by his particular focus on veterans' benefits as a major locus of fiscal indiscipline. The legendary Hundred Days of the special session of Congress that began a few days after Roosevelt's first inauguration are most famous for banking and securities exchange reform, the creation of the first federally funded relief programs, the National Industrial Recovery Act, the Agricultural Adjustment Act, and TVA. These and other bold and eventually expensive new initiatives (which for a time succeeded, as John Maynard Keynes was then predicting, in lifting the American economy out of the doldrums) have obscured in the popular mind a very different aspect of Roosevelt's political agenda. He had campaigned in 1932 on the need to balance the federal budget, which seems remarkable and even hypocritical in light of the expansive and expensive programs that followed.

However, Roosevelt, who was no Keynesian, was sincere about the budget, and within a day of the convening of the special session, as the next order of business following the Emergency Banking Relief Act of March 9, 1933, he asked for quick passage of an Economy Act aimed at large-scale reductions in federal outlays. One of the major targets was federal salaries, but the largest by far was veterans' benefits. Roosevelt knew that throughout the 1920s the latter had absorbed more than a quarter of the federal budget, and in 1931, immediately following the expansion of "compensation" to those with non-service-related disabilities, spending on veterans topped $1 billion for the first time, amounting to 29 percent of all federal expenditures.[39] Here was meat (or perhaps one could say fat) for the budget cutter's cleaver.

The Economy Act revoked the laws and regulations that defined "compensation" benefits for World War I and Spanish-American War veterans and gave the president wide latitude in determining new ones. Within a few weeks the first executive orders appeared, dramatically reducing non-service-related pensions (and calling them "pensions" for the first time) and cutting costs to lesser degrees in other parts of the benefits program. The scale of the overall reduction was very large—between 1932 and 1934 veterans' benefits declined by more than 40 percent, from just under $1 billion to less than $560 million.[40] The American Legion and its congressional allies strenuously opposed the cuts, and in 1935 Congress enacted a new law (over Roosevelt's veto), one that reestablished Congress's primacy in setting veterans' benefits, restored many benefits to veterans with service-related disabilities, and, once again, substituted "compensation" for "pension."[41]

Nonetheless, Roosevelt had won the battles over non-service-related pensions and the overall levels of veterans' benefits. Even with the restoration of various cuts, the cost of veterans' programs remained stable into the early years of World War II; thus, the seemingly inevitable march toward a general-service pension for World War I veterans had been halted. Roosevelt had broken a long-established historical pattern.

The post–World War I period is indeed a notable one in the history of veterans' benefits in the United States and not merely for this successful resistance to expanding pensions. Critical to the struggle against vigorously defended interests and traditions were, after all, a variety of programmatic innovations and proposals more or less responsive to Progressive Era concepts of social insurance and public sector planning, which were intended to replace the pension monolith. Most of these were introduced and fought out on the national level, although parallel battles took place on the state level (twenty states, for example, enacted bonuses), and occasionally a state went beyond the federal government, as did Colorado, Wisconsin, and Oregon when they enacted programs of educational stipends or loans for veterans.[42] These state programs could be significant—Wisconsin's subsidy, which was available for veterans from the state attending school at any level, amounted to $30 per month, an amount equal to most doughboys' army pay.[43] Whatever the legislative venue or size of the program, new thinking was being brought to bear on the issue of veterans' benefits, and it was clear even before the armistice of 1918 that postwar policymaking would never again be the same. Indeed, the innovations of the interwar period form an immediate and influential background to the proposals that would find their way into the GI Bill in 1944.

Some of these innovations, as we have seen, served to limit veterans' benefits rather than to expand them, while several others of a more generous nature were not enacted. One major new idea—adjusted service compensation—became a source of political contention that was not resolved until nearly two decades after the end of the war. In all of these ways, the experiences of American veterans of the twentieth century's two major wars were extremely different. The debates and laws of the post–World War I period departed dramatically from traditions that stretched back to and beyond the Revolution and provided a number of ideas that could be drawn upon in the future. Still, as the former doughboys would be—and were—the first to argue, they did not provide a new model for the aftermath of the next war. The conflicts and failures of this era, as much as its success in responding to the perceived excesses of a still more distant past, helped make the Servicemen's Readjustment Act of 1944 unique.

TWO

FDR and the Reshaping of Veterans' Benefits, 1940–1943

In his fireside chat of July 28, 1943, President Franklin D. Roosevelt announced his commitment to a comprehensive set of benefits for veterans of World War II. (Courtesy Cornell University Library)

A s WAS THE case in the longer history of veterans' benefits, policy innovations and debates during and after World War II were closely bound up with evolving institutions in and outside government and with a changing array of political forces. As we have seen, a number of new contexts framed the debate over benefits for veterans of World War I, chief among them the size and disrepute of the preexisting pension program for Civil War veterans. Still earlier programs had occasionally produced justifiable charges of corruption and fiscal irresponsibility, but these were largely forgotten in the post–Civil War era, when the political climate greatly favored the enactment of increasingly generous pension laws for Union veterans. From the World War I veterans' point of view the saviors of the Union had succeeded all too well. Former doughboys who looked to their government for material recognition of their wartime sacrifice faced five straight presidential administrations determined to lower costs and deny the special claim of veterans upon the U.S. Treasury. Aided by allies in Congress, the veterans did win some battles, but many of them believed they had fared very poorly—and unfairly so—in comparison with those of earlier wars.

This meant that the debate over benefits for veterans of the *next* war would occur in a very different political environment. If the doughboys suffered from the excesses of the post–Civil War pension system, the GIs of World War II would benefit from the far less generous treatment of those who had fought the War to End All Wars. It was not a privileged, pampered class that had tasted General MacArthur's tear gas and borne the brunt of President Roosevelt's Economy Act, nor was it an aging, diminishing, and easily ignored cohort. More than half a century had elapsed between the end of the Civil War and the engagement of U.S. troops in World War I. For many years Civil War veterans, individually and as members of the Grand Army of the Republic, had successfully pursued their political interests, but by 1917 death and old age had vastly reduced their numbers and their influence over national policy. Woodrow Wilson need hardly have considered the Civil War veterans' response to war-risk insurance and other attempts to control the cost of new veterans' benefits. The interval between the two world wars, on the other hand, was much shorter (only twenty-three years between the 1918 armistice and the Japanese attack on Pearl Harbor), which is a significant but generally overlooked factor that affected the debate over the shape and extent of postwar benefits for veterans of this latest—and biggest—war.

When this debate began in the early 1940s, World War I veterans were in their forties and fifties, little diminished in their numbers, and at or near the peak of their activity and influence in their communities and in the larger world of Washington politics. Moreover, they were better organized for the task ahead. The GAR was an organization limited to Union veterans of the Civil War and expressed no official interest in public policies toward veterans of other wars. The American Legion and the other new veterans' groups, by contrast, were intended to be permanent organizations open to veterans of all of the nation's future wars. Institutionally, they were as eager to be involved in debates over World War II veterans' benefits as they had been when the issues were their own bonuses and pensions; indeed, the Legion, the VFW, and the Disabled American Veterans (DAV) could expect to survive only if veterans of the next war were drawn to them as viable promoters of their own interests. What better way to attract new members than to speak out forcefully for the rights of those just now being sent off to war? The largest of the post–World War I veterans' organizations, the American Legion, vigorously carried forward the fight for the prospective veterans of World War II. This vigor reflected the numbers, the relative youth, and the still-developing influence of the World War I cohort no less than the institutional purposes of the organizations they had formed. Veterans' policy had never before been subjected to so strong an influence from the veterans of a previous war.

In addition, there had never been a political context for such policy quite like the one that had taken shape during the New Deal. Civil War pension laws reflected the increased capacities and ambitions of the post–Civil War state, and the various reactions against the pension during and after World War I manifested important elements of Progressive Era policy science. However, nothing before it had changed the institutions and practices of the U.S. government like the New Deal, and nothing before it had so influenced Americans' expectations concerning action from the public sector. New initiatives (conservatives called them "intrusions") in employment, agriculture, banking, industrial production, energy, social insurance, community development, and housing created an array of new federal bureaus and agencies and with them the widespread expectation of still more initiatives from this larger, more multifaceted, and more centralized state.

Within this altered framework of government action, some specific New Deal programs helped prepare the way for new departures in veterans' policy. Probably the most significant were new federal interventions in the market for home mortgages. Hoping both to relieve foreclosures and stabilize lending within a badly depressed housing market, Roosevelt had proposed, as part of the larger package of relief programs of the Hundred Days, a system of home-mortgage refinancing to be undertaken by a new public agency, the Home Owners' Loan Corporation (HOLC). Nothing like this had ever been attempted by the federal government, and it was followed a year later by the more permanent restructuring of the home mortgage market under the auspices of another new agency, the Federal Housing Administration (FHA). The lending program of the HOLC was terminated in 1936 as part of a larger retrenchment of early New Deal relief programs, but the FHA, its system of mortgage guarantees, and its rules and guidelines survived as part of an enduring shift in the interface between government and private markets in the United States. They survived, too, to provide the model for a significant component of the GI Bill.

On the other hand, the drafting of the GI Bill was affected by political factors quite different from those of the expansive early days of the New Deal and not merely because the war itself preempted further experimentation in domestic policy. The expansion of the New Deal had already been foreclosed by substantial Republican gains in the 1938 midterm election; indeed, the prospects for costly new programs had dimmed even earlier, as southern Democrats increasingly voted with Republicans in a conservative bloc that would only increase in strength through the late 1930s, the war years, and beyond. This conservative resurgence in Congress was echoed, moreover, within the administration. The president himself sponsored a significant retrenchment of various relief programs after the economic recovery of 1936 and 1937 and turned increasingly to more conservative advisors even as the recession of 1938 and 1939 seemed to call for more vigorous priming of the federal pump. Liberals did not disappear from the Roosevelt administration, but as Alan Brinkley has so ably argued, even they increasingly turned away from the idea of an "activist managerial state" toward a new liberalism "less inclined to challenge corporate behavior…and more strongly committed to the use of 'compensatory' tools—a combination of Keynesian fiscal measures and enhanced welfare-state mechanisms—in the struggle to insure prosperity."[1] This was a less aggressive (one might say more conservative) form of "liberalism," turning to the state primarily to foster full employment and economic growth while protecting individual rights and the well-being of the aged, the ill, and others less able than most to benefit from a prospering economy.

The expansion of public-sector capacities during the salad days of the New Deal may have altered the climate of policymaking by making vigorous and multifaceted public action much more commonplace than it had been in any previous period of U.S. history. But the politics of the late 1930s and the war years greatly complicated the outcome of any new domestic initiative. The prospective veterans of World War II could not be assured that (or in what manner) the post–New Deal state would be summoned to their aid.

The Roosevelt administration's early forays into postwar planning occurred in this mixed context of New Deal institutions, resurgent conservatism, and a determined and well-organized cohort of World War I veterans, and they were further complicated by the mind and methods of the president himself. Thus far, everything we have seen of Franklin Roosevelt on the subject of veterans' benefits would lead us to expect an administrative program that did not single out the veterans of this latest and largest of wars for special treatment. If anything, he would insist upon placing them on the same footing as other Americans facing the predicted difficulties of the immediate postwar period. However, Roosevelt's stand on this issue, from his early days in the Wilson administration to the bonus vetoes of 1935 and 1936, did not guarantee a particular course of action.

Temperamentally as well as tactically, FDR was notoriously difficult to predict, even when it came to apparently settled ideas, and his political genius lay in no small measure in keeping both his enemies and his friends off guard. Rexford Tugwell, who for a time was one of the president's closest advisers, spoke of his "almost impenetrable concealment of intention," and Roosevelt delighted in the bafflement he could create around him. "I'm a juggler," he once told Treasury Secretary Henry Morgenthau, "I never let my right hand know what my left hand is doing."[2] At times, as David Kennedy points out, the juggling consisted of "putting several people of incompatible views to work on the same project, none of whom knew what the others were doing."[3] The enigmatic Roosevelt could then take stock of diverse and sometimes conflicting ideas and fit the most persuasive of them both to his own goals and to current political conditions. He was at once a visionary and a pragmatist, a patrician reformer committed to improving the well-being and security of ordinary people, and a crafty and sometimes ruthless politician, skilled (but with notable missteps, as in the politically disastrous "court-packing" bill of 1937) in the art of the possible. "Take a method and try it," Roosevelt instructed. "If it fails, admit it and try another. But above all, try something."[4]

The president's formulations of postwar policy reflect both his ideals and his tactical flexibility, although at first there was no apparent compromise with his long-standing attitude toward special legislation for veterans and no attempt to trim other programmatic sails to prevailing political winds. Roosevelt recognized the need for a comprehensive postwar plan well before the United States entered World War II and as early as November of 1940 assigned the task to the National Resources Planning Board (NRPB), headed by his uncle, Frederic A. Delano. Neither Delano nor the NRPB are among the best-remembered New Deal players, and planning for the end of a war that had not truly begun might not have seemed the most urgent of priorities. Nonetheless, this was by no means a trivial pigeonholing of a bothersome chore, nor was it a mere bone tossed to an otherwise unoccupied family member. Frederic Delano was a formidable figure with a distinguished career in business and public service. Even before the New Deal era he had accumulated a great deal of executive experience in city and regional planning and thus was the logical choice to head the National Planning Board created by Secretary of the Interior Harold Ickes in July 1933 under the authorization of the National Industrial Recovery Act (NIRA). Delano's NPB was an important behind-the-scenes force in the early New Deal, giving specific direction and shape to vast numbers of public works projects. When its status was threatened by the Supreme Court's overturning of the NIRA, President Roosevelt reconstituted it first as the National Resources Committee and then as the NRPB within the executive office itself. There it remained as one of the last major refuges of New Deal planners, still headed by Frederic Delano and still ably assisted by his long-time vice chairman, Charles E. Merriam, himself one of the nation's outstanding theorists of public planning.[5]

The NRPB entered into the postwar plan with gusto and over the following two years prepared a number of reports. The most general of them, *National Resources Development Report for 1943*, Part 1, *Post-War Plan and Program*, was delivered to the president in December of 1942. It briefly summarizes a long list of planning proposals for postwar demobilization, economic growth, urban services, transportation, land and water use, energy production, and social services and articulates a bold set of national goals that, for the most part, fit well with Roosevelt's long-held views toward veterans as ordinary citizens— full employment above all but also equal access for all citizens to security, health and nutrition, education, and good housing.[6]

The report also includes a small opening toward a separate policy for veterans. The very first area of substantive discussion, demobilization, begins with reference to jobs for veterans and notes with approval that the Selective Service Act of 1940 had included provisions for returning veterans to their old civilian jobs. It also observes that Roosevelt had used the occasion of the signing of a November 1942 revision to this act, which extended the draft to eighteen- and nineteen-year-olds, to address steps that might be taken "to enable the young men whose education has been interrupted to resume their schooling and afford equal opportunity for the training and education of other young men of ability after their service in the armed forces has come to an end."[7] It is hardly surprising that Roosevelt had recognized the problem of interrupted schooling as he signed this act, but his reference to "other young men of ability" suggests something larger. Could Roosevelt have already been thinking of a more comprehensive educational plan for veterans? Was this short phrase the harbinger of a new attitude on his part toward veterans as a group with special needs?

At the very least, Roosevelt was opening up new possibilities in the formulation of policies aimed at veterans of the new war, and he did so with more than just a few words in a speech. At the time of the signing of the 1942 Selective Service Act, the president appointed the Armed Forces Committee on Postwar Educational Opportunities for Service Personnel. Placed under the auspices of the war and navy departments, the committee was headed by Frederick Osborn, a wealthy and talented businessman and social scientist (Osborn was a prominent eugenicist who attempted to rescue this controversial discipline from Nazism and other forms of racism) and for the last year a brigadier general heading the army's Morale Branch. The Osborn Committee was actually the second such group authorized to develop policies for the education of veterans. In July of 1942, Roosevelt had approved a request from Frederic Delano for a demobilization planning committee within the NRPB, and Delano quickly created the Conference on Post-War Readjustments of Civilian and Military Personnel (more often known as the Post-War Manpower Conference, or PMC), a group with a somewhat broader portfolio that included veterans' education. Characteristically, Roosevelt set two different sets of policymakers to work on the same problem and sat back to await the results.

Having established a separate subgroup to work on veterans' policy, Delano's NRPB did not build a case for it in its general reports to the president. The *National Resources Development Report* makes no other reference to veterans aside from the one already noted, and the subject of postwar veterans' benefits is explicitly excluded from the much larger and more significant NRPB report, *Security, Work, and Relief Policies*, which Roosevelt released to the public in March of 1943.[8] Leaving not only veterans' benefits but also matters such as economic and natural resource management to other committees, the authors of this report focused on what they called "public aid," the proper object of which is "the assurance of access to minimum security for all our people, wherever they may reside, and the maintenance of the social stability and values threatened when people lack jobs or income."[9] Following this simple statement was a series of proposals for expanding "public aid" in the form of federal work programs, unemployment compensation, old-age and disability insurance, public assistance to poor people, and "social services essential to the health, education, and welfare of the population."[10] Most of these proposals were barely sketched out, but they were impressive in their sweep and constituted a veritable manifesto for reinvigorated public social planning.

Liberals immediately hailed the report as "the American Beveridge Plan," referring to the ambitious proposals for expanding the British welfare state put forward only three months earlier by a commission headed by Sir William Beveridge of the London School of Economics.[11] The latter had also been hailed upon its public release. There was, however, a very significant difference between the reception and fate of the two national programs. In Britain, praise issued from across nearly the entire political spectrum, and, as historian Paul Addison has written, the Beveridge Plan served not only as a domestic program for the postwar Labour government but also as the vehicle for the forging of a new and quite durable political consensus.[12] The NRPB reports, however, found no such consensus. American conservatives denounced the board's proposals, along with the very idea of a postwar society so comprehensively planned by the central—and Rooseveltian—government. Conservatives in Congress quickly killed the NRPB reports. Then they killed the NRPB itself by denying it funding for the next fiscal year. By the end of 1943 this central New Deal planning agency had ceased to exist.[13]

But what of that small opening for a postwar policy specific to veterans and of the efforts of the two committees working on education and other demobilization issues? With or without the NRPB's guidance, congressional conservatives were far more amenable to planning for massive military demobilization than they were for the "American Beveridge Plan." They knew that 15 million men and women, more than one in ten of the entire American population, would eventually be demobilized. They accepted the idea that wartime spending had brought the economy out of the deepest depression in U.S. history and shared with many Americans the fear that the depression would resume with the end of the war. In particular, conservatives worried about the political consequences of massive unemployment, when hordes of young men, skilled in the use of firearms, would begin to roam the streets, angry over their inability to regain a foothold in the civilian world. World War I had spawned major revolutions in Russia and Germany. Would hard times following World War II trigger a new one in the United States? These fears gave a new kind of urgency to the question of what the government ought to be doing for its latest—and largest—crop of veterans. And they gave FDR an opportunity to shape postwar domestic policy in ways the broader NRPB reports did not.

Both of the demobilization committees authorized in 1942 issued reports to the president in the summer of 1943. The NRPB Post-War Manpower Conference had debated two very different approaches to the problem of mass demobilization: slowing the pace of demobilization itself so the economy could more effectively absorb the influx of new workers or easing the effects of rapid demobilization with financial support for the unemployed and for veterans returning to school or entering job training. In the end, fearing an uproar from the GIs and their families, the PMC decided against a gradual demobilization and proposed several measures for coping with the veterans' rapid return: a three-month paid furlough before each serviceperson's discharge (in effect granting a government subsidy to the new veterans while they searched for work); a federal unemployment compensation system available to veterans and others to supplement those provided by the states; and aid to veterans for one year of education or training, extended to four years for a much smaller group through competitive scholarships.[14]

The Osborn Committee, which focused entirely on the question of schooling and job training, had consulted with the PMC and issued very similar recommendations for educational and training subsidies. Its report, though, revealed more explicitly how well the goals of each group meshed with conservatives' fears and principles and with Roosevelt's own resistance to treating veterans as a separate class of citizens. Educational subsidies were not to be regarded as a reward to veterans or as a program to underwrite their individual ambitions. "We have regarded any benefits which may be extended to individuals in the process as incidental," wrote the committee. "The primary objective...of all the efforts of our committee is to do what is necessary to overcome the educational shortages created by the war."[15] In concert with this focus on the economic consequences of rapid demobilization, both groups recommended that educational subsidies be directed toward specific manpower needs in the U.S. economy.[16]

A year earlier, Roosevelt had resisted going public with proposals for postwar demobilization and development. In a letter to Frederic Delano written around the time of the creation of the PMC, he noted that the public's focus must remain on winning the war and offered the opinion that "any publicity given at this time to the future demobilization of men in the armed forces or industry would be a mistake."[17] Now, however, he clearly felt the time was right and that the proposals for veterans' educational benefits, along with mustering-out pay and unemployment compensation, represented his best chance to frame policy for the immediate postwar period. Roosevelt knew that the broader NRPB proposals were dead, and he sensed both the political feasibility and the likely popularity of more limited measures of immediate benefit to returning soldiers and sailors. Thus, FDR's embrace of the PMC's and the Osborn Committee's proposals suggested a reversal of his long-held convictions on veterans' legislation.

Roosevelt was famously adept at sensing the direction and size of a political opening, and he was also skilled at passing through that opening while preserving other policy options. Samuel Rosenman offers an old New Dealer's interpretation of Roosevelt's intentions: that federal financing of education for GIs would be an "entering wedge" that would garner wider acceptance of federal aid to education of all sorts and for all Americans. In his memoir, *Working with Roosevelt*, Rosenman traces this striking policy shift to FDR's earliest exposures, during therapeutic trips to Warm Springs, Georgia, to poor schools of the rural South. "In private conversations," writes Rosenman, the president made clear his unhappiness with regional and local disparities in the quality of schooling, as well as his conviction of the need to equalize educational opportunities "through the resources and Treasury of the United States." Roosevelt well understood that educational policy had always been the prerogative of the individual states and that federal aid to education would be fiercely resisted by "states' righters," an understanding that goes a long way toward explaining why there had been no attempt to construct such an aid program even in the most expansive days of the New Deal. "But he was also sure that even the most rabid opponent of federal aid to education would not dare raise his voice against federal financial aid for educating GI's [*sic*]." Hence, the "entering wedge": "If he could once get this piece of legislation on the books it would be much easier thereafter to get more and more federal aid for all children in states that could not provide decent educational facilities out of their own resources."[18]

Rosenman's interpretation is underscored by Roosevelt's public statements about postwar policy, which frequently, if sometimes subtly or ambiguously, joined proposals for veterans' benefits to broader goals. When the president submitted the major NRPB reports to Congress on March 10, 1943, he observed: "Men in the armed forces and those engaged in the war effort rightly expect us to be considering their future welfare." Even apart from his inclusion of the phrase "those engaged in the war effort," which referred to vast numbers of civilians, he preceded this sentence with a statement of still broader import: "We can all agree on our objectives and in our common determination that work, fair pay, and social security after the war is won must be firmly established for the people of the United States."[19] In a July fireside chat announcing the newly crafted veterans' initiatives (an address to which we will return), Roosevelt quickly added: "Your government is drawing up other serious, constructive plans for certain immediate forward moves. They concern food, manpower, and other domestic problems that tie in with our armed forces."[20] And in a press conference two days later, in which he discussed the PMC proposals for veterans, he noted that "the report places strong emphasis on the importance of bringing about a rapid conversion of industry from a wartime to a peacetime basis, and in establishing full employment as one of the objectives of the demobilization process."[21] These statements and others like them kept before the public the prospect of domestic policy that transcended veterans. Even with the American Beveridge Plan torn from his book of recipes, Roosevelt could stir a pot in which veterans' benefits were but one ingredient.

There are other indications that, despite the pressures and preoccupations of war, FDR was thinking in quite fundamental terms about American society and of government's role in shaping and securing social well-being in the years to come. At a press conference on December 28, 1943, the president, having been pressed by a reporter at the previous conference about the fate of the largely moribund New Deal, launched into his well-known tale of Dr. New Deal and Dr. Win-the-War. The first of these medical "men," a few years back, had administered strong remedies to a patient suffering from numerous internal disorders. In the process of recovery, the patient "had a very bad accident" that required the services of an orthopedic surgeon, Dr. Win-the-War, who had just about put the patient back on his feet. Was the patient then almost fully cured and in need of no doctor at all? Here Roosevelt dropped his droll metaphor and spoke directly to the imperatives of the coming peace:

> It seems pretty clear that we must plan for, and help to bring about, an expanded economy which will result in more security, in more employment, in more recreation, in more education, in more health, in better housing for all of our citizens, so that the conditions of 1932 and the beginning of 1933 won't come back again.[22]

Dr. New Deal was, at the very least, still on call, and his patient was not merely the coming cohort of World War II veterans but "all of our citizens" as well.

Two weeks after this press conference, FDR delivered a far more important address, a State of the Union speech that, because the president was ill and could not journey to the Capitol, was also broadcast as a fireside chat. In it Roosevelt articulated a theme that harkened back to many of his previous statements, including his famous Four Freedoms address of 1941, and expressed the core of his thinking about domestic policy: the need for what he called a "second Bill of Rights." What Roosevelt had in mind were the economic rights that would guarantee freedom from want and fear—a "useful and remunerative job," an adequate income, a decent home, medical care, protection from the "fears of old age, sickness, accident, and unemployment," and a good education, among others—and the president clearly meant them to belong to every citizen.[23] It was at precisely this moment that the GI Bill of Rights was taking shape in Congress; indeed, within a few days FDR would be meeting with a committee of the American Legion to discuss the organization's proposals for the bill. Roosevelt was thinking of a bill of rights, too, but one with a much more general application.

These broader statements help us understand Roosevelt's thinking as he introduced his own proposals for benefits designed specially for veterans. Having received the report of the PMC (and a little later, the Osborn Committee) in the midst of the conservatives' assault on the NRPB, he decided to present his package of veterans' benefits not to Congress but to the American people. On July 28, 1943, he broadcast a fireside chat devoted ostensibly to progress in the war and in particular to the good prospects for victory in Italy in the wake of the news of Mussolini's resignation, which Roosevelt called the "first crack in the Axis." Then, unexpectedly, he turned to the veterans. We must plan now, he argued, for "the return to civilian life of our gallant men and women in the armed services," who "must not be demobilized into an environment of inflation and unemployment, to a place on the breadline or on a corner selling apples." Roosevelt acknowledged the sacrifices made by civilians during the war, but he now emphasized, as he never had done before, that "the members of the armed forces have been compelled to make greater economic sacrifice and every other kind of sacrifice than the rest of us" and proposed that Congress enact laws (he was not necessarily thinking of a single GI bill) that would provide veterans with mustering-out pay, educational assistance, unemployment insurance, and other benefits. Significantly, there was no call for educational assistance or any other benefit for civilian war workers or for citizens generally.[24]

Roosevelt's proposals were interpreted by some as a political triumph. *Newsweek* called their insertion into a speech supposedly on the military aspects of the war "a shrewd maneuver" and "a coup that caught the President's political foes flat-footed." Republicans could only fume. Senator Styles Bridges of New Hampshire complained that Roosevelt "had dangled before the eyes of the soldiers the gift of their own tax money," and Republican national chairman Harrison Spangler, who spoke loftily of "the dangers to our democratic institutions of the Commander-in-Chief stooping to this type of politics among those who, instead of thinking of him as a cunning political leader, should have confidence that he is thinking only of winning the war." *Newsweek*, which noted that there had until then been little leadership on this issue, characterized Spangler's comment as "the anguished outcry of a politician who sees a political plum snatched from under his nose."[25]

Three months later the president followed up on this speech by presenting the Osborn Committee's proposals to Congress (and avoiding any mention of the NRPB's PMC report). On October 27, 1943, he asked Congress for legislation that would finance one year of college education or vocational training for all World War II veterans with an unspecified minimum time of military service and up to three years of additional education or training for "a limited number of ex-service men and women selected for their special aptitudes." He went beyond the Osborn report in proposing that educational and vocational opportunities "should be of the widest range" and not limited to or focused on areas of the economy determined by others to have special manpower needs. Roosevelt's own focus, indeed, was on the veterans themselves, as it had been in his July address, and he was emphatic in asserting their special claim to government assistance. "We, at home," he intoned, "owe a special and continuing obligation to these men and women in the armed services.... It is an obligation which should be recognized now; and legislation to that end should be enacted as soon as possible.... We have taught our youth how to wage war; we must also teach them how to live useful and happy lives in freedom, justice, and decency."[26]

A second message went to the Hill a month later, calling for the remainder of the proposals he had outlined in July—mustering-out pay, unemployment allowances, and credit toward Social Security, old age, and survivor benefits for time spent in the military. These were "a minimum of action to which the members of our armed forces are entitled over and above that taken for other citizens." Roosevelt hinted once again at more general domestic policies, and while he continued to elevate the veteran to a position above all others, his vision of the purpose and result of a veterans' benefits program was stated finally in terms of the broadest realization of the freedoms and rights that were the deepest preoccupation of Dr. New Deal: "The goal after the war should be the maximum utilization of our human and material resources. This is the way to rout the forces of insecurity and unemployment at home, as completely as we shall have defeated the forces of tyranny and oppression on the fields of battle."[27]

However, Dr. Win-the-War had not yet finished treating his patient. Roosevelt had clearly seized the initiative in the articulation and promotion of a program of benefits for World War II veterans and with his messages to Congress established himself as the conceptual father of the GI Bill. But the war itself was still his primary preoccupation, and he would provide little evident further guidance as Congress began to consider his and others' proposals. His early steps, taken in the inhospitable political climate in which the NRPB had withered, were significant and not only because they placed the issue—and specific policy proposals—on the legislative agenda well before the end of the war. Roosevelt's initiative was also noteworthy because it signaled a new direction in the history of veterans' legislation. Congress and the American public now understood that the treatment of World War II veterans would differ from that of so many embittered veterans of World War I and, indeed, that it would differ in form and purpose from any that had followed every previous American war. A dramatic departure from a very long history was about to occur.

In the late autumn of 1943, when FDR returned from Congress to get on with winning the war and the American Legion prepared to send a veterans' legislation committee to Washington, no one could predict what shape the package of new benefits would assume. That would be the work of the next six months. There would ultimately be more than one bill, but one, the Servicemen's Readjustment Act of 1944—the GI Bill—would encapsulate nearly all of the new policy departures and begin its long march into American legend. It was signed into law as American soldiers were still scrambling off the beaches of Normandy.

THREE

"Mission Accomplished"

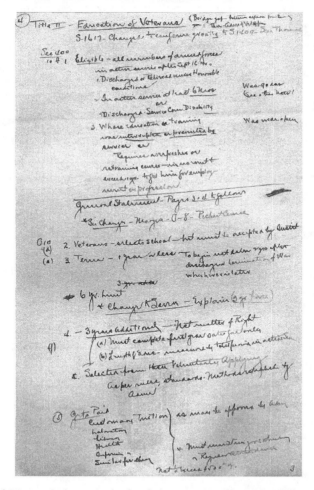

A page of Harry Colmery's draft of the veterans' benefits bill proposed to Congress by the American Legion. (Courtesy American Legion Library)

B Y THE FALL of 1943 Roosevelt understood that Congress would not pass an American Beveridge Plan. The election of 1942 had been a disaster for his Democratic Party. With Republican gains of forty-seven seats in the House of Representatives and seven in the Senate, Roosevelt faced the most conservative Congress of his presidency. Since southern Democrats could now join Republicans to form a majority coalition, the prospects for maintaining New Deal social programs, let alone expanding them, appeared dim.

The expectations for legislation that would integrate the veterans of World War II into American society, however, remained far brighter. Following Roosevelt's fireside chat on veterans' benefits in July and his two addresses to Congress in October and November, more than two dozen bills had been introduced into the House and the Senate, ranging from mustering-out pay to educational assistance to unemployment compensation. However, none of these bills emerged as more likely to pass than the others. Preoccupied with winning the war, the president seemed content to allow the Democratic congressional leaders, Sam Rayburn (D-Texas) and John McCormack (D-Massachusetts) in the House and Alben Barkley (D-Kentucky) in the Senate, to move the veterans' agenda in a decisive direction. A bipartisan consensus existed to do something for the GIs. What benefits they would receive was not yet clear.

Enter the American Legion. Founded in 1919, the organization aspired to speak for all American war veterans. By 1940, it boasted more than one million members, far more than its competitors, the Veterans of Foreign Wars and the Disabled American Veterans. Many members of Congress on both sides of the aisle were active members of the organization. In December 1943 the American Legion stole a march on the VFW, which five months earlier had called attention to delays in treating soldiers with disabilities. Releasing the results of a nationwide survey to 1,537 veterans, the legion's national commander, Warren Atherton, charged that "jurisdictional bickering," "official red tape," and "just plain official incompetence and indifference" meant that blind, paralyzed, and paraplegic soldiers were waiting three to eight months between the filing of compensation claims and the initial payment.[1] Atherton demanded that by Christmas Congress provide mustering-out pay for every discharged serviceperson and that the VA eliminate bottlenecks in payments to soldiers with disabilities, enlarge hospital bed capacity, and hire additional trained personnel.[2]

To enlist public support, American Legion leaders joined forces with the national newspaper chain of William Randolph Hearst, an outspoken critic of Roosevelt and the New Deal. The *Chicago American*, the *Boston American*, and the *New York Journal American* assigned correspondents full time to the controversy over America's "unwanted battalion" and commissioned cartoonists to expose the "Shame of a Nation." Daily editions of Hearst papers supplied readers with clip coupons urging their representatives in Congress to act. And Hearst turned loose his editorial cannons. On January 12, 1944, the *Journal American* blasted "procrastinators" in Congress for failing to meet the Christmas deadline: "There is nothing to DEBATE about, nothing to BARGAIN about, nothing to justify a further WASTE OF TIME." Why make veterans "bear the brunt of the New Deal Administration's sole economy?" opined the *Journal American*'s editors less than a month later.[3]

Blowing the whistle on the neglect of soldiers who had incurred disabilities burnished the legion's credentials as the champion of World War II veterans—and emboldened officers of the organization to push for comprehensive legislation for GIs in the postwar world. As he released the results of the legion's survey of veterans with disabilities, Atherton appointed a committee to draft a master plan for the demobilization, rehabilitation, and reintegration of the more than 15 million World War II service personnel. Democrat John Stelle, a former Illinois governor who had ties to the Roosevelt administration, served as chairman. Other members included past national commander Harry Colmery of Topeka, Kansas; Sam Rorex of Little Rock, Arkansas, a U.S. attorney; W. B. Waldrip, of Detroit, Michigan, a banker; and R. W. McCurdy, of Pasadena, California, vice chairman of the legion's National Rehabilitation Committee. By "raising enough hell right now," one legion official wrote, the organization could extend the claims of the disabled to able-bodied veterans, keep the pressure on Congress, and prevent the passage of one bill from diminishing support for the others.[4]

Though committee members had been working on GI benefits for months, they began formal deliberations on December 15, 1943. Much of the work fell to Colmery. A graduate of Oberlin College and the University of Pittsburgh Law School, Colmery had served as an instructor and a pursuit pilot in the Army Air Service while stationed in Texas during World War I. A successful attorney who specialized in contracts, insurance, and business law, Colmery was a staunch Republican who had served as a delegate to the GOP National Convention in 1936 and as chairman of the Willkie War Veterans National Committee in 1940. But his greatest love, except for his college sweetheart, Minerva Hisertodt, and their three children, was the American Legion, which he had served virtually full time since 1937.[5]

Drawing on pending legislation, the recommendations of the Osborn Committee on Postwar Educational Opportunities for Service Personnel, the American Council on Education, the National Education Association, and conversations with leaders in the House and the Senate, Colmery stitched together an "omnibus bill." Members of Congress and the administration may have been most concerned about the dangers of massive unemployment among veterans, but the American Legion committee cast its argument largely in terms of what the nation owed to the men and women it had trained in the art of destruction and put in harm's way. Every veteran, John Stelle proclaimed, would return home handicapped in some way: "It might be a physical handicap, or an educational handicap, and generally it would be an economic handicap." The government must "take them back sympathetically, away from the horrors and stark reality of war and give them every opportunity to become disciplined forces for progress."[6]

Committee members insisted that benefits for World War II veterans should in all respects equal or exceed those granted to their World War I counterparts. One agency, the Veterans Administration, ought to assume responsibility for the entire program, which should help service personnel resume their civilian lives at the point at which induction had interrupted them. The war, the Legionnaires emphasized, had stopped "the normal development and growth of the skills and potential leadership" of the nation's most patriotic men and women. In contrast to the shabby treatment accorded the doughboys, the American Legion's bill gave veterans "a decent break, a chance to stand on their feet and be master of their own fate," work out their own plans of life, and not have to sit and wait for a pension check for the rest of their lives."[7]

Cartoon from the front page of the *National Legionnaire*, January 1944. Priorities changed dramatically soon after the publication of this image, which places a limited educational goal near the end of the list, and makes no mention of loans for homes, farms, or businesses. Muster-out pay, the first item listed, was enacted by Congress as a separate measure before passage of the comprehensive GI Bill. (Courtesy American Legion Library)

The organization proposed six categories of veterans' benefits:[8]

1. To ensure that veterans' claims were processed expeditiously, all soldiers should be informed of their rights before they were discharged. Funds were provided to construct hospitals and other rehabilitation facilities. To expedite care, especially for GIs with nervous disorders and tuberculosis, the Veterans Administration would have priority second only to the War and Navy departments in requisitioning building materials.

2. To ease the transition from military to civilian life, service personnel would receive mustering-out pay of up to $500, depending

on length of service. As the Stelle Committee knew, a Gallup poll indicated that 88 percent of Americans supported a lump-sum payment for every veteran, and the administration supported similar legislation with a maximum of $300 to be remitted in monthly installments. The U.S. Senate had unanimously passed a mustering-out bill on December 17, 1943, but the Military Affairs Committee of the House of Representatives had recessed for Christmas without taking action.

3. To assist veterans who wished to resume their education, the Stelle Committee borrowed key provisions of a bill proposed by Elbert Thomas (D-Utah), a former political science professor, staunch New Dealer, and chairman of the Committee on Education and Labor in the Senate. Under the plan, veterans whose education or training had been interrupted by induction into the armed services, who had served for at least nine months, and who had been honorably discharged would be entitled to one full year of benefits. The Veterans Administration would pay tuition and fees of as much as $300 to educational institutions. Single full-time students would receive $50 per month as a subsistence allowance; married students would receive $75. After a year, the VA might grant three more years of financial aid to students with "exceptional ability or skill."

4. Although armed services personnel had been paid far less than civilians who worked in the defense industry during World War II, the American Legion did not endorse adjusted service compensation. Instead, the organization's bill provided government-backed loans to veterans who wanted to purchase homes, farms, or businesses, while the states and the VA would share the costs. For homes, the program was authorized to underwrite a bank loan of 95 percent of the appraised value, with $7,500 as the maximum. For farms the ceiling was $12,500. In no case could the interest rate exceed 6 percent. To make certain that financially strapped states did not impede the flow of funds to needy veterans, the bill allowed the VA to advance the entire amount, and the states would be required to supply their share by July 31, 1949.

5. The American Legion placed all activities related to employment under the purview of the Veterans Administration. The Veterans Employment Service, established in 1933, was thus transferred to the VA. In an attempt to weaken the U.S. Employment Service, the legion mandated de facto control by the states.

6. Finally, the American Legion authorized payment to unemployed veterans of up to $25 a week for a maximum of fifty-two weeks. The VA was empowered to deny benefits to former GIs who participated

in strikes, were suspended or fired from jobs for misconduct, failed to accept suitable work, or refused to attend training sessions designed for them.

Although the legion's omnibus bill would be rather substantially modified before Roosevelt signed it, many of its essential features remained intact. Supporters lauded the legislation for opening up "such opportunities as the nation's fighting men of all other wars never dared to imagine in their fondest flights of fancy." The bill conferred benefits on more people than had any New Deal measure, including Social Security. The legion upped the ante on mustering-out pay, opened the door to funding higher education for four years, and even flirted with a weekly unemployment stipend of $35 a week. Subcollege training and loans for homes, businesses, and farms were designed to help millions of men and women enter the middle class. The benefits would be costly, Warren Atherton acknowledged, but constituted "a sound investment. If we can spend hundreds of billions to wage war, we should be able to spend a few billions to make that war worth winning for those who [will] win it."[9]

In some respects, Suzanne Mettler has pointed out, the bill was not an extension of New Deal largesse. "Unless something is done soon in the legislation of returning soldiers," Harry Hopkins, Roosevelt's aide, had warned the president, "the opposition may steal the thunder." And to a considerable extent, the Legionnaires, some of them implacable opponents of the New Deal, did indeed fill a political vacuum created by the election of 1942, the demise of the NRPB, and Roosevelt's role as "Dr. Win-the-War." The president had taken the initiative in 1943, and in several provisions of the omnibus bill, as well as amendments added to it, a New Deal agenda is readily apparent. At the same time, we can be sure that Harry Colmery and company did not see their proposals as catalysts for expanding federal domestic programs for all Americans. The American Legion's legislation was aimed exclusively at the citizen-soldiers of World War II and would grant benefits to them regardless of whether they went abroad or fired a gun in anger. The bill was self-liquidating, not open ended, and veterans were required to use its provisions within a few years of discharge. In addition, it was hostile to federal government bureaucracies (except for the VA) and to interference with state's rights.[10]

Members of the Stelle Committee envisioned the legislation more as a safety net (and a return to the prewar status quo) than a stepladder. In other words, GIs, Colmery maintained, "should be aided in reaching that position which they might normally have expected to achieve had the war not interrupted their careers." In important ways, the American Legion was fighting the last (post)war. Expecting veterans to return to an economy with high unemployment and inflation, they conjured up images of social unrest, as Roosevelt had, with uniformed men standing in breadlines or on street corners, selling apples, and a new generation of bonus marchers descending on the nation's capital. Many Americans agreed. In a Gallup poll released in July 1944 almost 50 percent of respondents anticipated that 7–20 million of their fellow citizens would be jobless when the war ended, some 14–34 percent of the civilian workforce. Labor Department projections were similar, with worst-case scenarios of an unemployment rate of about 25 percent. For this reason, the American Legion opposed "the outright demobilization of those in service unless a proper job is awaiting them upon their discharge." Moreover, they were willing to use government resources, albeit temporarily, to provide veterans—and American society—a soft landing.[11]

Some supporters of the omnibus bill sought to prevent New Dealers from using soldiers' benefits as a springboard for social reform. "The thing we have to fight down," Republican congressman Bertrand Gearhart declared, "is the crafty effort of so many different groups to use the war for the reorganization of the world."[12] Agreeing with Gearhart's viewpoint was J. Bennett Clark, a senator from Missouri and a founder of the American Legion. "I have never seen the veterans' organizations of the United States so much wrought up, as unanimous, and as bitter," he wrote, as they were over "the proposal to take a simple matter of veterans' rehabilitation and pitchfork it into a general scheme of social rehabilitation affecting all of the people of the United States."[13]

These barbs had been aimed at the now defunct NRPB, but anti–New Dealers were also concerned about augmenting the power of the Department of Labor and the U.S. Office of Education, both going concerns. In preparing the bill's sections on job placement and unemployment insurance, the Stelle Committee relied on Stanley Rector, chairman of the legislative committee of the Interstate Conference of Employment Security Agencies and a militant foe of "federalizing" labor policy. The omnibus bill "should be labeled plainly for what it is," Rector advised, "namely a temporary program of definite duration to meet the special problems of a special group." He pushed for a five-year time eligibility limit for unemployment compensation, a "system of disqualifications designed to give teeth to the work test," and investigations to make sure that claimants were trying to get jobs. "Otherwise," Rector concluded, "any system of liberal allowances may well be perverted into a pension system or extended furlough pay system."[14]

Equally dangerous was the prospect of expanding federal control over higher education. Given the likelihood of government subsidies that would permit millions of veterans to get undergraduate, professional, and graduate degrees, historian and social critic Bernard DeVoto predicted in the May 1943 issue of *Harper's Magazine* that Congress might create a federal bureau of education empowered to dictate curricula and pedagogy and perhaps even to influence admissions and the hiring of faculty. "The power to subsidize, they say, is the power to destroy." If big government called the shots, DeVoto concluded, colleges and universities would "gradually lose their autonomy."[15]

Sharing this concern, Harry Colmery bypassed the U.S. Office of Education in his bill. "It was not even a matter of five or ten minutes, or even a day, in working that out." In addition, the American Legion declined to support pending education bills in the House and the Senate. The House bill, drafted by Graham Barden (D-North Carolina), was particularly dangerous because it used the vague—and expandable— term "war service person" to describe beneficiaries. Barden's bill, Governor Stelle suggested, would create in the director of War Service Education and Training a "federally controlled Little Caesar, with absolute power over the destinies of our state schools." Americans were on the verge of handing over the future of the nation's armed forces and the next generation of young men and women to a higher education "bureaucrat" who would be empowered to "take any measures he finds necessary" to train veterans.[16] Samuel Rosenman may have been correct in detecting a plan to expand the federal role in American education in Roosevelt's October 1943 message to Congress. The American Legion and some of its allies in Congress were determined to prevent just such a perversion.

Legion leaders deemed it essential to grant the Veterans Administration exclusive jurisdiction over GI benefits. After all, the package was "temporary and exclusively for veterans." As the Osborn Committee had acknowledged, shunting GIs from agency to agency made little sense. With Frank Hines as VA director, moreover, "crackpots, long-haired professors, and radicals" were unlikely to influence policy. A veteran of the Spanish-American War and the Filipino insurrection, Hines had been appointed head of the agency by Warren Harding. However, his penchant for pinching pennies was more reminiscent of Calvin Coolidge. Dubbed the "bald-headed fox from Utah" for his canny command of the poker table, Hines traveled to work by bus and stayed in the office from seven in the morning to six at night. Petrified that extravagant experiments for veterans might trigger another Economy Act, Hines could be counted on to tread cautiously and oppose any measure to extend benefits to civilians.[17]

The American Legion released its bill to the public on January 8, 1944. Recognizing that legislation titled "the Omnibus Veterans' Relief Bill" or "the Serviceman's Readjustment Act of 1944" had "all the political sex of a castrated mule," Jack Cejnar, the legion's acting publicity director, suggested "a Bill of Rights for GI Joe and GI Jane"—and then the catchier "GI Bill of Rights." To millions of Americans, journalist David Camelon has written, "to the parents, wives, sweethearts and friends of the veterans, and to the veterans themselves, it was the GI Bill of Rights—then and ever afterward."[18]

On January 14 Atherton and Stelle spent forty-five minutes at the White House explaining the provisions of the bill to Roosevelt. The president expressed support for a package of benefits for veterans but did not endorse the legion's bill, perhaps because he did not want to antagonize the authors of other measures. By the winter of 1943–1944, moreover, Roosevelt was not well. In March he would be diagnosed with congestive heart failure. He was, no doubt, already conserving energy for meetings to plan the Normandy invasion and for postwar conferences with Churchill and Stalin. This was not the time—or the place—to spend his political capital. Without the president's "general blessing," historian Davis Ross has concluded, no GI bill would have passed. Once the American Legion bill was introduced into Congress, however, Roosevelt let legislators work their will.[19]

The legion, however, conducted a massive public relations campaign. "We didn't organize the American Legion to be a savings bank for a last man's club," Atherton exclaimed. "The best way to use every dime in our treasury is in the assistance to the veterans coming out of this war." Department commanders and adjutants in 12,000 posts and 9,500 auxiliary units distributed petitions, cards, letters, and telegrams that urged Congress to pass the bill. Hearst helped by assigning three savvy journalists to the legion. Roy Topper of the *Chicago American* handled promotion. David Camelon of the *New York Journal American* prepared feature stories, and the *Boston American*'s Frank Riley canvassed members of the House of Representatives and the Senate, recording their attitudes on a huge chart that ran the length of the room from floor to ceiling in the American Legion's Washington offices at 1608 K Street NW. One observer dubbed the operation "the most powerful lobby that has ever been organized."[20]

The lobbyists stressed the sacrifices soldiers had made and warned of the consequences of inaction. "Have you ever looked at the eye of a boy who has been in the front line, who really has witnessed the glare of a sub-machine gun which he carried?" Governor Stelle asked. Battle hardened veterans—boys who had been taught to kill—would soon return to the heartland, "millions of them, to walk your streets of Lafayette, Bloomington, Chicago," and "God knows what will happen" if, like the boys of 1920, they were forced to "sell shoestrings or apples." Veterans of World War I and "you mothers who have boys," Stelle asserted, must demand that their elected representatives see to it that this time the GIs make a smooth transition to civilian life. Only then could everyone be certain that "we will have a peaceful nation."[21]

More than four hundred radio spots and dozens of motion picture "trailers" prepared by the American Legion and sometimes narrated by wounded soldiers, sailors, or marines sang the praises of a "Magna Carta" for veterans based on rights they had earned "the hard way—in the training camps, on the battlefields, and in the hospitals." These GIs did not want "gratuities." "They want only what is justly due them." The legion's package of benefits was the least a grateful country could do for those who had "borne the brunt of a score of Pearl Harbors, Salernos, and Tarawas."[22]

Although almost one million soldiers had already been demobilized, the legion pointed out, the Veterans Administration was "still on a peacetime basis, kicked around like a stepchild, while other government agencies are competing for the right to look after various interests of the veterans." Those with disabilities were getting "shabby, indifferent, and lax treatment." Since political demagogues were using "the veteran problem" to feather their own nests—and more than a thousand GIs were getting discharged each day—time was running out. Congressional dithering "piles on added misery to brave hearts already wrung by the tortures of war." Telephone, telegraph, or write right now, the promos prodded, "and you will have the thrill of reversing the usual order for once and reporting to our fighting forces: MISSION ACCOMPLISHED!"[23]

Already substantial, support for veterans was growing. Nonetheless, GI Bill sponsors knew the devil was in the legislative details and worked to build momentum for quick passage. The agreement of a House-Senate conference committee in late January on a mustering-out bill helped. Congress provided $200 for all military personnel and $300 for anyone who had served overseas—far less than the $500 Warren Atherton had demanded. The legislation, Davis Ross has noted, left the American Legion in an enviable position: It could claim paternity for mustering-out pay and remove it from the omnibus bill, while reserving the right to join Congressman William Lemke (R-North Dakota) in chastising Congress for being "too peanutish" with veterans when "America's generosity was on trial."

Through luck and lobbying, the GI bill received the most favorable committee assignments. Deluged by postcards and petitions from legion members, the House Rules Committee chose the World War Veterans Legislation Committee, chaired by John Rankin (D-Mississippi) over the Invalid Pensions Committee, chaired by John Lesinski (D-Michigan) and the Military Affairs Committee, chaired by Andrew May (D-Kentucky), which had been slow to act on mustering-out pay.[24]

A lawyer and World War I veteran, John Rankin came to the House of Representatives in 1921 and became chairman of the Veterans Committee ten years later. A "little man with bushy hair and a Hallelujah voice," he quickly established a reputation for white supremacist, anti-Semitic, anti-Communist, xenophobic, and union-baiting bombast. During World War II, he lambasted a proposal that the American Red Cross abandon the practice of labeling blood to indicate whether it came from black or white donors as a conspiracy by "the crackpots, the Communists and parlor pinks...to mongrelize the nation." Although he cosponsored the bill that created the Tennessee Valley Authority, Rankin was no friend of the New Deal, but he was a champion of veterans of the armed forces. He led the (unsuccessful) 1935 fight to override Roosevelt's veto of the bill for cash payment on World War I veterans' bonus certificates. In 1942 he introduced legislation to increase the base pay of soldiers from $21 a month to $50. Rankin's racist rants masked a mastery of House rules.[25]

Edith Nourse Rogers (R-Massachusetts), the ranking Republican on Rankin's committee, was equally enthusiastic about veterans' benefits. A volunteer in hospitals in Europe and the United States for the YMCA and the Red Cross during World War I, Rogers became known as "the Angel of Walter Reed." Elected to fill the House seat of her deceased husband in 1925, she asked to be assigned to the Committee on World War Veterans Legislation. Rogers sponsored bills to construct a network of hospitals for veterans throughout the United States and to create a Nurses Corps in the Veterans Administration. She would not refuse to "spend more money," she told her constituents, "when I know that people need it." In 1941 she introduced legislation to establish the Women's Army Auxiliary Corps (WAAC) and guaranteed women the same pay as members of the "regular" army. Rogers reflected—and reinforced—bipartisan support for the GI bill.[26]

In the Senate, the GI bill was referred to the Finance Committee's Subcommittee on World War Veterans Legislation, chaired by J. Bennett Clark (D-Missouri). The son of a former Speaker of the House, "Champ" Clark had opposed America's entry into World War I but then enlisted, attained the rank of colonel, and, as chairman of an organizational meeting in France, helped found the American Legion. Elected to the Senate in 1932, Clark opposed many New Deal measures. An isolationist until the Japanese attacked Pearl Harbor, he opposed the repeal of neutrality legislation and voted to restrict military spending and limit the president's power to initiate hostilities. When Roosevelt shifted control over federal patronage in Missouri to Clark's rival, Harry Truman, the Champ's influence declined. He eagerly embraced an opportunity to burnish his image—and flex his muscles—by shepherding the GI bill through the Senate.[27]

Conducted in January, February, and March, hearings in the House and the Senate committees revealed virtually unanimous support for aid to veterans. They demonstrated as well that no one, including the drafters of the GI Bill, knew which benefits soldiers would use, how many would use them, or how much the legislation would cost, and their guesses ranged from $3.5 billion to $10 billion. Witnesses, congressmen and -women, and senators tended to overestimate the number of GIs likely to request unemployment insurance and underestimate the number of soldiers who would enroll in education and training programs. This uncertainty gave New Deal Democrats an opportunity to expand benefits. As the GI Bill raced toward a final vote in each chamber of Congress, they would slip under the radar of politicians determined to ensure that federal largesse to veterans was an exception that proved the rule: that social welfare programs tended to subvert freedom and individual initiative. If the New Dealers had their way, Senator Alexander Wiley of Wisconsin warned, the GI Bill would become a Trojan horse: "The Federal Government was liable to use this as an opportunity to open up the whole scope of Federal jurisdiction."[28]

As the hearings got under way, sponsors of the GI Bill scrambled to mollify the Veterans of Foreign Wars, the Military Order of the Purple Heart, the Disabled American Veterans, and the Regular Veterans Association, which had all felt upstaged by the American

Legion. Omar Ketchum, the legislation representative of the VFW, which had been working on a veterans' education bill with the American Legion in November 1943, reminded senators that the legion had no monopoly on concerns for GIs. The omnibus bill, he claimed, was not "a miraculous cure-all which has suddenly been discovered." On February 16 officers of the four organizations wrote a stinging letter to Senator Clark and Congressman Rankin, in which they complained that "everything that glitters is not gold." The nation's first responsibility was to veterans who had sustained physical and psychological injuries. Legislation as costly as the Servicemen's Readjustment Act might well "jeopardize the entire structure of veterans' benefits and provoke another Economy Act."[29]

Six days later Millard Rice, national service director of the Disabled American Veterans, sent the committee chairs an even blunter assessment. The omnibus bill, Rice snorted, "is more appropriately described as ominous." It would necessitate a vast bureaucracy, interfere with states' rights, and generate a "revulsion of feeling" among taxpayers. Rice considered the unemployment provision particularly odious. Paid to GIs even if they had served only three months, the legislation rewarded "the lazy and chisely types." Simple justice dictated that Congress address the needs of veterans with disabilities before considering, let alone conferring, any other benefits on World War II personnel.[30]

The American Legion's competitors preferred a bonus that would be based on length of service. This approach, they emphasized, minimized administrative costs. However, when they introduced a bill in March, they overreached in specifying a maximum payment of $5,000 per individual, at a cost of $25–$30 billion, many times the projected cost for the GI Bill. The American Legion commanders breathed a sigh of relief. There would be no bonus bill. By then, moreover, they had secured the support, albeit grudging, of the VFW. Millard Rice continued to take potshots at the "mis-named GI Bill of Rights," but a potential obstacle to passage had been removed.[31]

The House and Senate committees turned to the specific provisions of the legislation and devoted most of their attention to unemployment compensation and education and training. The exchanges, especially in the House, reflected an animus against the federal government, as well as appropriations for poor or jobless citizens. Apoplectically opposed to any legislation that would grant African Americans in his state an unemployment stipend equal to that of whites, Rankin feared that the GI bill might make it easy for millions of men "to get on Federal relief, which we call unemployment compensation." He preferred a lump sum to assist recently discharged veterans until they found work. His plan, he boasted, would not reward shirkers or make it possible for a farmer in Mississippi, struggling to make $50 a month, to "see his neighbor, who was in the same company with him, down on the creek fishing at $100 a month." One-time adjusted service compensation would not require additional government personnel, while unemployment allowances "would probably turn loose on this country a swarm of bureaucrats that would almost equal the locusts of Egypt."[32]

In even more colorful language, Rankin defended administrative jurisdiction of the provision for loans to help GIs purchase homes, businesses, and farms from being turned over to the Federal Housing Administration. He strongly supported the notion that "a man ought to be able to own his own home from the ground to the sky" and advocated raising the maximum loan guarantee. But the FHA, Rankin announced, mocking Roosevelt's rhetoric, had "virtually said one-third of the ill-fed and ill-clothed ought to live in Government houses." Nor had he forgotten that, during the Great Depression, the New Deal Department of Agriculture had issued the "uneconomical, unsound, discouraging, dishonest, and immoral" order to farmers to plow up their cotton and kill their pigs. Rankin did not want "any such agency as that trying to go out and teach our farmers to milk ducks or try to teach the people to live in trunks. I want these men to invest in the kind of homes they want; if they want to put the smokehouse in the kitchen that is their business."[33]

A coalition of Republicans and southern Democrats agreed. Fearing that the Senate would accede to the demand of Robert F. Wagner (D-New York) to assign the veterans' job-placement responsibilities to the U.S. Employment Service, they rang alarm bells against centralization and New Deal bureaucracies. If, as many suspected, the economy plunged into a recession in 1946, Errett Scrivner (R-Kansas) predicted that Americans might say, "All right. We have done it for those men in uniform, and they are not entitled to any more than anybody else, and therefore let us give these benefits to everybody else."[34]

Colmery, who had written a draft of the GI Bill on the back of "Alfred Landon for President" stationery, addressed these concerns by assuring House members that the legislation would not give big-government liberals a foot in the door. To make sure that unemployment compensation did not serve as a precedent, he had refused "to throw it into the Federal Security System" and placed a time limit on benefits so that taxpayers did not give veterans "anything except a chance to get back to the place they otherwise would have been."[35] "You are making a contrast," Colmery told his colleagues, "between the indolent and lazy man and the self-reliant man who has fought for his country" and "doesn't want to live on his country." Workers who had never served in the armed forces (and augmented their skills, salaries, and security during the war) were entitled to unemployment compensation under ordinary circumstances. Did GIs not deserve at least as much? "These men are going to be the greatest bunch of individualists that this country ever had." When Rankin implied that anyone might game the system, Colmery countered, "I have not lost confidence in them."[36]

Like unemployment compensation, education and training benefits in the GI Bill were designed in no small measure to mitigate the impact of postwar recession or depression without breathing new life into the New Deal. Education facilitated economic readjustment for individual veterans and society in general, Warren Atherton argued. In all likelihood, millions of demobilized soldiers would not find work "tomorrow, next week, or the week after." As some of them took time off to complete their education, pressures on the job market would ease. Atherton did not want to make educational provisions a "sinecure," with too many using them "just to sit around." Moreover, Colmery fretted as well about authorizing "a vast scheme of education" without any relationship to the veterans' academic ability. Benefits that were "too liberal," he suggested, might result in a backlash.[37] The hearings consequently focused on eligibility for education and training. Should the benefit be conferred only on those whose education had been interrupted? Should every veteran—or only those under twenty-five—be eligible for four years of higher education? After one year, should government officials in the VA or the U.S. Office of Education select the best students in fields (like engineering) where shortages were anticipated—and authorize them to complete undergraduate, professional, or graduate degrees?

Legislators assumed that enrollments depended on economic conditions. If jobs were scarce, GIs might go to school. Nonetheless, virtually no one predicted a flood of applications. In September 1943 Edith Jones, president of the National Education Association, had reminded the national convention of the American Legion that not all that many veterans had the requisite qualifications for college. About 25 percent of World War II GIs, she reported, had completed high school. Another 14 percent had attended or finished college. A U.S. Army survey conducted at the same time found that only 7 percent of enlisted men intended to apply. In December 1944, six months after he had signed the GI Bill, Roosevelt believed "hundreds of thousands" might matriculate. Frank Hines put the number at 700,000, distributed over several years. And as late as March 1945 Earl McGrath, a dean at the University of Buffalo and later U.S. Commissioner of Education, opined that GIs wanted to get a job and a wife and start a family as soon as possible. Many of them would take short vocational training courses, but "in no academic year will more than 150,000 be full-time students in colleges and universities."[38] "The vast majority of the men who are fighting this war never saw the inside of a college and probably never will," Rankin declared.

Moreover, that was not at all a bad thing from his perspective. Colleges had become "denaturing institutions," with professors teaching young men and women "how to select the right spoon, or drive ducks, or things like that." Nonetheless, as long as the federal government did not hold a "club" over colleges and universities "for the purposes of control," Rankin believed veterans deserved "just as much training as if they were going to Harvard and studying all the sociology and other ologies that might be afforded to them."[39]

An exchange during the Senate hearings captured politicians' thinking out loud about an educational entitlement. Senator Clark asked W. E. Givens, executive secretary of the National Education Association, whether the government should offer tuition and a living stipend for four years of college to every veteran:

DR. GIVENS   "If they want it."

SENATOR ERNEST MCFARLAND (D-ARIZONA)   "You mean, if they need it."

SENATOR CLARK   "I have a boy in the Marines who is 20 years old, who was a senior at the University of Missouri studying journalism."

DR. GIVENS   "He will not want it, will he?"

SENATOR CLARK   "There is no rhyme or reason to say he is entitled to four years, that the Government should send him to school for four years more. He can go ahead and get an A.B., an A.M., and possibly a Ph.D. and several other things in four years, but I do not think he is entitled to that."

DR. GIVENS   "I believe, Senator, a boy who has offered his life to defend his country and who desires further training, I think that is the best investment the Government could make. I do not think your boy would need it. He probably will not need it, anyway."

SENATOR CLARK   "I want to give every boy that has been in the Army, the Navy, or the Marine Corps all possible opportunities."

DR. GIVENS "That is all we want."

SENATOR CLARK "At the same time I do not want to build up the idea of a kid living off the Government and going to school instead of going to work."[40]

These sentiments invited members of Congress to conclude that they might have their cake and eat it, too: offer education and training without incurring substantial costs because the vast majority of "the boys" would not "want it" or "need it." They gave Senator Ernest McFarland the opening for which he had been waiting. Born in Earlsboro, Oklahoma, in 1894, McFarland had served as a seaman second class in World War I. A rural school teacher, lawyer, county attorney, and member of the American Legion, he was elected to the Senate in 1940 in a stunning upset over twenty-eight-year incumbent Henry F. Ashurst. A progressive Democrat who advocated extending educational benefits and home and business loans to GIs as early as 1942, McFarland believed that the provisions in the omnibus bill were "not adequate." He worked closely with American Legion leaders on an ad hoc committee to strengthen the legislation and bided his time.[41]

On January 28, 1944, he introduced the amendment that earned him the right to claim the title "Father of the GI Bill." Endorsed by the American Legion, McFarland proposed to make education and training benefits available to virtually all returning veterans who had not been dishonorably discharged and had served for at least six months. Those who satisfactorily completed a first year and whose continued education would "contribute to the national welfare" would receive tuition and a living stipend for another three years. The monthly allowance, which was kept at a meager $50 per individual and was combined with the requirement that veterans would have to meet the high educational standards prevalent in colleges and universities, McFarland suggested, "will be quite a limitation." And so would the desire of GIs, single as well as married, to get on with their lives.

As a result, GIs would no longer have to prove that their education had been "interrupted." Defining—or deciding—whose education had been delayed or prevented, Colmery had testified, would be difficult. Would eligibility extend to young men and women who had dropped out of school because they knew they would be drafted and preferred to work for a while rather than start a new semester? What about those who had been forced by family circumstances to "interrupt" their education for a year or two—or were too poor to begin at all? Should education and training be denied to veterans whose outlook changed while they were in uniform and now wished to enter a new career or profession? No single term or concept covered these situations. The nation, Colmery concluded, had a "very compelling obligation" to take soldiers from "the horrors and stark reality of war" and provide them with the skills to flourish in "the peaceful pursuits of American life."[42]

Since virtually no one wanted to give a battalion of bureaucrats discretion over eligibility and almost everyone accepted Colmery's assurance that "their numbers will be curtailed," the Clark Committee adopted McFarland's amendment. With no fanfare and no revised estimate of costs, the lawmakers had moved beyond rehabilitation and readjustment and provided veterans an opportunity to make a fresh start.[43]

The full Senate passed the GI Bill unanimously on March 24. The House took until May 18, as colleagues wrangled with Rankin over the education and unemployment benefits. The compromise legislation, which also passed unanimously, assumed that all veterans under twenty-four at the time of induction had had their education "interrupted" and were eligible for education and training beyond the one-year minimum. Everyone else would have to provide evidence to qualify. Unlike the Senate measure, the House bill slashed the maximum duration for unemployment compensation from fifty-two to twenty-six weeks and created a new job placement division inside the Veterans Administration.[44]

Nonetheless, the GI Bill was not yet ready for Roosevelt's signature. The House-Senate conference committee appointed to resolve differences between the two bills agreed rather amicably on education and training and loans for homes, farms, and businesses. However, Rankin renewed his objections to unemployment compensation. Although both houses had granted states substantial discretion over eligibility and the size of monthly allotments for the "idleness benefit," he remained convinced that, given the Senate's "generous" provisions, a vast majority of the fifty thousand black veterans in Mississippi would remain unemployed for the whole year. The Congress of Industrial Organizations, Rankin fumed, was pushing unemployment compensation "for all it is worth" and "undoubtedly" would demand that benefits be extended. Despite charges by the American Legion that he was "stalling" and Clark's claim that resistance to compromise was "based entirely upon the hatred of certain Congressmen for the colored portion of our armed forces," Rankin dug in his heels. Clark's remarks, he shot back, came "with poor grace" from a senator who was taking up Congress's time during a war in a futile attempt "to harass the South over the poll tax issue." Accusing any Southern politician of "hatred for colored troops" was a "gross mis-statement." Rankin and his colleagues were willing to give blacks "justice as we have always done, but we are not willing to put them or any one else on a dole" or encourage idleness "by paying them $60 to $100 a month for twelve months to the exclusion of the industrious white veteran and the industrious colored veteran" who tried to earn their own living.[45]

Rankin pressed his demand that the Senate limit unemployment compensation to twenty-six weeks and locate job placement services in the VA rather than the U.S. Employment Service. He wanted educational benefits that would be granted to each GI to be subtracted from the unemployment compensation subsequently available to that veteran. Three congressmen on the conference committee, Augustine Kearney (D–New Jersey), A. Leonard Allen (D-Louisiana), and J. Hardin Peterson (D-Florida), were willing to accept the Senate's position. Two representatives, Paul Cunningham (R-Iowa) and Edith Nourse Rogers (R-Massachusetts) stuck with Rankin. The seventh member, John Gibson (D-Georgia) was ill and had returned to his district. Under congressional rules, a bill would die if a majority of the seven representatives from each house could not agree. On June 5 Gibson sent Rankin a telegram, granting him "full authority to cast such ballot as you think best." Two days later he had a change of heart and wired Rankin to record him "in favor of the Senate's unemployment version." Rankin refused to do so. Conference committee votes, he had now decided, had to be cast in person. The conferees, it appeared, might report to their respective houses that they were unable to agree.[46]

With a final vote scheduled for June 10, officers of the American Legion tried frantically to track Gibson down. It was not easy. Stymied by a five-hour delay on phone circuits between Washington, D.C., and the congressman's home in Douglas, Georgia, they used the telephone priority of the *Atlanta Constitution*. Nonetheless, Gibson was not at home. So the Legion broadcast bulletins on WSB in Atlanta and WGOV in Valdosta, asking listeners to contact Operator 2 with information about his "whereabouts," and enlisted the assistance of the Georgia Highway Patrol. When Gibson was finally located, returning home from a doctor's appointment, Legionnaire Clark Luke drove him to the Army Air Force Base in Waycross. No army plane was available, however, so Gibson was then hustled into an army car driven by Corporal Jack Hunter, a former Notre Dame track star. Escorted by Georgia police on motorcycles, Hunter raced through a storm at speeds approaching ninety miles an hour to deliver the congressman to Jacksonville, Florida, some 150 miles away. An Eastern Airlines commercial airliner, scheduled to depart for the nation's capital at 2:20 A.M., was waiting, kept on the ground by order of the airline's traffic manager. The plane landed at Washington National Airport at 6:37 A.M. Less than four hours later, Gibson broke the deadlock. Rankin, Cunningham, and Rogers then made it unanimous. Within a week, the House and the Senate had affirmed the revised bill.[47]

In its final form, the GI Bill appropriated $500 million for the construction of facilities for veterans, including hospitals; authorized unemployment compensation of $20 per week for a maximum of fifty-two weeks, with job placement services available under the U.S. Employment Service; provided up to four years of education and training at an annual tuition rate of as much as $500 (and a monthly stipend of $50 for single men and women and $75 for those with dependents) to GIs who had served at least ninety days, with the presumption that the schooling of all veterans who enlisted or were drafted before their twenty-fifth birthdays had been interrupted; and guaranteed 50 percent of farm, home, and business loans up to $2,000—much less than the maximum amount originally proposed by the American Legion—at an interest rate no higher than 4 percent.[48]

Roosevelt signed the bill on June 22, with most of the House-Senate conferees and representatives of the American Legion and the Veterans of Foreign Wars in attendance. In a bow to bipartisanship (and perhaps a swipe at Rankin and Clark), he handed the first pen to Edith Nourse Rogers. Speaking briefly at the signing, Roosevelt claimed paternity for a measure his administration had neither introduced to nor steered through Congress, noting at the outset that it "carried out most of the recommendations" he had made in three speeches to the nation in 1943.[49] More important, perhaps, was the president's notion of the core idea among the bill's various programs. To Roosevelt, this was neither educational opportunity nor government-guaranteed residential loans but the successful transition of millions of veterans from military service to civilian work. He singled out "satisfactory employment" as the most urgent need of service personnel and concluded that the GI Bill would help meet that need. It was for this reason, above all, that the bill delivered an "emphatic notice" to veterans "that the American people did not intend to let them down."[50]

The passage of the GI bill was, of course, covered by the popular press. However, the legislation did not receive editorial comment in the *New York Times, Washington Post, Baltimore Sun, Chicago Daily Tribune, Des Moines Register, San Francisco Chronicle*, or *Los Angeles Times*.

The White House signing ceremony competed with news about the allied invasion of Europe, which had occurred less than three weeks earlier. More important, along with the nation's politicians, journalists did not deem the bill "historic" or "iconic" but rather, as a writer for the *New Republic* put it, a largely temporary measure designed "to facilitate, as quickly as possible, the readjustment of veterans to civilian life." With the return of a robust economy, few GIs would request unemployment compensation and job placement. Provisions for education and training were "sound and generous," but at most, the *New Republic* predicted, 800,000–1,000,000 returning soldiers would use them.[51]

With an assist from veterans' organizations, the Veterans Administration scrambled to inform GIs of their rights. As they were discharged, soldiers and sailors received a VA pamphlet, *Going Back to Civilian Life*, and a *Handbook for Service Men and Service Women of World War II and Their Dependents*, which laid out the key provisions of the GI Bill. The American Legion distributed 2.7 million copies of *Gateway to Opportunity*, which contained capsule descriptions of all of the benefits, and a half million "Open Letter to GIs" folders, which reviewed the loan provisions.[52]

Nonetheless, a little more than a year after its enactment, the GI Bill seemed to be a disappointment, and its provisions underutilized or ineffective. Criticism of job placement services was virtually unanimous. "At the beginning of 1945," wrote Major General Graves Blanchard Erskine, director of the Retraining and Reemployment Administration of the U.S. Department of Labor, "it looked pretty much as though we had made a complete mess of the program which, next to getting home, meant most to America's fighting men." Jurisdictional disputes between the VA and the U.S. Employment Service (USES)—and conflict between the federal government, states, and localities—undermined the efforts of the VA and the American Legion to simplify the process of getting GI Bill benefits. Many veterans were not sure where to go for assistance. The staff of the USES, moreover, was no match for the herculean task they had been given. As late as 1946, the USES placed only twenty-eight GIs for every hundred who filed applications. Furthermore, many of them, critics charged, were offered low-paying, undesirable work. "This employment game isn't won yet for G.I. Joe," members of the Employment Committee of the American Legion reported to the National Executive Committee.[53]

Unemployment compensation came under fire as well. In an article in the *Ladies' Home Journal*, Henry Pringle argued, as Rankin had, that it was not wise "to set an identical scale, by Federal law, for village and city, farm and small town, in widely different areas of a big nation." Government handouts, Pringle wrote, encouraged veterans to game the system. Almost three hundred thousand GI farmers who had not yet marketed their crops were collecting allowances of up to $100 a month from Uncle Sam. Unpublished writers, a government official told Pringle, might well be entitled to unemployment compensation if they produced rejection slips: "It's not our function to say that a veteran is not qualified for the career he wants." In addition, "high rewards for doing nothing" prompted GIs to quit or be fired more often than civilian workers. The GI Bill was an invitation to idleness, one veteran proclaimed. "You apply for every job the USES refers you to, of course," wrote Pringle, "but you have a few beers on the way and then blow your breath in the boss' face. Or maybe you talk a little Red. He don't want you, naturally."[54]

These criticisms were potentially explosive since the main motivation of the GI Bill was the provision of jobs for veterans when they returned to civilian life. However, American free enterprise had come to the rescue by converting with surprising ease from a government-driven war economy to a consumption-based, peace-time economy. It was, as Roosevelt had predicted, the pent-up demand of fifteen years of depression and war in combination with widespread wartime personal saving that kept the economy from slipping back into depression. When wartime government controls on domestic production came to an end, long-deferred spending on automobiles, homes, and household appliances was unleashed, and many businesses actually expanded. There would be, after all, no wandering armies of unemployed veterans. Within six months of discharge, about 70 percent of veterans without disabilities had found full-time employment. Another 8.8 percent had regular work in less than a year. Thus, "52–20" and job placement services, which sponsors and supporters of the GI Bill, including Roosevelt, had thought its most essential provisions, would seem less pressing by the end of 1945 and more susceptible to criticism by those who feared bureaucracy and a federal dole.[55]

By almost all accounts, the legislation's loan provisions were a disaster. During the war, the construction of new residential houses had declined precipitously. Yearly housing starts, which had reached almost 937,000 during the Roaring Twenties, plummeted during the early years of the depression, rose gradually between 1934 and 1941, and then declined again to only 142,000 in 1944. With the army estimating that 41 percent of service personnel planned to purchase a home after demobilization, a housing crisis was imminent. To make matters worse, *American Legion Magazine* reported, "restrictions and red tape" had kept eligible veterans from closing deals. Of 208,000 private nonfarm homes built in 1945, only 6,000—fewer than 3 percent—were sold on VA mortgages. Veterans who were buying into the nation's preexisting housing stock with VA-backed loans in 1944 and 1945 numbered only thirty-seven thousand.[56]

Horror stories abounded. "Six months ago I was piloting a B-29 against the Japs," a veteran wrote to President Truman. "Now I am trying to build a home in my own home town. The first fight was easier.... A simple concrete unfurnished house of three rooms and bath would cost $8,500"—far more than the amount covered by the government guarantee. In a slashing exposé in *Collier's*, Frank Gervasi recounted the experience of Earl Eng, a bomber pilot who lived with his parents in Saint Paul after his discharge and then relocated to Chicago with his wife and baby. In the Windy City the Engs encountered "racketeering landlords" but continued to rent an apartment because even fairly modest homes were priced at $10,000. Bankers did not much care that Eng had fought fascism. Since he had not yet found a job, they deemed him a bad credit risk, leaving the young man "bitter, disillusioned, and angry." Millions of veterans faced the same problem. Frustrated at his inability to find a place to live, one GI had decided to reenlist: "The Army, at least, would shelter, clothe, and feed him." "If the government continued to temporize," Gervasi concluded, few veterans would have "any assurance of sound roofs over their heads and weather-proof walls around them for years to come."[57]

In 1945 shortages in construction supplies and inflated prices, as demand outstripped supply, seemed to stretch far into the future. The boom in marriages and babies, competition from civilians who had squirreled away savings during the war, and a series of work stoppages in the fall made the market even tighter. "You must remember," President Truman wrote, "that there isn't any possible way of waiving [*sic*] a wand and getting houses to spring up." These realities, wrote Henry Schubart, rendered "the limited" government home loan guarantees in the GI Bill "meaningless." Mrs. Samuel Rosenman, the chair of the National Committee on Housing, made an equally caustic assessment. Because of the $2,000 maximum set by Congress, she claimed, thousands of former soldiers "are being gypped with overpriced matchbox houses which won't last as long as their mortgages." They felt compelled to "mortgage their future," she added, because the GI Bill provided no benefits for renters.[58]

Even worse than the early returns on home loans were reports on the provisions for purchases of farms. "Most of the Congressmen who voted for the G.I. Bill," Harvard economists John Black and Charles Hyson had declared in November 1944, "were apparently not thinking very hard about the problem of helping ex-servicemen become farmers." The guaranteed loans would enable few ex-servicemen without substantial savings of their own to purchase family-sized farms. If any use was made of this "benefit," they concluded, "it will be to purchase small, cheap farms, mostly in the South, and in the poorer sections of other states." The GI-farmers would pay off their mortgages slowly, if at all, and "only if they are very prudent and thrifty, will they own the farms at the end of twenty years." When they added the specification for farm loans to the GI Bill, Black and Hyson speculated, members of the American Legion, the House, and the Senate may have thought subsistence farming a viable alternative for veterans if recession or depression settled over the country at the end of the war. Given current conditions, "servicemen seeking farms on which to support their families...will do well not to use the guaranteed loans in the GI Bill."[59]

Black and Hyson did not study any other provisions of the GI Bill, but they felt compelled to comment that the specifications for loans for GIs going into business were "even more tricky than for those going into farming." Since 52 percent of all new businesses failed within two years, Frank Hines acknowledged, government-backed venture capital for ex-servicemen, many of them inexperienced, was "hazardous." As a result, the Veterans Administration was extremely reluctant to encourage GIs to borrow money "to undertake any business venture which appears foredoomed to failure." Hines directed VA personnel to check character and credit references—and strictly enforce regulations against using loans to buy merchandise or to use as working capital.

The VA's tight-fisted policies, Frank Gervasi pointed out in another scathing critique in *Collier's*, included a tacit endorsement of the criteria bankers traditionally applied to loan applicants. Despite the good intentions of the GI Bill, character, educational background, ambition, and war record counted little or not at all. Those GIs who were without a credit history did not have much of a chance. To be sure, Gervasi wrote, many returning soldiers were asking for loans "to finance juke joints, hamburger heavens, tourist camps and other impractical ventures in which the birth rate is only decimals above the mortality rate." Still, the VA was throwing healthy babies out with the bathwater. As of June 15, 1945, VA officials had approved a grand total of 823 business loans, about four-tenths of 1 percent of the requests by veterans that reached their desks. By March 1946 the number was unlikely to exceed 3,000. During that period, moreover, fifty thousand GIs had started businesses without assistance from the government, most of them doomed to failure. Those GIs "who desire independence and a chance to be their own bosses" needed a lot more help than they were getting from the VA—or the GI Bill. Most of the VA staff members lacked expertise to give practical advice about equipment purchases, personnel, potential markets, private sources of funding, and long-term financing. "Obviously," Gervasi concluded, "the boost to our economy which the government had hoped would be provided by the influx of GI brain and brawn into small businesses simply hasn't materialized."[60]

Although job placement and loans brought the major fire from critics of the GI Bill, concerns about education and training were raised as well. Some observers joined Stephen Thompson of the *Baltimore Sun* in hailing the provision as "one of the most remarkable milestones in public education in America." The GI Bill, Thompson exulted, "not only paves, it literally carpets the way for every G.I. Joe and G.I. Jane." In the *New York Times*, journalist Edith Efron reveled as veterans stormed the academic beachheads previously reserved for children of privileged parents. With neither a colonel nor "a bomberater in sight," Efron wrote in August 1945, the New York University campus was "a thing of beauty" to the 1,957 GIs who had enrolled as full-time students. Indistinguishable from other undergraduates "save for the small golden eagle in their civilian lapels and a few tell-tale crow's feet around the eyes," the GIs were still "untensing" but were learning to love their newfound freedom. Furthermore, they were not at all self-conscious about enrolling at taxpayer expense. After all, a former sailor told Efron, "not too long ago we did something for Uncle Sam."[61]

Some educators, however, did not greet them with open arms. The GI Bill, thundered Robert Maynard Hutchins, president of the University of Chicago, was a "reckless" measure that "threatens to demoralize education and defraud veterans." Tens of thousands of demobilized soldiers will matriculate, Hutchins predicted, "only because they cannot get jobs." Because college and university administrators "cannot resist money," academic institutions might well find "themselves converted into educational hobo jungles" and degenerate into vocational training programs. Since industrial managers had simplified most industrial operations "to the point where they can be performed by a twelve year old," such programs were "education for slavery," unnecessary—and a waste of public resources. Even worse, the GI Bill was bound to encourage unscrupulous entrepreneurs to make their fortune by buying up "the charters of half a dozen bankrupt colleges."

Convinced that the "real danger" in the postwar era was "that college may be made so attractive that you may go there even if you should not," Hutchins recommended national examinations to identify GIs with the aptitude to succeed. The federal government, moreover, should advance no more than 50 percent of tuition to the veteran, while the colleges themselves would pay the balance (to ensure that they chose only the most qualified applicants). Higher education, Hutchins concluded, should not be used as "a substitute for the dole or for a national program of public works."[62]

Using somewhat less inflammatory rhetoric, James Bryant Conant, president of Harvard, worried about the consequences of basing educational opportunity on length of military service rather than "demonstrated ability." Given "sentimental pressures and financial temptation," Conant claimed, "we may find the least capable among the war generation, instead of the most capable, flooding the facilities for advanced education in the United States." Conant recommended that Congress revise the GI Bill by restricting access to "a carefully selected group" and confining the length and type of study "to the national educational deficit caused by the war."[63]

Hutchins and Conant could be dismissed as elitists. Nonetheless, they attracted the attention of the popular press. Moreover, many observers shared their conviction that veterans would make poor students. The GIs would use college as a stopgap, Major S. H. Kraines suggested, and be restless, rowdy, and ready to depart for greener pastures. Willard Waller, a professor at Columbia University, believed that "by and large, the veterans who should go to college are the same boys who ought to have gone if there had been no war." Many of the others, he stated, "are pitifully in earnest and try tragically hard, wearing shabby clothes, living in somebody's basement, eating a few cents worth of bread and milk and sometimes growing hungry while they beat their brains out trying to master college algebra or English. Others are aimless drifters with no purpose in life." If an ex-serviceman was in the top fifth of his high school class, Waller opined, he could probably do college work. "The second fifth is doubtful and the third fifth very doubtful indeed." Veterans, who have "lost so much time already," should not risk losing more "merely in order to live at Government expense." In addition, GIs who were married should recognize that the rhythm of college life "leaves little time for the enjoyment of domestic felicity." Even if they had outside income, college should be "almost out of the question" for GIs with babies. "For a great many veterans," Waller concluded, "the scales are heavily weighted against college attendance. They will do better to give up the idea."[64]

And it appeared that they had. After spending several weeks overseas talking with soldiers, Stanley Frank reported in the *Saturday Evening Post* that the GI bill had "only one conspicuous drawback. The guys aren't buying it." As of February 1, 1945, only 12,844 of the 1,500,000 discharged World War II veterans—less than 1 percent—had used the education benefit to enroll in a college or university. Army officials told Frank they were disappointed—"the understatement of the decade"— but insisted that this cohort was not typical. It included wounded soldiers and those who had left the armed forces because of physical or mental disabilities. When the war ended, they suggested, young, able-bodied veterans might be more responsive to higher education.

Frank found little justification for this optimism. The longer the war lasted, the more anxious soldiers would be to "make up potential wage earning time spent in the Army." Education, moreover, remained Americans' "favorite whipping boy, ranking one cut below fearless condemnation of wife-beating and the tax structure." Only 23 percent of U.S. troops, he maintained, had graduated from high school, and a mere 3.6 percent had college degrees. Those who returned from the front with "the swagger of survival" tended to look for "short cuts to self-advancement and happiness—manifest in hasty marriages." They had decided that "the four years reserved for sitting and thinking are too often largely devoted to sitting." Even though higher education could be a bridge to transport them from military to civilian life, Frank concluded, GIs would continue to reject it because it was "too slow, too uncertain, offering no tangible rewards."[65]

In his column "The Veteran" in the *New York Times*, Charles Hurd agreed that the educational benefit was not "realistic." Eager to settle, most GIs, Hurd implied, would opt for short, vocational courses of study rather than full-time, four-year degree programs, especially given the difficulty of housing and feeding themselves on $50 or $75 a month. Hurd did not argue that these allowances should be increased, but "they furnish another very good argument against the expectation that 600,000 to 1,300,000 veterans will be flooding the schools of higher education after the war."[66] Although the GI Bill was still ballyhooed by politicians and Veterans' Administration publications, Hurd asserted in March 1945, the legislation was now widely recognized to be "faulty, loosely drawn, and unrealistic...a make-shift piece of business that needs considerable revision." Warning of dire consequences if the "disillusion already being experienced by many veterans" spread to millions of GIs about to be discharged, Hurd lamented that no responsible group in or outside government was crafting legislation to address the bill's deficiencies.

Two months later Hurd was more encouraged. The Veterans of Foreign Wars and the American Legion, he reported, were pushing Congress to act, and committees in both houses were drafting amendments. While the bill's basic philosophy was sound, legislators understood that the loan provisions "simply have failed," the reemployment rights of veterans needed clarification, and the educational benefit did not cover the vast majority of discharged soldiers who wanted short and intensive training courses to prepare them for specialized jobs such as commercial photography. A "congenially workable" GI Bill was within reach. Failure to act, Hurd warned, would result in the "extension of demagoguery" in the name of the veterans; eventually there would be another bonus march on Washington.[67]

House and Senate committees held hearings during the summer and fall of 1945 that revealed how much the emphasis on the various provisions of the GI Bill had changed. With the economy absorbing most of the returning veterans, unemployment compensation had become far less controversial and job placement services less important. Legislators still sought ways to grant "seniority rights" to discharged GIs, but fears of massive joblessness, with soldiers selling apples on street corners, had receded. There would be no bonus march on Washington. Liberal legislators could now continue to redesign legislation, once intended to provide a safety net, into an engine of economic opportunity and social mobility. Conservatives remained concerned about costs and the growth of a federal bureaucracy. Paul Cunningham (R-Iowa) advocated leaving loan programs to bankers lest money be "poured down a rat hole" in overhead costs paid to the ballooning number of VA personnel. "What do you know about the value of homes in Des Moines?" he asked a VA official. "You do not know anything about them, any more than I know about them in Brooklyn, where you come from." However, the overriding concern of legislators across the ideological spectrum in 1945 was not that too many GIs were availing themselves of government largesse but too few—and the possibility that millions of disappointed veterans might take out their frustrations at the next election.[68]

The House hearings opened with testimony by Frank Hines. The unemployment allowance was working, the VA director claimed, while educational benefits and loans, "in my judgment, are going fast enough, but they are not as fast as some think they should go." Hines and his colleagues acknowledged that inflation had wreaked havoc with the cost of homes—and made administrators reluctant to certify that some asking prices were at "normal market value," as required by the GI Bill. The result, according to Omar Ketchum of the VFW, was that ex-servicemen "feel they have been sold down the river, that they were promised a loan and cannot get a loan." Although the VA was reluctant to endorse a substitution of the term "reasonable market value," fearing it would put veterans—and government-backed loans—at risk of default, a bipartisan consensus quickly developed around such a change.[69]

Farms and business loans presented far more intractable problems. With good-paying jobs readily available, farm income difficult to predict, and the number of family farms declining, veterans seemed uninterested in opting for life on the land, where the only certainty was hard work. Given inflation, moreover, few viable farms were on the market at reasonable prices. In Mississippi, much to Representative Rankin's regret, only eight GIs had applied for farm loans. In New York, twenty former servicemen had done so. The alternatives laid out by Farm Security administrator Robert Hudgens were grim: "We can say, 'sorry, no farm.' Or we can say, 'All right, we will lend you money, and we know you will be busted, but somebody will buy it after you are washed out, and he will get some security.' Or we can say, 'We will take your name and address. Come back in about ten years, and we will look you over.' "[70]

The maximum guarantee of $2,000 was inadequate for most business loans, witnesses told committee members. Still, they did not recommend a substantial increase because GIs lacked the skills to succeed as proprietors. Their "business prudence," Harold Breining of the VA testified, often was not equal to "their fighting ability." To date, only 535 GI Bill business loans had been granted throughout the nation. Gresham Griggs, director of the Community Advisory Center in Bridgeport, Connecticut, articulated the pervasive concern that the overwhelming majority of business loans were economically unsound. The veteran, Griggs believed, "hasn't the capital. He can take a job in that industry and learn something about it. He can go to night school.... I tell those boys that they shouldn't any more want to go into business with the equipment they have than they should want to fight Japs without training." Some witnesses recommended revising the GI Bill to allow veterans to use loans for working capital, as well as for purchases of buildings, equipment, and furnishings. Even so, virtually no one expected—or wanted—large numbers of veterans to avail themselves of the business loan provisions.[71]

Education and training, Griggs emphasized, "is worth a good deal more than the business loans or the home loans." Most members of Congress now seemed to agree. Shrugging off Rankin's testy request that his committee not "take all summer arguing about those fellows going to college and leaving out those nine-tenths" who want a job, they searched for ways to encourage veterans to take advantage of a benefit that was emerging as the principal pillar of the GI Bill. Noting that the measure had been "largely crucified by certain interested persons," A. Leonard Allen (D-Louisiana), a former teacher, principal, and superintendent, was "rather alarmed" that such a small percentage of ex-servicemen had gone back to school. Allen urged veterans' organizations to "hammer home" the message to GIs that education and training would enhance their lives, personally and professionally.[72]

Exhortation, they sensed, was not enough. So they revisited the "allowance" granted to full-time students. In 1944 Congress had set the stipend at $50 a month to discourage veterans from flocking to colleges and universities. Now, to boost enrollment, legislators considered a substantial increase. "You need have no fear," Ralph McDonald, an officer in the National Education Association, assured them, that with a grant of $80 a month (and an additional $20 for the first dependent and another $10 for each additional family member) the average veteran "will have any money left over for movies or luxuries."[73]

Educators also suggested ending the age limit on GIs assumed to have had their educations "interrupted." About 50 percent of the men and women in the armed forces, testified Francis Brown of the American Council on Education, were twenty-five or older when they were inducted. Since this cohort was deemed least likely to spend four years in a classroom, the consensus was that eliminating restrictions on their enrollment would increase applications by no more than 10 percent. Given the anemic response of veterans thus far, this estimate made a believer out of Congressman Allen. "In other words," he announced, "were we to strike out the age limitation entirely, we would eliminate a lot of worry that they have been having, and might not materially increase the burden of education on the government."[74]

Finally, witnesses recommended that Congress overrule the Veterans Administration directive that correspondence courses were ineligible from GI Bill benefits because students did not "attend" classes. However, when Errett Scrivner agreed that a veteran "cannot attend school any more through the mails than I could attend church through the mails," Congressman Cunningham demurred. "You might be able to attend church through the mails," he suggested presciently. And John Gibson, the self-proclaimed hero of the first GI Bill, had the last word: "It is totally unreasonable to exclude correspondence schools."[75]

In the waning days of 1945, the House and Senate agreed on substantial revisions to the GI Bill of Rights. The legislation, signed into law by President Truman, made no substantive changes in unemployment compensation or job placement. The new law based government-sponsored loans for the purchases of homes, farms, or businesses on an assessment of "reasonable value" instead of "reasonable normal value"—to account for inflation in the postwar era—and raised the limit on the guarantee for realty loans from $2,000 to $4,000. In addition, GIs could apply for these loans any time within ten years. The bill granted them up to twenty-five years to pay off home loans—and forty years to retire farm loans. Veterans could also use loans as working capital for the businesses or farms they purchased.

The most significant changes came in benefits for education and training. Congress extended the period at which a GI could begin a program of study from two to four years after discharge; lengthened the period during which benefits could be used from seven to nine years; dropped the requirement that soldiers over twenty-five prove their education had been "interrupted"; included correspondence courses in the education and training title; eliminated the stipulation that sums paid for education and training be deducted from future bonuses; and authorized the VA to pay the actual cost of education, up to $500 a year, if it exceeded tuition—a provision that allowed research universities, for example, to charge out-of-state tuition to in-state students. Finally, Congress raised subsistence allowances from $50 to $65 a month for unmarried veterans and from $75 to $90 a month for those with dependents.[76]

The GI Bill was now largely in place. The measure was a far cry from the temporary expedient that had been hastily cobbled together by the American Legion to ease the veterans' transition to an uncertain postwar American economy. As revised in 1945, it became an "opportunity" bill, although its benefits did not—and would not—extend from soldiers to civilian workers to citizens in general. Far from being the end-product of a grand design, the GI bill grew in fits and starts. The legislation drew on the reports commissioned by Roosevelt, was modified by opponents of "big government," and was then changed again by New Dealers and their allies. The bill had almost universal support because virtually everyone feared a repeat of the aftermath of

World War I and because virtually no one expected millions of GIs to trade their firearms and fatigues for caps and gowns.

Perhaps it was the 1945 amendments; perhaps the GI Bill just needed more time. Whatever the reasons, the disappointing early start to the bill's history quickly evolved into a substantial success. Between August 1945 (V-J Day) and New Year's Eve, 5.4 million soldiers and sailors were demobilized, double the number officials had predicted for the calendar year. Millions more donned their "civvies" the next year. These veterans would begin, almost immediately, to use their GI Bill benefits. On average they drew unemployment compensation for fewer than twenty weeks, and only 14 percent of them exhausted their maximum entitlement of fifty-two weeks. Over the next few years, however, 29 percent received government-backed loan guarantees, which enabled some 4 million vets to buy homes at low interest rates and 200,000 to purchase farms or businesses. Education and training became the great surprise of the GI Bill. A whopping 51 percent of GIs took advantage of this provision: Altogether 2.2 million attended college or university, and 5.6 million opted for subcollege training, usually in a short course or certificate program.[77]

Although scholars disagree about its inclusiveness and democratizing impact, the GI Bill was, without question, one of the largest and most comprehensive government initiatives ever enacted in the United States. A large majority of veterans who used it to buy homes or go back to school would say of it: "The GI Bill changed my life." And in the process of changing so many individual lives, it helped alter the institutional and physical landscapes of postwar America. The irony in this larger, less immediate result lies in the relation between the GI Bill—limited at first in focus and duration by congressional conservatives—and the more expansive agendas of New Deal liberals. Roosevelt did not live long enough to use this exclusive package of veterans' benefits to build support for more inclusive federal programs that would affect education, the workplace, home ownership, and the shape of American cities and towns. Nonetheless, the GI Bill did enable his successors—and the successors to John Rankin, Champ Clark, Ernest McFarland, and others who shaped the bill as it made its way through Congress—to apply the powers and resources of the federal government to all of these areas of American life with less controversy and less restraint. It might not be entirely accurate to say that the New Dealers had lost the battle but won the war, but the extent to which the lives of all Americans and not merely the nation's veterans were changed vindicated their fondest hopes.

FOUR

"SRO"

Veterans and the Colleges

Former GIs register *en masse* for college classes. (Courtesy Cornell University Press)

B Y THE SPRING of 1946, *Time Magazine* reported, it was "stand-ing room only" in many of the 2,268 universities, colleges, and junior colleges approved by the Veterans Administration as eligible for reimbursement under Title II of the GI Bill. Three hundred thousand World War II veterans had enrolled, more than three times the number of matriculants in the entire year of 1945. Millions more were on the way. In 1945, 88,000 of 1.6 million students were GIs. By 1947, 2.3 million men and women had enrolled in colleges and universities, 1.15 million of them veterans of World War II. The dilemma of administrators in higher education, wrote Milton MacKaye in the *Saturday Evening Post*, was akin to that of the family "who inherited a herd of elephants: where to put them.... The bitter tea of the educators is this: the dream of opportunity is at hand, and the colleges do not have the facilities, the housing, the instructors or classrooms to handle it."[1]

With a big assist from federal and state governments, institutions of higher education struggled to meet the challenge. The impact on American society and culture cannot be measured with precision, but by all accounts the investment in human capital made through the GI Bill yielded enormous dividends. Hundreds of thousands of Americans who otherwise would not have returned to school completed under-graduate and graduate degrees. Along with the GIs who would have resumed their education without the legislation, they added 450,000 engineers, 180,000 doctors, dentists, and nurses, 360,000 teachers, 150,000 scientists, 243,000 accountants, 107,000 lawyers, and 36,000 clergymen to the ranks of the nation's professionals. As this chapter demonstrates, the benefits fell disproportionately on white males. Nonetheless, although the GI Bill was, at best, a mixed blessing for women and African Americans, it clearly sustained postwar prosperity, fueled a revolution in rising expectations, and accelerated the shift to the postindustrial information age.[2]

Less noted was the impact of Title II on institutions of higher edu-cation. The massive influx of veterans resulted in changes—some of them permanent and profound—in the physical plants, admissions procedures, guidance and testing services, curriculum, pedagogy, and relationship to the government of American colleges and universities. Most important, the GIs' academic achievements enhanced the prestige, practical value, and visibility of a college diploma. Harold Stoke, president of the University of New Hampshire, was perhaps too sanguine in proclaiming that the GI Bill had "unwittingly imposed compulsory education on the nation." The legislation, however, did help forge a consensus that the number of college-caliber candidates, drawn from all socioeconomic and ethnic groups, was far larger than previously thought. Americans began to perceive undergraduate and graduate degrees as gateways to the professions, the new route to the American Dream.[3]

In 1946, Title II of the GI Bill remained an experiment with an uncertain outcome. Considering it "their bounded duty to open the doors of opportunity to the multitudes"—and not unmindful of the tuition pouring into bursars' offices—colleges and universities scrambled to accommodate as many students as possible. Enrollments on many campuses exploded. At Purdue University, degree matriculants jumped from 5,628 in 1945 to 11,462 in 1946. The enrollment at Syracuse University in 1945 was 4,391; a year later it had swelled to 15,228. Most institutions aided and abetted GIs in their sprint toward the degree. They granted academic credit for experience, training, or education in the armed services. They ran short courses and summer sessions and used the quarter system. The University of Louisville instituted a "twilight division," with a night shift that offered introductory courses, and the University of Pittsburgh added a two-year Associate in Arts degree. Four years, Dean Stanton Crawford explained, delayed veterans "more than we feel is justified."[4]

Housing the veterans was the most pressing problem. Of one hundred colleges polled by the American Council on Education in 1945 (before eligibility under Title II was liberalized), eighty-seven reported shortages. These institutions alone needed 47,300 single rooms and an additional 22,120 apartments (to accommodate the families of married veterans). At first, the Veterans Administration refused to help with housing because it segregated veterans from civilian students and put them "in a special category." Congress raced to the rescue. In a series of amendments to the Lanham Act of 1940, which authorized the federal government to construct public housing to facilitate the nation's defense, the House and the Senate authorized the National Housing Agency to rent housing to veterans, construct temporary units for them, move facilities to sites approved by colleges and universities, and reimburse institutions that had already incurred expenses in doing so. Congress appropriated almost $450,000,000 for these initiatives. When the funds ran out in August 1946, 101,462 accommodations had been transferred to institutions of higher education.[5]

An additional 100,000 units came from government facilities located near college campuses. Just about anything with four walls, including Quonset huts and mess tents, sufficed. Quarters once utilized by bachelor officers at Kirtland Field housed students at the University of New Mexico; barracks at Camp Kilmer and a prefabricated steel factory, about to be delivered to the Soviet Union, were turned over to Rutgers University; Hiram College in Ohio gained access to apartments at the Ravenna Ordnance Plant; Rensselaer Polytechnical Institute leased LSTs (landing ship tanks), floating in the Hudson River, to accommodate 600 veterans; and the government converted thirty-nine prisoner-of-war barracks from Weingarten, Missouri, into 117 housing units for veterans enrolled at Notre Dame. At peak enrollment, historian Keith Olson has estimated, perhaps 300,000 student veterans lived in facilities acquired under the Lanham Act amendments.[6]

Colleges and universities also used their own resources to add housing stock. In addition to the "East Vetsburg" and "Tower Road" complexes on its Ithaca, New York, campus, for example, Cornell University leased the Glen Springs Hotel in Watkins Glen, a once luxurious facility with a country club, health resort, and golf course that had been unoccupied for four years. Cornell converted the hotel into apartments for 135 married veterans, an infirmary, a sun porch, and a recreation lounge for dancing. Meals were served in a cafeteria set up in the main dining room. Although New York State provided assistance for the project, the university's contribution included $50,000 for furnishings and equipment and about $26,000 a year to bus the students to Ithaca, a round trip of more than fifty miles.[7]

Many of the living units were permanent residence halls that were erected with an understanding that, after the veterans graduated, enrollment at many institutions would remain far larger than it had been in the prewar years. In the immediate aftermath of the war, dormitory construction was hampered by a housing boom, which inflated prices and created a shortage of building materials. Nonetheless, hundreds of colleges and universities built dorms—or made plans to do so. At Notre Dame, a residence hall named for Father John Farley went up at a cost of almost $730,000. Penn State authorized construction of two new buildings, each accommodating 1,000 students. They were completed in 1948 and 1949, when ground was broken for three more residence halls designed to house 1,500 students at an additional cost of $6 million.[8]

In addition to housing, colleges and universities provided more classrooms, laboratories, libraries, and offices for faculty and administrators. Convinced that the battle of the (enrollment) bulge would last no more than four years, Veterans Administration director Frank Hines insisted that permanent additions to the physical plant constituted "expansion to destruction." In August 1946, with the Veterans' Educational Facilities Program (VEFP), Congress amended the Lanham Act yet again to permit and pay for the disassembly, transportation, and reassembly of surplus military buildings on the campus of any Title II institution facing a temporary shortage of floor space. At a cost of about $80 million the government moved 5,920 structures, including ordnance depots, military barracks, and Quonset huts, to more than seven hundred colleges, where they became makeshift classrooms and faculty offices. Two other provisions of the VEFP permitted educational institutions to acquire without cost or purchase in advance of public sale surplus government property, including furniture, textbooks, cars, lockers, electronics equipment, air conditioners, chemicals, and medicine. By the end of 1948, assets valued at almost $125 million had been transferred.[9]

Without the additions to their physical plants authorized by the Lanham Act amendments, colleges and universities would not have been able to serve nearly so many World War II veterans. However, according to the U.S. Office of Education, the structures supplied by the federal government met only 78 percent of "urgently needed" space—and 51 percent of the space that was "justifiably needed." Thus, ignoring the admonitions of Hines, many institutions embarked on aggressive construction programs. David Marsh, president of Boston University, defended his decision to expand—and relocate the central campus from Copley Square to Commonwealth Avenue—with an argument embraced by many of his counterparts throughout the country: "While we have been lengthening the ropes of our educational tent to make it larger, we are at the same time strengthening the stakes—and strengthening the stakes in every way: teaching and research personnel, library and laboratory equipment, financial security, and physical plant." In 1940 colleges and universities had spent $73 million of their own resources on plant operation and maintenance. New construction, of course, screeched to a halt during the war, but in 1946 expenditures reached $111 million. By 1948, the year GI Bill enrollments crested, they skyrocketed to $202 million.[10]

Public colleges and universities sought state appropriations to fund construction—and private institutions tapped their endowments and borrowed money. Tuition revenues, however, were essential. With applications at record numbers—and Uncle Sam on the hook for up to $500 per student—institutions raised their rates in the second half of the 1940s by an average of 25–30 percent. The University of Wisconsin, for example, increased its fee from $48 a semester in 1945 to $60 in 1947 and $75 in 1949. Nonresident tuition rose from $148 to $225 during these years. Most important, since the nonresident tuition more nearly approximated the actual cost of education, the Veterans Administration allowed the university to charge nonresident tuition to Wisconsin citizens covered by the GI Bill. This decision provided university administrators a windfall of almost $1 million for the fall semester of 1946 alone and nearly $10 million by the early 1950s.[11]

Such arrangements, as President Stoke realized, aroused "dark fears about the corrupting effects of public subsidy." What would happen, *Time Magazine* asked in 1947, when the economic nest egg cracked because the federal government "stopped ladling out millions of dollars under the GI Bill of Rights?" Would classrooms, labs, and residence halls lie idle, with maintenance deferred and colleges mired in debt? Administrators in higher education, in essence, were betting the farm that enrollments would not decline in the 1950s—and giving themselves an incentive to make a college education more desirable, necessary, and possible for young people from every segment of the population.[12]

This same belief—"if we build it, they will come"—shaped faculty recruitment in the postwar period. With the sudden and steep increase in enrollment, most institutions searched frantically for qualified teachers. Colleges and universities in California, for example, needed to add at least 5,820 instructors to its faculty of 7,802 just to accommodate the GI matriculants in 1946. Moreover, search committees found that the pickings were slim. Given low salaries and a booming economy, a substantial number of the college professors who had served in the armed forces decided not to return to the classroom. In addition, the disruption of graduate education during the war had left the pipeline of PhDs cracked and leaky.[13]

Colleges and universities improvised. At Penn State, high school teachers moonlighted by teaching fully accredited courses to nine hundred students at extension centers in State College, Bellefonte, Philipsburg, Lewiston, Sayre, Shamokin, and Somerset. The University of Iowa adopted practices that were replicated throughout the nation. In the fall of 1946, Iowa's College of Liberal Arts hired ninety-one temporary instructors, many of them graduate students who agreed to postpone research on their master's and doctoral theses. Thirty-eight of them had no prior teaching experience. These young teachers joined the tenured faculty in offering large lecture courses, leading discussion sections, and counseling veterans. Large courses became the norm, as did multiple-choice exams that were graded by machine. Personal contact between professor and student was minimal, *Life Magazine* reported, but veterans eager to "speed up their education" did not much mind.[14]

At the same time, however, colleges and universities made substantial additions to the permanent faculty. Scrambling to hire unprecedented numbers of new professors, department chairs, deans, and presidents could no longer rely exclusively on "old-boy" Anglo-Saxon Protestant networks. In the 1930s, elite research universities began hiring some of the 1,684 faculty members, including five Nobel Prize winners, who had been dismissed from institutions of higher education in Nazi Germany. Established in 1933, the graduate program of the New School for Social Research in New York City welcomed many of them. After the war, both public and private universities sought the services of refugee-scholars, including recent arrivals from Eastern Europe and the Soviet Union, even if their command of the English language was less than impeccable.[15]

The doors swung open as well, at least halfway, for Jewish academics. Before the war Brahmins in the humanities and social sciences excluded Jewish scholars as radical, deficient in gentility, and incapable of understanding the essence of American culture. The war against Aryan supremacy and the exigencies generated by the GI Bill silenced some of them and drove others underground. In hiring faculty, as well as in admitting students, talent increasingly trumped heredity. Following assurances that "he has none of the offensive traits which some associate with his race," Oscar Handlin became the first Jew in Harvard's History Department. Louis Hartz, a brilliant political theorist and expert in comparative politics, became the first Jewish senior appointment in the Government Department at Harvard. At Cornell University, trailblazers included M. H. Abrams in English, Alfred Kahn in economics, and Milton Konvitz in industrial and labor relations. The dike broke in other institutions as well, especially those with large numbers of Jewish undergraduates.[16]

The dike would never be rebuilt. In the ensuing decades, the faculty at public and private universities grew larger and ever more diverse. In the 1940s, however, the increase did not match the growth in the number of students. In all institutions of higher education, Keith Olson estimates, enrollment climbed 75 percent between 1940 and 1948, while the number of faculty members increased by 52 percent. Nonetheless, the latter figure—which represents more than one hundred thousand men and women—is impressive, especially in the context of shortages of qualified candidates and concerns that enrollment would drop, perhaps precipitously, at the end of the 1940s.[17]

As postwar realities compelled administrators and professors, old and new, to readjust pedagogy, they prompted them as well to reassess the curriculum. In 1944 Francis Brown of the American Council on Education predicted that the vast majority of GIs would seek vocational, technical, and professional training: "No exhortation," he insisted, would get them to major in the liberal arts. Writing in the *Journal of Higher Education* two years later, Argus Tresidder agreed that most beneficiaries of the GI Bill would search for "specific skills and a steady point of view" and find them in engineering, medicine, and business. Determined veterans—who "didn't fight in a foxhole to live in a rat hole"—could not be convinced that reading Beowulf and Shelley or conjugating vulgar Latin verbs would help them climb into a higher income-tax bracket. With the exception of Robert Hutchins at the University of Chicago, who wished that vocational instruction would disappear from the curriculum, most college and university presidents, Tresidder reported, were preparing for a massive shift from general education to applied subjects. At the University of Kansas, Chancellor Deane Waldo Malott asked his faculty why English composition was the only course required of every student. Wasn't mathematics now as essential a tool in communication as the spoken and written word? Anticipating a revolution in higher education, President Edmund Ezra Day of Cornell believed that "the interest of individuals, as well as the security of the commonwealth," demanded that the intellectual focus "of the great numbers be scientific, commercial, and industrial, rather than literary."[18]

It did not work out quite that way, however. A high percentage of GI Bill students did choose professional and preprofessional majors. About a quarter of them sought degrees in engineering, architecture, physical sciences, and allied professions. A large—and growing—percentage prepared for careers in education, law, medicine, and business. In 1952, for example, about a quarter of Title II beneficiaries (including nondegree matriculants in training programs) opted for a curriculum in business administration or management.[19] Nevertheless, a mass exodus from the liberal arts in colleges and universities did not occur. Stimulated in part by the importance attached to the

Three World War II veterans being briefed about GI Bill educational benefits. The magazine article accompanying this photograph informs us that two of the three used the GI Bill to attend college. (*The Saturday Evening Post*, August 18, 1945)

study of foreign languages and "area studies" (especially Asia) during the Cold War and in part by curiosity to learn more about the people and cultures they had encountered as soldiers, returning veterans were no more likely than nonveterans to choose "practical" courses of study. "Alive to the ferments now at work in civilization," Walter Spearman and Jack R. Brown suggested in the *South Atlantic Quarterly*, GIs were interested in "developing their powers to think, feel, and act, acquainting themselves with the best that has been thought and said in the world," and satisfying "an insatiable hunger to know the why and how of international cooperation."[20] The more "selective" the school, moreover, the more robust the interest in the humanities and social sciences. Table 4.1 summarizes enrollments by the Class of 1949 at the University of Wisconsin.

In 1949–1950, the disparity between the majors of veterans and nonveterans continued, with 61.7 percent of the former and 51.0 percent of the latter in the liberal arts. The School of Commerce reported registrations by 1.4 percent of former soldiers and 4.5 percent of nonveterans.[21]

Table 4.1.   Enrollments by the Class of 1949 at the
University of Wisconsin

College	Veterans (2,652)	Nonveterans (825)
Liberal Arts	38.1 percent	25.5 percent
Education	10.3 percent	6.1 percent
Commerce	13.9 percent	44 percent
Engineering	27.6 percent	16.0 percent
Agriculture	10.1 percent	8.4 percent

In 1945 and 1946, of course, no one knew the courses of study GIs would select or how well they would adjust to campus life. Most observers agreed with the American Council on Education that student-veterans would benefit from guidance and testing to measure academic aptitude, provide up-to-date vocational information, and ease the transition to civilian life. With support from the Veterans Administration, colleges and universities provided counseling services that served more than a million former soldiers by 1951. These advisement centers, historian Kathleen Frydl has demonstrated, gave rise to the "student personnel movement," which, in the second half of the twentieth century, became a fixture in higher education in the United States.[22] Before 1945, few institutions had provided academic, vocational, or personal "advisement centers." Toward the end of World War II, the Veterans Administration required that service personnel who had incurred disabilities take a battery of tests to delineate options for training and employment. With passage of the GI Bill, the VA began to provide counseling to "able-bodied" veterans. To save money, advisement centers were located on college and university campuses, even though testing and vocational guidance was available as well to veterans who did not intend to return to school. The first center, located at City College in Manhattan, used both VA and college staff. The model was deemed a success. By 1946, 323 advisement offices were located in institutions of higher education throughout the country. The VA covered the costs of many tests that measured interest, intelligence, aptitude, personality, and achievement.[23]

Even before the financial support furnished by the VA was discontinued, testing, counseling, and placement had become the responsibility of colleges and universities. Located initially in admissions offices, trained professionals in ever-increasing numbers were assigned to dormitories, dean of students' and academic advising offices, and psychological services. For better and worse, thanks in no small measure to the GI Bill, generations of students—and their parents—came to expect assistance with study skills; emotional, social, sexual, and marital problems; and employment.

With or without counseling, GI Bill students were remarkably successful learners. About a quarter of the veterans who enrolled in a college or university did not complete a degree, a much smaller drop-out rate than in the civilian population. Exit interviews suggest that most of those who left prematurely did so for financial reasons. Few GIs "flunked out." Moreover, a surprisingly small percentage of veterans failed to adjust to campus life. "Where are the psychiatric problems we had been led to expect?" an instructor at Princeton asked. "Our veterans are normal, fine youths."[24]

Veterans quickly acquired a reputation as mature, serious students. Instead of "taking a ride on Uncle Sam's generosity," they attended virtually every class, intently took notes, and asked questions. "The window-gazers and hibernators have vanished," one Harvard professor exclaimed. "This crowd never takes its eyes off you." Civilian-students did not disagree, though they did not always share the faculty's growing enthusiasm for academically oriented veterans. "They're grinds, every one of them," a civilian senior at Lehigh University in Bethlehem, Pennsylvania, complained, "It's books, books, books all the time. They study so hard we have to slave to keep up with them."[25]

The veterans' performance helped shape popular perceptions of the GI Bill as far-sighted legislation by making equal opportunity a reality and challenging assumptions about who could benefit from a college education. By mid-1946 even James Bryant Conant, Harvard's president, the one-time critic of federal funding of higher education for World War II veterans, was eating some crow. The GI Bill, Conant now believed, was "a heartening sign that the democratic process of social mobility is energetically at work, piercing the class barriers which, even in America, have tended to keep a college education the prerogative of the few."[26]

Concerns that the GI Bill would lower academic standards proved groundless as well. In fact, students at the University of California referred to veterans as "D.A.R.s (Damned Average Raisers)." "The G.I.s are hogging the honor rolls and the Deans' lists," Benjamin Fine reported in the *New York Times* after a nationwide tour of college campuses in the fall of 1947. That spring a mere 35 of the 6,010 veterans at the University of Minnesota were dismissed because of poor grades, one-twentieth of the discharge rate to which the institution was accustomed.[27] A slew of studies demonstrated that veterans failed less often, earned higher grades than their civilian counterparts at the same institutions, and, contrary to conventional wisdom, ascribed slightly less importance to grades. Perhaps because they were more motivated, veterans also did better relative to their ability than did nonveterans— by about a fourth to a third of a letter grade. The best students tended to be those who had been away from school the longest, were older, and married. These veterans may have been the least likely to complete college but for the GI Bill. Their impressive achievement, Fine concluded, provided a definitive refutation of the skeptics who had predicted they would be "an educational problem."[28]

Even more than good grades, the ease with which veterans adapted to campus life assumed almost mythic dimensions. Profiles of GI Bill students were ubiquitous in the nation's newspapers and magazines. They did not always follow Norman Rockwell, who depicted a former grunt, perched in the shuttered windowsill of his college dorm room, overlooking the clock tower on the quad, puffing on a pipe while reading a book, with his golf bag leaning against the wall. However, virtually without exception, student-veterans were portrayed as gracious and grouseless white males. These images became iconic—and shaped popular perceptions of the GI Bill for decades.[29]

About half of the GI Bill students in college were married, and their travails and triumphs dominated media coverage. At the University of Iowa, according to a *Life Magazine* article, accompanied by photographs taken by Margaret Bourke-White, about 170 married veterans rented furnished trailers for $25 a month. While they waited for a barracks or a Quonset hut with running water, the families used communal baths and washrooms at the Hawkeye Trailer Camp. When the men studied or went off to class, the "wives cheerfully wash, starch and iron their babies' white ruffles, hang bright chintz curtains and wax the trailer floors." With the families sharing washrooms, clotheslines, and garbage disposals, the article reported, "there are no secrets, no differences, and no Joneses to keep up with." With cooperation a necessity, the families established their own governing councils, which met in a washhouse or a boiler room to discuss sanitation, rent, and camp welfare. Many GIs took part-time jobs to supplement their incomes, working in Iowa City's junkyards, soda fountains, and grocery stores, driving cabs and taxis, or serving as assistant policemen. Barely making ends meet, the *Life* article suggested, the families had little time for parties—and yet the article featured a snapshot of a surprise birthday party for former navy pharmacist and premed student Donald Sonius.

As they crowded around a table, sharing coffee and home-baked cake, the Hawkeye campers seemed quite content.[30]

References to the GI Bill as an experiment in democratic governance, however, were far less prevalent in the popular press than success stories of individual veterans. In "Meet a Student Veteran," for example, C. S. Forester—author of the celebrated Hornblower novels—introduced readers of the *Ladies Home Journal* to Philip Gray, a disabled ex-corporal in the army air force with a bum knee, a punctured ear drum, a baby boy, and a pregnant wife. Gray was studying to be a research chemist at the University of California, Berkeley. "Brainy, introverted, capable of great concentration," he could not have dreamed of a college degree if the government had not provided tuition and a monthly stipend. The son of an auto mechanic and logger, Gray had lost his mother in 1936. At fourteen, he had hired out at a chicken ranch in Snohomish, Washington, so that he could buy clothes and school supplies, then joined the CCC camp near Seattle. "Character as well as ability," Forester emphasized, got him through high school. After graduation, he took a job at a filling station before enlisting in the army.

Stationed in Albuquerque, New Mexico, Gray was assigned to radio school before his honorable discharge. By then he was married. In search of a career, he took aptitude tests paid for by the VA and learned he would be good at teaching science or in production management: "It was at this moment that Gray discovered that Uncle Sam was prepared to make the dream a reality; that any veteran of promise could claim the right to complete his education at the expense of the Federal Government." At Berkeley, Philip, Mary, and Gary moved into a white clapboard "beehive rooming house," with a common tub and no refrigerator or icebox, that accommodated nineteen families. The beehive, according to Forester, "was astonishingly congenial: mothers looked after other babies indiscriminately with their own; or stood stoically in line to use the one sink or stove; while nineteen husbands tried to keep sixteen infants from becoming too restive under the spur of appetite." After two months, the Grays relocated to a two-bedroom bungalow about a mile from campus, where only seven people resided. Their one-bedroom apartment, with kitchen privileges, cost $25 a month plus $10 for utilities. "I guess we can get through seven more semesters," said Mary Gray as she gazed around "their incredibly crowded room." After Gray graduated as a first-rate physical chemist and began earning $250 a month, Forester predicted, he "will not remember anything about the rooming house on Haste Street, and I shouldn't be surprised if Mary smiled when she remembered it."

The Grays could not quite make it on the monthly allowance supplied by the government, so Philip worked two jobs to make an additional $10 a week. He took candid shots at parties and dances and sold them for seventy-five cents apiece to Berkeley undergraduates. And along with two buddies he repaired radios and rented out amplifiers, record players, and records. Still, the family did not always stay solvent until the end of the month. Mary offered to put Gary in a nursery and go to work, but "Phil thinks she has a plenty big enough job already." Should the government increase their allowance? Forester did not think so. However, he hastened to deny that this opinion was based on "bland indifference" and pointed out that 22.7 percent of families in the United States had incomes of $1,000–$2,000 a year. Workaday worries, he wrote, were "a stimulus as well as a sedative. The contemplative life is not good for the returned soldier, however much he may yearn for it."[31]

Neither Phil nor Mary Gray complained about the GI Bill's living stipend—at least not to Forester. Perhaps they feared the kind of response they would get or thought it likely that they would be told to stop wasting time griping, much as a dean at Purdue warned engineering students who protested the VA ruling that restricted them to Pickett and Eckel slide rules. Even worse, they risked the sarcasm of a John Rivoire, a student-veteran who "dared" the *Cornell Daily Sun* to print his assessment of GIs trying to live on a "mean and miserable sixty-five dollars a month." After listing his expenses, which included (in addition to food, clothes, and lodging) a car, insurance, a beer a week, a weekly movie (and a ticket for his date), a coupon book for athletic contests, toothpaste, shaving cream, Listerine, and Quinsana (for his athlete's foot), a subscription to the *New York Times*, a slide rule, notebooks, and a Parker 51 pen, Rivoire gibed: "To support me in the manner to which I am accustomed would take more than I care to tabulate now.... Even if I work for some of my expenses—unthinkable thought—I cannot possibly hope to balance my budget. Sometimes I wish I had never been born."[32]

Most GIs, of course, supported the adjustments in the living stipend enacted by Congress after 1945, but they did not take the lead in public discussion of them and rarely complained about any VA or college regulation or requirement. When a counselor told Frank Holt he could not enter Purdue because he had not established residence in Lafayette, Indiana, the former flight engineer went to Evansville for two years before transferring to his first choice. Whatever the motivation, such deference contributed to the growing appreciation of GIs as stoic and even heroic.[33]

The veterans' quiet determination helped make the VA—and the federal government—almost invisible. The VA did, on occasion, micromanage. Government bureaucrats decided whether to pay for caps and gowns, the binding of dissertations, and research trips for graduate students. Moreover, there was petty graft at bookstores that charged full price for texts normally sold at a discount, for instance, and for purchases of supplies that were not actually required for courses. Abuses were minor, however—and neither the veterans nor the college officials called attention to them. Even the big-ticket item, tuition, caused few problems, with only about 1 percent of $2 billion in dispute. "To enter college under the G.I. Bill of Rights," boasted Bristow Adams, an emeritus professor at Cornell University who served as counselor in the Veterans Education Office, "involves little red tape and formality. The only form the applicant is required to file is the simplest government form I have ever seen." Equally important, Title II offered the same benefit to all veterans whether they were "grunts" or generals. Applicants were not screened or means-tested. Grants and stipends were awarded directly to veterans, who were empowered, as consumers, to choose where—and what—to study. And so the college program was hailed in the 1950s by the VA, the General Accounting Office, a House Select Committee, a presidential commission, and the vast majority of Americans as the jewel in the crown of the GI Bill, which existed well within the traditions of individual responsibility and equality of opportunity and offered greater benefits for less money than any other provision of the landmark legislation.[34]

Most of all, student-veterans wanted to get into a good college— and to complete a degree. Existing colleges and universities were able to accommodate them, but what would have happened had they been unable to do so? Were "emergency colleges" a feasible and perhaps even less expensive alternative? The response of politicians and academic administrators in New York State provides some answers to these questions. Home to about 10 percent of the nation's population, New York faced an educational crisis in 1946. The only state without a public university, New York relied on private colleges and universities, and the surge in enrollments overwhelmed them. With the draft about to be curtailed, the normal flow of high school graduates was about to resume. If these young men and women enrolled in colleges and universities at the pre–World War II rate, about 105,000 of them would be full-time students, only 37,000 short of the maximum capacity of every two- and four-year institution in the state. At the same time, however, as many as 100,000 veterans were preparing applications for admission. The situation, Governor Thomas E. Dewey proclaimed, posed a "serious threat to the whole future of trained leadership in our State, and to the personal lives and ambitions of tens of thousands of our youth."[35]

Dewey was not just another governor. With a nationwide reputation as a "racket-busting" district attorney, he had won statewide office in 1941. Three years later he was the Republican candidate for president of the United States but lost in a landslide to Franklin Roosevelt. Dewey anticipated easy reelection as governor in the fall of 1946 and was already preparing to run against President Truman in 1948. Though critical of the New Deal, he supported government action in domestic affairs. The looming crisis in education for veterans, he recognized, was a potent political issue.

In March 1946 Dewey presided over an "emergency conference" attended by the presidents of eighty-five colleges and universities in New York State. He announced that he had set aside $15 million for the construction of temporary housing for twenty thousand veterans on their campuses. In addition, this was only the beginning. Dewey demanded that academic administrators increase their "educational facilities" by 26 percent and their housing stock by at least 30 percent. Colleges should begin double sessions, establish extension centers, and use classrooms from early in the morning to late at night.

Several presidents pushed back. If colleges were forced to double enrollments, President Alan Valentine of the University of Rochester warned, the quality of education would deteriorate. Qualified faculty were hard to find, Valentine maintained. "The bottom of the barrel has been scraped." Dewey believed some additional instructors could be hired but urged that all faculty teach extra classes. Such sacrifices were as much "a part of winning the war" as "pressure teaching" had been before the surrender of Germany and Japan. "We don't want to perpetrate a fraud in education," Dewey acknowledged. "Yet I think it would be better to give the veterans the best that you can than to keep them out. You cannot have one hundred thousand veterans walking the street, saying that colleges have refused to admit us. Let's get them in this year even though you will have to sacrifice some of your standards."

The governor knew that creating new institutions "overnight" was impossible. At best, they would be "jury-rigged" schools "which no student would care to attend and no student ought to attend." Nonetheless,

Dewey raised the possibility of using the physical structures on military bases to provide education and training for the influx of veterans. If operated by the great established colleges of the state, these installations, Dewey suggested, could put in place educational essentials.[36]

Within twenty-four hours, the presidents accepted the governor's challenge. They pledged to enroll an additional 31,000 students on their campuses. An additional 10,000 would be educated at emergency extension collegiate centers that would be set up jointly with public high schools. In addition, 19,000 more would be admitted to rehabilitated military installations. In June, the Education Department of New York State announced that in the fall of 1946 junior colleges would open colleges in three locations under the auspices of a temporary corporation called Associated Colleges of Upper New York (ACUNY), a consortium of seventeen private institutions. Champlain College, housed at the Plattsburgh Barracks, a 727-acre campus, opened in September 1946 with 1,101 students. A month later, Mohawk College, housed in the buildings of the army's Rhoads General Hospital in Utica, began teaching 1,323 students. And Sampson College, the largest ACUNY institution, with an initial enrollment of 2,825, held its inaugural convocation on the 2,597-acre Sampson Naval Training Center on the shores of Seneca Lake. In early 1947 ACUNY added a fourth unit, the Middletown Collegiate Center, in Orange County.

The ACUNY colleges offered the standard freshman and sophomore curriculum in the liberal arts, business administration, and engineering. On each campus, barracks or hospital rooms had been converted to dormitories, and some apartments for married students were available. Tuition was set at $150 per quarter, though within a year the institutions switched to a semester system. The hallmark of the admissions policy was "flexibility and even deviation" from published standards, dictated by the "enormous emergency"—even if it meant admitting a larger percentage of students below the scholarship average. Applicants were admitted without examinations on presentation of a high school transcript. Mature veterans who showed "other evidence of being qualified for college work" were admitted conditionally. In addition, some credit was granted for training received while in the service. After two years, students who did satisfactory work were eligible to transfer to colleges throughout New York State as soon as space became available.[37]

In the fall of 1947 Benjamin Fine hailed ACUNY in the *New York Times* as an "educational miracle." With the leadership of President Asa Knowles, former director of extension at Rhode Island State College,

ACUNY completed the herculean task of converting three military installations into college campuses within a few months and hiring a staff of 550, many of them leaders in their fields. At Sampson, the largest ACUNY college, the last vestiges of military life were rapidly disappearing. Repainted inside and out, the barracks were now comfortable dormitories. The cafeteria seated 2,500 diners, the library had study spaces for 1,300, and a 600-foot gymnasium would soon host physical education classes. Fine was most impressed by the semimicro chemistry and physics laboratory at Sampson, perhaps the first of its kind in a college or university. More accurate than standard equipment, the miniature devices might well "revolutionize" pedagogy in the sciences. Although started as "an overflow center for veterans," Fine concluded, Sampson—and the other ACUNY colleges—were "among the top institutions of higher learning in the country."[38]

The Associated Colleges of Upper New York were impressive in other respects as well. In classes ranging from ten to forty, students received careful attention from their instructors. Each institution, according to Amy Gilbert, the official ACUNY historian, quickly and competently assembled basic library holdings. Although "the partitions were thin, ventilation was a problem, and the painted blackboards were not replaced by slate until 1947–1948," the classrooms were "amazingly satisfactory." The laboratory equipment, including microscopes, were "especially remarkable at a time when shortages of apparatus were pressing." Moreover, student life was varied and vibrant. Each college had a campus newspaper, a radio workshop, dozens of clubs, a concert band and brass ensemble (with instruments provided to the students), and a big social weekend at the end of which a campus queen was crowned. The intramural sports program was extensive, with the colleges offering equipment for football, basketball, boxing, badminton, handball, volleyball, and golf. With the exception of Middletown, ACUNY institutions competed with each other and with neighboring colleges in twelve sports. In 1946–1947 ACUNY won 91, lost 101, and tied 6 events.

Of course, ACUNY faculty and staff were proudest of their students' academic record. By the spring of 1947, a total of 7,375 students had taken some classes at Sampson, Champlain, or Mohawk. Of these, 898 had withdrawn because of poor grades, financial difficulties, unsatisfactory college conditions, unavailability of desired curriculum, illness, family problems, or reenlistment in the armed forces. This dropout rate compared favorably with four-year institutions throughout the country—and was quite striking, given the flexible admission standards employed by the "GI colleges." Even more remarkable was the transfer rate. By 1949, more than 7,000 students who had attended ACUNY for various lengths of time had transferred to degree-granting colleges that stretched from Maine to California and as far away as Geneva, Switzerland. With the assistance of advisers in the transfer office, 100 percent of applicants who had completed their course of study with a grade point average of 2.0 or better gained acceptance.[39]

Beneath the surface, however, the ACUNY colleges were beset with problems. One of the most vexing challenges concerned a non-academic matter, the State Education Department reported in 1947. After numerous complaints about meals—and cost overruns at the cafeterias—the contract with the food services company was terminated. Still, the next firm was no better. Furthermore, janitorial services were just as bad. In a visit to a dormitory at Sampson, investigators found rooms littered with discarded clothing, empty milk and soft drink bottles, and overflowing ashtrays. Filthy shower rooms and toilets, they warned, "could jeopardize the health of the residents."[40]

Officials of the State Education Department had good reason to be concerned about "an adverse effect on the morale of the student body." Sampson College, wrote Bill Beeney, an investigative reporter for the *Rochester Democrat and Chronicle*, was "a dreary, drab, depressing place." Despite the recent renovations, "many of the buildings show the ravages of disuse—and vandalism. The dormitory rent is cheap; it should be. It looks like a breeding ground for unrest." Students were afraid to speak out because administrators brooked no dissent. If the identities of "troublemakers" were known, they claimed, "we'd be out of here in five minutes." Beeney acknowledged that some of the grousing was trivial—and typical of students living on a former naval base far from a town or city. Nonetheless, he concluded that "there's a kettle of fish on the fire at Sampson."[41]

The quality of the faculty was yet another kettle of fish. Although members of the visiting committee of the State Education Department concluded that instructors were "well prepared for teaching in junior college," their report made clear that the academic experience at ACUNY institutions was, at best, uneven. With teacher shortages throughout the state and competition from established colleges, recruiting capable candidates constituted quite a challenge. The 425 instructors on hand in 1947 were a mixed bag. Fifteen percent of them had completed doctorates; 49 percent held master's degrees; and 36 percent a BA or BS. Positions in mathematics, engineering, physics, chemistry, and biology proved especially difficult to fill. Since many instructors had no teaching experience, department heads prepared syllabi, assignments, and examinations for each course and distributed guidelines for grading.

In-service training helped, but serious problems remained. Some instructors in engineering exhibited "rigid and inflexible routines in following lesson plans" and even refused to stop when clarification was necessary. The visiting committee was also "unenthusiastic" about the teaching of English composition at Champlain College, where instructors filled classes with "drill work and review of material which should have been covered in junior high school." There was evidence as well of grade inflation at ACUNY. "It is entirely possible that such courses as Accounting, Chemistry, Mathematics 53, Modern Languages, and Pre-Engineering 101 may have an unusually high percentage of A and B students," the committee noted. However, since most of the students have been away from school for a long time, "this is not likely." Nor was there a satisfactory explanation for the relatively small number of Ds and Fs at Champlain. Education Department officials reminded the faculty that C was an average grade, acceptable for promotion, graduation, and transfer. They also reminded themselves, a bit defensively, that ACUNY was not a four-year college and "probably should not be compared with a junior college at this time since they are offering only a full freshman program plus electives."[42]

The report of the State Education Department was silent on the greatest disappointment at ACUNY: enrollment. Despite a vigorous publicity campaign—and a decision to admit nonveterans—the total registration at the four ACUNY colleges never came close to the system's overall capacity of 9,942 students. It appears that ACUNY was the last choice of most GIs. As of January 1947, for example, 23,065 individuals had requested application forms, but only 8,174 actually applied. The enrollment for the winter quarter was only 5,768. Many of the accepted students had withdrawn because they had been admitted elsewhere. In public, ACUNY administrators remained resolute. "We want students who have the academic qualifications for Yale, Harvard, or Princeton but who cannot gain admission there because of the heavy enrollment," announced Howard Thompson, dean of the faculty at Sampson. Yet it was increasingly clear, Gilbert acknowledged, "that those who would be available in 1948 might be substandard students." Therefore, ACUNY redoubled its efforts to attract high school graduates. Enrollments, however, continued to decline precipitously. Mohawk closed its doors in September, and the following June Sampson followed suit. Of the first-year students at Champlain and

Middletown in the fall of 1949, only 45 percent were veterans. On March 31, 1951, ACUNY went out of business.[43]

The "GI university" had been a costly experiment. New York State spent nearly $10 million to convert military installations into college campuses and acquire new equipment that would be used for less than three years. For the more than seven thousand students who transferred from ACUNY to degree-granting institutions, Governor Dewey's initiative had no doubt been a success. In the speed with which it opened for business, ACUNY was indeed a miracle. Still, veterans had voted with their feet, and their application forms, and existing institutions had stretched and strained to absorb virtually all of them.[44]

By the early 1950s, Title II had about run its course. In 1953, World War II veterans constituted only 6.1 percent of enrollments in colleges and universities. It was time to ask what had been wrought. In response, the GIs answered with one voice. "I can say this honestly," Robert Booth recalled many years later, "I'd never have gone to college without it." Born in Omaha, Nebraska, in 1926, Booth began washing dishes in restaurants when he was twelve to help his family through the Great Depression. With a knack for mathematics and engineering, he enlisted in the navy after graduation from high school. Under the navy's V-12 program, Booth spent two semesters at the University of California–Berkeley before shipping out to chase German U-boats in the Atlantic. The war ended before he saw action—or got his officer's commission, so he returned to Novato, California, where his family had relocated, and got a job repairing tractors. Married, with the first of his five children on the way, Booth asked an old high school teacher about courses on engine theory. "You ever heard of the GI Bill?" the instructor asked. Booth had not. The following Monday he was back at Berkeley as an engineering student, with his V-12 courses counted toward the degree. He graduated in 1949, then worked for Boeing and Lockheed Aircraft, helping design B-52s, state-of-the-art helicopters, and Polaris missiles. But for the G.I. bill, "I'd have stayed on the farm, fixing tractors."[45]

Most observers echoed these sentiments then, thereafter, and now. In 1965 John Emens, president of Ball State Teachers College in Muncie, Indiana, celebrated the GI Bill for giving veterans "an opportunity to find lost paths." It was, Emens noted, the gift that kept on giving. In 1965 veterans enjoyed an average annual income of $5,100, compared to $3,200 for nonveterans; their unemployment rate was about half that of nonveterans. Furthermore, education begat education. The children of college graduates are far more likely to continue their studies after high school—and the sons and daughters of World War II vets were no exception. "Only God knows what would have become of me if it had not been for the GI Bill," Herbert Edelman of Brooklyn told Ball. Well into the new millennium, the GI Bill had not lost its luster. Title II, proclaimed journalist Edward Humes, made possible the education of fourteen future Nobel laureates, two dozen Pulitzer Prize winners, three Supreme Court justices, three presidents of the United States, and hundreds of thousands of skilled professionals. "All would owe their careers" to the bill that "transformed America and rewrote the American Dream."[46]

These assertions, however, did not go unchallenged. Had there been no GI Bill, some scholars asked soon after the legislation was enacted, would veterans have gone to college anyway? How much of the post-war college admissions crush resulted from pent-up demand created by the war itself rather than from new federal legislation? With financing from the Carnegie Foundation for the Advancement of Teaching, two educators, Norman Frederickson and William Schrader, surveyed 10,000 students at sixteen universities in 1946 and 1947 on this very issue. About 10 percent of the veterans, they concluded, almost certainly would not have enrolled without Title II. Another 10 percent "probably would not have." The GI Bill, then, deserved credit for about 446,000 of the veterans in college in the postwar period.[47]

This, of course, is not a small figure. It approaches the number of college degrees lost to the nation between 1942 and 1946. As Suzanne Mettler has pointed out, no government initiative in the history of higher education in the United States, including the Pell Grant program of the late twentieth century, has been as generous—and therefore no initiative, either before or since, has come close to the impact on the recipients' lives. Mettler has also provided good reasons to regard the Frederickson-Schrader estimates as conservative. Omitted from their sample were the kinds of institutions likely to be popular among veterans from less prosperous families—junior colleges, teachers colleges, business colleges, and less prestigious local colleges. A survey conducted in 1946 and 1947, moreover, may have oversampled more privileged veterans who were completing degrees interrupted by military service while undercounting those who had not given college much thought and were somewhat slower to enroll.

Subsequent studies, including Mettler's own comprehensive survey of more than two thousand veterans, conducted in 1998 and with an astounding return rate of 74 percent, provide additional evidence of the GI Bill's role in increasing access to higher education. Fully 54 percent of Mettler's nonblack, male veterans agreed that they could not have afforded college without the Title II benefits. For some, like Jim Murray, the GI Bill drew attention to an option never before considered. Discharged from the air force, Murray took his old job in the steel mills until his wife urged him to "take advantage" of the GI Bill and get a degree from Penn State. Without the push, Murray was not at all sure he would have mustered the will to do so. Many others—75 percent of college users in Mettler's sample—indicated they would have gone to school only part-time or at night but for the GI Bill's provisions for tuition and a living stipend. Not all of them, we can guess, would have completed degrees without it.[48]

The GI Bill also helped veterans stay in school longer. On average, according to one study, beneficiaries gained 2.7–2.9 years of education. Three hundred and fifty thousand of them enrolled in graduate and professional degree programs. The bill also appears to have boosted occupational status. A much smaller percentage of those who did not use Title II to go to college became business executives, stockbrokers, lawyers, or doctors. In addition, GIs who went to college, Mettler concludes, "enjoyed more frequent and greater leaps of social mobility." They had higher incomes, more job security, better health and pension benefits, and enhanced status.[49]

An examination at ACUNY's Mohawk College conveys something of the scale of higher education in the years following the GI Bill. (Courtesy Cornell University Press)

Equally important, since the bill paid full tuition up to $500 a year, many veterans expanded their educational horizons and matriculated at the best schools in the country. In 1946, 41 percent of student-veterans had enrolled in 38 schools, with the remainder spread thinly among 712 other fully accredited colleges. While prestigious institutions were beginning to burst at the seams, the American Association of Colleges Conference indicated that its member-colleges still had room for 250,000 students. A modified version of this pattern persisted throughout the life of the legislation. "Why go to Podunk College when the Government will send you to Yale?" *Time* magazine asked. With—and without—advice from the VA, hundreds of thousands of World War II veterans knew the answer, for 52 percent of them enrolled in private colleges and universities under the GI Bill. By contrast, 80 percent of veterans of the conflicts in Korea and Vietnam used their more meager tuition stipend at public colleges and universities.[50]

"Heinz" Kissinger was one of the veterans who "traded up" because of the GI Bill. Born in Furth, Germany, in 1923, Kissinger fled to New York City with his family in 1938, as the Nazi crackdown on Jews intensified. An excellent student at George Washington High School, Heinz entered City College to prepare for a career as an accountant. "For a refugee it was the easiest profession to get into," he remembered later. Drafted by the army in 1943, he completed basic training at Camp Croft in Spartanburg, South Carolina. Heinz became Henry, a naturalized U.S. citizen, and a private first class. With high scores on an IQ test, Kissinger was sent to Lafayette College in Pennsylvania to study engineering. In November 1944 he shipped out to Europe, where he served in his native country as a translator in a counterintelligence unit and as administrator of Krefeld, a city in Westphalia, where he helped restore civil government. Sergeant Kissinger received his honorable discharge in May 1946 but remained in Germany for a year as an instructor in the European Command Intelligence School in Bavaria. In September 1947, as Kissinger prepared to return home, his army buddy Fritz Kraemer, another German émigré, advised him to finish his undergraduate degree at an elite college. As a result, he applied to Harvard as a sophomore on the GI Bill of Rights, with a New York State scholarship to boot. Gaunt, bony, bespectacled, and poorly dressed, Kissinger impressed his professors as hardworking and smart. He submitted a 377-page honors thesis to complete his government major and graduated near the top of his class in 1950 with a Phi Beta Kappa key. He remained at Harvard for his PhD in international relations and then became a member of the faculty before beginning his long, distinguished, and controversial career in the foreign policy establishment of the Nixon and Ford administrations.[51]

Whether they worked in the public or the private sector, Mettler has shown, veterans who received education and training through the GI Bill participated more actively in the civic and political institutions of postwar America, joining 50 percent more organizations than non-users. Other variables, including level of education and socioeconomic circumstances, do not account for these differences in rates of participation. "Something about the program itself," Mettler concludes, prompted the exemplary citizenship of the beneficiaries. The longer they used Title II benefits at the college or subcollege level, the more active they tended to be.[52]

Not surprisingly, GIs gravitated at first to churches and veterans groups, especially the American Legion and the Veterans of Foreign Wars, but over time they joined a diverse array of organizations such as the PTA, the Elks, the Chamber of Commerce, and the AFL-CIO. Along with higher rates of affiliation, veterans were also more likely to take active roles in local posts or chapters, raise money for special causes, and become officers. Like other Americans, they joined to enhance their professional status, enrich their social life, and help their kids. Having benefited from a program that gave them a leg up, they seemed to be attracted as well to associations that improved the community—and the larger society—by providing opportunities to less fortunate individuals. What is more, 90 percent of the organizations they joined reached beyond the locality by providing access to regional, national, and even international meetings. This rich associational life allowed veterans to accumulate "social capital"—and sometimes to reduce class cleavages.[53]

These skills and interests contributed to greater political involvement as well. Here as well, Mettler's survey shows, the GI Bill proved to be a formative experience by evoking in beneficiaries the feeling that they were part of a benevolent political system and thus had some responsibility to keep it vital and vibrant. Most of the veterans did not view the bill as an entitlement but saw it instead as a privilege. Those who made the most extensive use of its benefits felt the strongest obligation to give something back to society in return for their education and training. "It was a hell of a gift, an opportunity, and I've never thought of it any other way," remembered Luke LaPorta, a native of Queens, New York, who earned a bachelor's, a master's, and a doctorate on the GI Bill. Even now, LaPorta wonders "if I really earned what I've gotten."[54]

Title II veterans also tended to have a positive view of government. After all, the GI Bill provided evidence that policies that were initiated in Washington could be effective without being intrusive or bureaucratic. They appreciated its simple, standardized procedures, which were applied equally to all of the recipients. With eligibility rarely questioned and applicants treated with respect, Title II gave veterans a sense that they were honored members of a grateful nation. In the 1950s the perception that usually "government will do what is right" was pervasive in the United States as millions of Americans entered the middle class, but for Title II GIs that perception was stronger—and it lasted far longer.[55]

Veterans were neither more liberal nor more conservative than their contemporaries. They were, however, more knowledgeable about politics, more inclined to join a party, work on a campaign, and vote in primaries and general elections. They were also far more likely to run for political office. In the 1940s, "GI Joe" tickets promised to end "politics as usual." In 1960 veterans accounted for about 60 percent of the members of the U.S. House of Representatives. Throughout the 1970s and '80s, while younger Americans lost their faith in government, political leaders, campaigns, and elections, World War II veterans remained steadfast citizens.[56]

With the passing of "the Greatest Generation," civic and political participation has declined. The impact of the GI Bill on higher education in the United States was more permanent. By the 1950s, Keith Olson has observed, large colleges, large lecture classes, and the employment of graduate students to teach discussion sections had become the norm. In 1948 only 10 universities enrolled more than 20,000 students. Two decades later, 55 universities did so—and more than 60 increased the number of degree matriculants past 10,000 for the first time.[57]

Campus life changed as well, though not always in accord with the predictions made in the '40s. The refusal of "GI grinds" to submit to hazing, paddling, and freshmen beanies—and their apparent lack of interest in football and frat houses—created expectations that colleges might become "book factories," with fewer extracurricular activities and less school spirit. It did not happen. The image of the student-veteran who was contemptuous of extracurricular activities and school rituals is something of a myth. Many GIs enjoyed fraternity beer parties, played golf, and goofed off. In any event, panty raids and "dinky caps" proliferated in the 1950s—and fraternities and football remain defining features of many colleges and universities.[58]

Some changes ushered in by the GI Bill became part of the college fabric. The legislation, as we have seen, gave a big boost to "the student personnel movement," which came to include aptitude tests, vocational guidance, residential hall professionals, peer counseling, and mental health clinics. Career-oriented GIs may have helped accelerate the trend toward vocationalism among college students. Moreover, married students, once shunned by colleges and universities, were now welcomed. The example of veterans, who balanced academic and family responsibilities so well, made the difference. As the marriage age plummeted in the 1950s, hundreds of colleges and universities built low-cost apartments for them on or adjacent to the campus.[59]

Most important, of course, the bill demolished the contention that the core constituency of higher education was young men and women from affluent families and helped usher in an era of greatly expanded access to America's colleges and universities. Articles on GIs in colleges, historian Daniel Clark has indicated, reveled in stories about average Americans storming ivory towers. By the late 1940s, advertisements for consumer products had democratized the image of higher education. More middle-class Americans embraced college as an important—and a reachable—goal. The GI Bill, Clark concludes, helped open "a new route to the American Dream" to a wide segment of the population.[60] "This much has been revealed," Donald Moyer, director of Veterans Education at Cornell, wrote in 1947. "College enrollments will be permanently higher. The so-called G.I. Bill of Rights has enabled qualified students to come to college who formerly, because of their low economic status, would have been denied the privilege." How higher education faced this challenge, Moyer concluded, "is one of the most significant questions confronting us today."[61]

To help set the agenda, Truman appointed a Commission on Higher Education in July 1946. As chairman of the twenty-eight-person commission he chose George Zook. A native of Fort Scott, Kansas, Zook had been president of the University of Akron and U.S. Commissioner of Education under Roosevelt. As president of the American Council on Education, he had worked closely with the American Legion and politicians on both sides of the aisle in formulating the higher education provisions of the GI Bill.

The Truman Commission's six-volume report, *Higher Education in American Democracy*, issued in December 1947, set forth a bold blueprint for the future. Influenced no doubt by the experience of the first wave of GI Bill students, the commissioners asserted that, since higher education was becoming a prerequisite to occupational and social advance, "it is obvious, then, that free and universal access...in terms of the interest, ability, and need of the student" must be a major goal in American education. They were confident that at least 49 percent of the current college-age population could complete at least fourteen years of schooling and about 32 percent had the ability to finish an advanced liberal or professional undergraduate degree. Convinced as well that greater access need not be accompanied by a dilution of academic standards either in admissions or scholarly attainment, they urged an increase in enrollment in higher education from 2.3 million in 1947 to 4.6 million by 1960.

The commission's report contained four fundamental reforms: (1) Each state should develop a master plan to build and staff new institutions of higher education; (2) since the ratio of "semiprofessional" occupations that required two years of education to professions that necessitated a four-year degree was about five to one, a dramatic expansion in the number of junior colleges should begin. These institutions, which the commission called "community colleges," should offer terminal vocational degrees; (3) the federal government should grant need-based scholarships to deserving undergraduates and graduate students; and (4) federal legislation should end discrimination based on race, ethnicity, gender, and income.[62]

The Truman Commission report added momentum to the movement to expand access to higher education. Nonetheless, not all of its recommendations were implemented immediately. Since education at all levels had traditionally been the responsibility of states and localities, Congress held no hearings and passed no legislation. The federal government did not provide financial assistance to scholarship students until the passage of the Higher Education Act of 1965, which also set aside funds for the purchase of library, laboratory, and instructional materials.[63]

Statewide planning had begun even before the Truman Commission was created. In California, two master plans, issued in 1948 and 1953, set up a three-tier system of higher education. Some seventy junior colleges, open to any graduate of an accredited high school, would develop a largely vocational curriculum leading to an Associate of Arts degree. Twenty state colleges, with students drawn from the upper third of high school students, would offer liberal arts and occupational studies leading to bachelor's and master's diplomas. Nine campuses of the University of California composed the top tier and offered admission to young men and women who ranked in the top 12.5 percent of their high school classes. These institutions developed the full range of liberal arts and sciences, preprofessional, graduate, and professional studies.[64]

While not nearly as ambitious—or as structurally differentiated— plans generated by many other states also called for expanding public education, opening new campuses that offered two- and four-year degrees, and establishing administrative infrastructures to sustain large and complex "systems" of higher learning. In New York, for example, the GI Bill served as the catalyst for the creation of the State University of New York. In February 1946, at the request of Governor Dewey, the legislature established a Temporary Commission on the Need for a State University. Two months later, the State University of New York was founded. A central administration based in Albany supervised thirty-two units, including teachers colleges, two-year agricultural and technical institutions, the Maritime Academy, and the so-called contract colleges located at Alfred, Cornell, and Syracuse universities. The legislation authorized SUNY's board of trustees to add, as needed, new colleges, medical schools, and "an integrated university on a single campus." In 1950 the federal government transferred Champlain College to SUNY as a four-year college. That same year, community colleges were added to the system, and Middletown Collegiate Center was among the first to open. With the end of GI enrollments, however, politicians became cautious. Consequently, SUNY did not add any more engineering or four-year colleges of arts and sciences, law schools, or doctoral programs until the late 1950s and 1960s, when the state legislature, at the behest of Governor Nelson Rockefeller, directed the construction of an extensive state and college university system.[65]

As chapter five explains, neither the GI Bill nor the Truman Congress explicitly outlawed discrimination in higher education based on gender, race, and ethnicity. Nor did the government guarantee access to college based on ability rather than income. Nonetheless, the creation of new institutions—and the slowly changing admissions practices of some old ones—did make it easier for students from middle- and lower-middle-class backgrounds to extend their education beyond high school.

Here, too, the GI Bill was the catalyst. Not surprisingly, World War II veterans with the highest standard of living as children and those with the highest level of education prior to military service made the greatest use of the college provisions. Age made a difference as well, as younger veterans were more likely to pursue additional education. Nonetheless, socioeconomic status was not all that significant a variable, especially among veterans whose parents had encouraged them to stay in school. One example is Richard Colosimo. Raised in Depression-ravaged Pittsburgh, Colosimo often went to bed hungry. However, his father, who worked part-time in a tailor shop, often told him, "Dick, I don't know how I can ever help you, but get an education—that's the most important thing." After his military discharge, Colosimo entered the American Television Institute, a subcollege training program in Chicago. After a few months, he entered the University of Illinois, only to transfer to the University of Pittsburgh to complete his degree after he got married. The GI Bill provided him—and many other economically disadvantaged veterans—"a way out."[66]

For a time, it appeared that the bill would change admissions policies permanently, even at the most prestigious colleges, which had privileged the privileged. In 1945 officials in the president's office at Harvard overruled an administrator who had opposed "special advertising" for World War II veterans, reminding his colleagues that "We are not Pond's Cream or Kirk's Family Flakes." *What about Harvard?* was mailed to sixty-five thousand former soldiers and sailors. The GI Bill, Provost Paul Buck hoped, might "provide a new stamp and a new direction to the Harvard student body...to blend democratic selection into aristocratic achievement." Although the admissions office made the final decision, Harvard directed the veterans office to "pot" (i.e., rank) the candidates, who were placed in a pool separate from civilian applicants.[67]

Harvard did not come close to this egalitarian ideal, however. While GIs, who constituted more than half of the entering class of 1946, made it the most economically and ethnically diverse in the institution's history, fully three-quarters of the veterans had been admitted to Harvard before they entered military service. Those accepted who had no prior connection to Harvard were relatively affluent as well: Their parents' average income was 50 percent higher than that of the parents of scholarship students and three times greater than that of the typical American family. More than 40 percent of the veterans who entered Harvard in 1947 had graduated from private schools, including elite prep schools in New England. The nonveterans at Harvard, of course, were as privileged as ever. About 80 percent of those who applied from the top private schools were admitted, whereas only about a third of those who sought admission from three of the most highly selective urban public high schools in the northeast got in.[68]

After 1946, moreover, Harvard returned to past practices. Veterans constituted only 11 percent of the entering class in 1947—and a miniscule 3.5 percent in 1948. In the 1950s, Exeter, Andover, Groton, and other elite boarding schools continued to get preferential treatment, with about three-quarters of their applicants admitted. If prep school students constituted a third of each class or less, one dean opined, Harvard might "lose its social prestige entirely," as Yale, Princeton, and Williams became the first choice of gentlemen. In 1955 only 18 percent of applicants from Stuyvesant High School, Bronx High School of Science, and Central High School of Philadelphia got a thumbs up. The number of scholarship students was also dropping—from a high of 32 percent of freshmen in 1953 to 23 percent four years later. Harvard scholarship packages increased the amount of loans relative to grants, thereby making it increasingly difficult for students from economically disadvantaged families to attend. A decade after passage of the GI Bill, the vast majority of Harvard students came from the segment of the population in the top 10 percent of income. Their standardized test scores were higher, and they made a better impression in interviews. "The odds are pretty well stacked against the very needy student," concluded Richard King, director of the Office of Tests.[69]

After the surge of GI Bill students had ended, the nation's prestigious private institutions recruited their entering classes in much the same way as before. Scholarship students tended to come from middle-class rather than poor families. The percentage of undergraduates on financial aid in the 1950s did not differ dramatically from the pre–World War II era. State institutions—and especially the community colleges—absorbed most of the enrollment increases during the decade. Students from lower-middle- and working-class backgrounds made up at least a majority of matriculants in (low-tuition) public community colleges in the decade after the end of the war. As the economy expanded, along with jobs for college graduates, about a third of those who completed an Associate's degree transferred to four-year institutions. These students joined the largely middle-class constituency of state colleges and universities.[70]

Enrollment in institutions of higher education reached 3.2 million in 1959, far short of the estimate made by the Truman Commission. It would be during the following two decades that the doors to America's colleges and universities opened more widely. In 1970, 8.6 million baby boomers were in college. In 1980, 12.1 million people were degree matriculants. In no small measure, family income still dictated whether students would go to college—and which institution they would attend. However, thanks to financial aid provided by the federal government and the states, access to higher education was far greater than it had ever been.[71]

The GI Bill, of course, does not deserve the credit for these developments, and in this sense its influence on higher education has probably been overstated. It did nonetheless play a substantive and a symbolic role in American society and the history of higher education in the mid-twentieth century. The legislation replenished the human capital of the United States, which had been depleted by low college enrollments during the war and hundreds of thousands of combat deaths and disabilities. The number of conferred degrees, which peaked at 496,000 in 1950, was greater than the total in any single year before World War II. It would not be exceeded until the 1960s. This educated workforce helped the nation enter the postindustrial age. Title II also accelerated, albeit modestly, the expansion in higher education, both as a stimulus for the development of statewide systems of public colleges and universities and as evidence of the achievements of a diverse cohort of students. Its immediate and manifest successes spread the perception that higher education was the preferred path to economic mobility in the United States. For decades the bill served as a rallying point for reformers who were seeking to increase access to college. While Title II may not have been the watershed its most zealous partisans proclaimed, it was critically important, as one critic put it, "not just for what it did but for what so many Americans have lovingly believed it did." Designed as a temporary expedient, it did a good deal for individual GIs and the economy—and in legitimizing the notion that a college degree should be and actually was within reach for millions of Americans.[72]

FIVE

"The Most Inclusive Program"

Race, Gender, and Ethnicity in Title II

Instruction to a diverse class at an ACUNY college. (Courtesy Cornell University Press)

E DUCATION AND TRAINING became the vital center of the GI Bill, a certificate of admission to postwar prosperity in the United States. By 1950, the U.S. government had spent more money to educate veterans than it had on the Marshall Plan. Excluding no one who had been on active duty for at least ninety days and had not been dishonorably discharged, the benefit was acclaimed as "the most inclusive program provided for national heroes of any war." It did not discriminate between more or less privileged Americans. It made no distinctions between GI Joe and GI Jane. Moreover, although the armed forces remained segregated at the end of World War II, the legislation did not contain a "single loophole for different treatment of white and black veterans," exclaimed Charles Hurd in *Opportunity*, the magazine of the National Urban League, in 1945. Unlike Social Security, which did not cover farmworkers and domestics, jobs often filled by blacks, the bill was colorblind. "If someone was good enough to die for America," wrote journalist Michael Bennett, "he or she was good enough to enjoy all the rights of an American."[1]

The GI Bill did indeed provide educational opportunities to millions of women, blacks, and economically disadvantaged veterans that were not offered to non-GIs.[2] Many of them subsequently became active in civic and political organizations and helped advance the cause of equal rights in the United States. Nonetheless, as army nurse corps veteran Ann Bertini put it, "they really created it with men in mind, didn't they?" White men, she might have added. With the notable exception of Congressman Rankin, the authors and administrators of the bill did not consciously intend the legislation to be racist or sexist. Neither did they challenge dominant assumptions about race and gender in the 1940s or take into account the implications of a benefit conferred exclusively on veterans of the armed forces, a bastion of white male privilege.[3]

Like virtually all protracted conflicts, World War II provided employment and educational opportunities to women in the United States. With millions of men in uniform (and abroad), the demands of wartime production drew unprecedented numbers of women, both single and married, into the workforce. Women labored in factories and on assembly lines, jobs previously deemed beyond their physical capacities. They were also recruited as undergraduate, graduate, and professional students by colleges and universities who had lost their preferred customers to the draft. When the war ended, however, many Americans, including the sponsors of the GI Bill, expected most women to return—happily—to "normalcy."

During the 1930s, bleak job prospects kept many young people, especially young women, in school. In 1940, 642,757 women graduated from high school, some 52.3 percent of the total. In the '40s, the number of graduates continued to climb. The percentage of seventeen-year-old boys who finished high school rose from 48 to 54. Girls showed an even more impressive increase—from 54 to 61 percent. Cobbling together the resources for college entailed substantial sacrifices for most families, of course, and the majority of women chose a husband or a job over a bachelor of arts or science. Nonetheless, enrollments in higher education increased until the United States entered the war. The number of female matriculants climbed from 481,000 (10.5 percent of women aged 18–21) in 1930 to 601,000 (12.2 percent of that cohort) in 1940. Since the number of males in college rose even more rapidly, the percentage of women in higher education actually dropped—from 43.7 percent in 1930 to 40.2 percent in 1940.[4]

By 1942, with millions of young men marching off to war, institutions of higher education faced a crisis. To sustain enrollments (and tuition revenues), colleges courted women. Professors and administrators encouraged women to become leaders in student government and take editorial positions in student publications. To meet the national emergency, they admitted women into fields previously thought beyond their intellectual capacities. Between 1942 and 1945 a 29-percent increase occurred in women majoring in the sciences. Barnard students trained in meteorology and electronics. For the first time, Columbia University and Rensselaer Polytechnic Institute welcomed women into their engineering programs. Through an agreement with Radcliffe, Harvard opened its undergraduate curriculum to females (though their access to the Widener Library was restricted to Saturday afternoons). Preferring "very superior women" to an applicant pool of mediocre males, Harvard admitted twelve females to the Medical School in 1945. That year, women composed 14.4 percent of all first-year medical students in the United States.[5]

Assumptions about "women's place" were challenged in the social sciences as well. In the fall of 1942, the Department of Sociology at Syracuse University offered a course titled "The Status and Responsibility of Women in the Social Order." Students were asked to consider women as "creative personalities outside the home," as well as in their current status as wives, mothers, and homemakers. With the syllabus correlated closely to "present developments," the course contained a section on women in the defense industry, including information about the training required for specific jobs. At Syracuse, Dean of Women M. Eunice Hilton hoped that this class and others would begin to redress "the failure of women to fulfill the hopes of suffrage advocates."[6]

On many campuses, then, gender—and gender stereotypes—were bending. Still, the depth and permanence of the changes should not be exaggerated. A substantial majority of undergraduate women remained committed to general education and the humanities rather than to specialized or preprofessional instruction. Moreover, sex ratios in higher education did not shift significantly until the very end of the war. Some men received draft deferments to stay in school and study science, engineering, or medicine. Although the enrollment of civilian men declined 68.7 percent between 1939–1940 and 1943–1944, the army and navy contracted with colleges and universities to provide training in technical fields that ranged from meteorology to foreign languages to more than a million soldiers, sailors, and air force personnel. With 4,500 ex-GIs enrolled in 1942, Harvard became "one of the foremost military and naval academies in the U.S." The president of the University of California–Berkeley called that institution "a military tent with academic sideshows."[7]

Nor did women rush headlong into the groves of academe. Motivated by patriotism and/or financial considerations, many of them opted for work in the civil service, the defense industry, and nursing and also found employment as ambulance drivers. Others got married, had babies, and stayed at home. Between 1940 and 1944, in fact, the number of women in colleges actually declined by 25,000. And yet, the wartime proportion of women in academe could not help but grow. In 1944, when the military brought many more students in uniform to Europe and the Pacific, women approached 50 percent of college enrollments and received more degrees than men. In 1945, 55 percent of matriculants were female.[8]

Many women braced themselves for a "reversal of opportunity" when the war ended. By 1945, Helen Hosp, a staff member of the American Association of University Women, had already observed "a shift from excessive admiration for women's capacity to do anything, to the idea that women ought to be delighted to give up any job and return to her proper sphere." Veterans' preference, she predicted, would dominate hiring decisions. Hosp nonetheless hoped that the trend toward increased enrollment of women in colleges and universities would continue. She detected a "widespread belief" that educated women could help ensure "the richness and stability" of American culture, business, and civic life.[9]

With the passage of the GI Bill, however, the outlook for women in higher education grew dimmer. Merit-based criteria of admission to college, the AAUW reported, had become complicated by feelings of social obligation toward veterans, "a certain masculine jealousy of professional prerogatives," and the political pressure exerted by veterans and their organizations. During the war, wrote journalist Milton MacKaye, many coeducational institutions could not have survived without the enrollment of young women. Afterward, however, the wheel turned again. Speaking off the record, several college and university officials told MacKaye that many females of college age would not be able to matriculate. Housing was perhaps the greatest constraint. While men could be quartered "anyplace where walls can keep out the weather," female undergraduates were restricted to "supervised" housing. In what appeared to be a zero-sum game, women would have to wait their turn: "Servicemen—and service women—will be first; the promise has been made."[10]

As MacKaye suggested, one group of women, the GI Janes, did not have to worry. They constituted approximately 2 percent of World War II military personnel. Veterans in all of the major units—the Women's Army Corps (WACs), the Navy (Waves), the Coast Guard (SPARs), and the Marines (MCWR)—were eligible for Title II benefits.[11] Not subject to the draft, military women did not represent a cross-section of the American population. They were more affluent, had more highly educated parents, and had received more schooling than their male counterparts. About 62 percent of enlisted women, for example, had attained at least a high school diploma. The comparable figure for enlisted men was 39 percent. Nevertheless, as Suzanne Mettler has demonstrated, these women were less likely than men to use GI Bill benefits. While fully half of male World War II veterans used Title II, only 40 percent of females signed up for higher education and subcollege training. Women who used Title II spent less time in school—on average one or two years compared to three years for men. They were also far less likely than men to get a degree—about 63 percent of women and 79 percent of men completed their academic programs.[12]

Even with a grant from the government, going back to school proved to be far more difficult for women than for men. The postwar generation got married more frequently—and earlier—than any generation in U.S. history. Only 9 percent of Americans believed that a single person could be happy. A whopping 96.4 percent of the women and 94.1 percent of the men who came of age after World War II took the trip to the altar. Most of them were married by their mid-twenties. Almost immediately these couples began having lots of kids, often in rapid succession. They yearned for family stability, historian Elaine Tyler May has written, and imprinted a "powerful ideology of family domesticity" on their lives. Traditional gender roles, with the woman "homeward bound," became distinctive features of upwardly mobile, middle-class life. If a single woman went to school, she was advised to find a husband before she graduated. If a married woman wanted to be a student, she prepared to do double duty.[13]

One of 132,000 women who used the education benefits, Vivian Erickson Kingsley presents a case study of the challenges for student GI Janes. Born in Connecticut in 1920, she enlisted in the navy after her boyfriend was killed in the North Sea. Trained as a nurse, she was posted to St. Albans Naval Hospital in Queens, where she met Bill Kingsley, an enlisted man preparing to be a pharmacist. Married within the year, the Kingsleys had a son. When the war ended, Bill got his high school diploma and entered the University of Denver in 1947. A year later, Vivian was admitted as well—to the university's nursing program. The couple, now with two children and another on the way, lived in a Quonset hut, each working a part-time job to make ends meet. By taking a heavy course load each semester and attending summer sessions, Bill graduated in two and a half years. In 1950 he took a job as a high school teacher. Vivian did not get her degree for another ten years. Her family came first. "A lot of women dream of a great marriage," she recalled. "I got the dream."[14]

Two provisions of the GI Bill put veterans like Vivian Kingsley at a distinct disadvantage. Unlike men, women veterans did not receive a living allowance for a dependent spouse while they were in school. Veterans and college students Anne Bosanko and Ken Green got married in 1946. Their stipends totaled $145 a month—$90 for him, $55 for her. Bill sponsors had assumed that husbands could—and should—provide for themselves and their families. They had not contemplated providing childcare credits and facilities to student-veterans even though the federal government had made allowances for female workers in defense plants during World War II.[15]

Gender neutral on its face, the nine-year limitation on GI Bill benefits also fell disproportionately on women. Expected to raise the children or work while their husbands were in school, women tended to defer, delay, or drop their own personal and professional plans. As one WAC put it, my future "depends on his wishes." Ann Bertini did not go back to school until her children had left the house. At fifty and on her own nickel, she began training to be a funeral director. Indeed, while some 60 percent of female veterans received some education and training after their discharge, only 58 percent of this cohort used the bill to pay for it.[16]

The Veterans Administration, moreover, made no special efforts to inform women of the benefits to which they were entitled. While men were briefed about the bill when they were discharged, and were offered educational and vocational counseling, such services, according to Mettler, were "provided only sporadically to women." *Going Back to Civilian Life*, a pamphlet issued by the War Department, did not refer to women. Moreover, since women were far less likely than men to join a veterans' organization, they lacked access to another important source of information and encouragement.[17]

More than GI Bill regulations and administration, the ideology of domestic containment explains why so many women did not use the education and training benefits. Responding to Mettler's survey, more than a third of nonusers cited family obligations. One veteran got married and helped her husband run a bakery. Another took care of her father after her mother died—and then got married. About 28 percent of female veterans indicated that they "preferred to work." After a brief dip in the immediate aftermath of the war, nonetheless, employment rates for women actually picked up. More women entered the labor force in the 1950s than in the '40s. They often viewed their jobs as (temporary) extensions of their gender role, necessary to make ends meet or contribute to the upward mobility of their families. Finally, the "head-long rush into domesticity" lay just beneath the surface of the justification provided by 20 percent of nonusers: "I had all the education or training I needed."[18]

Education and training under the bill, then, were far less pivotal for female veterans than for males. In the 1950s, female college graduates encountered occupational segregation, wage differentials, glass ceilings, and hiring restrictions for high-status jobs. As a result, although many individuals praised the program for enhancing job opportunities and fostering personal and intellectual growth, Title II had a less significant socioeconomic impact on women than on men. A third of survey respondents identified themselves as housewives. Of those who worked outside the home, very few (except for teachers and social service providers) were white-collar professionals. Less involved as well in civic and political life, women veterans, Mettler concludes, did not "perceive the affirming messages of inclusion that so enhanced the participation rates of male beneficiaries."[19]

The for-men-mostly benefits of the GI Bill did not go unchallenged in the 1940s. In 1945, one hundred young widows founded the Gold Star Wives of World War II. Led by Marie Jordan, a twenty-four-year-old housewife from Tappan, New York, the organization established chapters throughout the United States and set up job-placement bureaus and childcare facilities. Members received legal aid and help in locating affordable housing. In 1947, the Gold Star Wives petitioned Congress to extend the GI Bill of Rights to 105,125 World War II widows. They wanted government guarantees of small loans; provision of medical and hospitalization benefits to families of slain servicemen; and tuition for four years of college education, with a $65 monthly subsistence allowance, to children whose fathers were killed in the war.[20]

Denying that their organization was "a pressure group," the Gold Star Wives nonetheless pushed for substantial revisions in the GI Bill in testimony to congressional committees. A survey of war widows, they reported, revealed an average income of $33 a week, "not a very high amount for the principal breadwinner of the family." About 13 percent of widows expressed a desire to return to college under an expanded GI Bill. Sixty-six percent planned to take a training course—at schools for beauticians, bookkeepers, and stenographers—for up to a year. Another 21 percent had no plans to further their education even if the government subsidized it. Estimating $1,180 per person for tuition and living expenses, President Ruth Dutcher put a price tag of $145 million on education and training for war widows. Four years of college for their children, "the dream of every parent," would cost an additional $321 million.[21]

Rather than charity, Helen Gooden testified, war widows wanted self-sufficiency. Some of them might well get by on their own resources, but the GI Bill had not intended that a veteran—or his family— "should just get along." The nation owed as much to war widows as it did to those veterans who came back alive. With a GI Bill grant, Gooden intended to put her twenty-one-month-old daughter in a nursery school, complete her master's degree, and teach French in high school. War widows who taught, she concluded, could be breadwinners and homemakers and would be able to spend time with their children and teach the next generation "the ideals for which their husbands died."[22]

The Gold Star Wives had been told, Marie Jordan acknowledged, "that it is too late, that this is an economy Congress." She recognized as well "that it is difficult to get anything passed now, unless you number 14 million veterans and not 101,000 widows. Numbers still matter." Defensively—and even somewhat desperately—Jordan and her colleagues questioned their own survey to demonstrate that "the cost in reality would be less than the amount which we estimate." Very few widows would actually enroll in college, they claimed, and a large majority of their children "will never meet the educational requirements."[23]

The proposed legislation never had a chance. Although the VFW was officially neutral, the American Legion opposed any extension of benefits to nonservice personnel. Speaking for the Veterans Administration, General Omar Bradley agreed, citing "tremendous additional cost to the government" and "the general basic policy of limiting such benefits to persons who rendered active service in the armed forces." Bradley questioned the "appropriateness and basic soundness" of departing from the original concept of the GI Bill.[24]

Full of compliments for "the girls," congressmen expressed sympathy, indicated a willingness to support an increase in widows' pensions, and turned thumbs down on education and training benefits for dependents of deceased veterans. Traditional assumptions about gender and concerns about costs lay behind their decision. Shouldn't widows be encouraged to remarry, they asked, and shouldn't their new husbands—and not the taxpayers—support them? Several bachelors quipped that they were not qualified to opine on the legislation before them. The bill did not survive its first reading. The GI Bill would not serve as a wedge to expand government social welfare benefits to any civilians. Furthermore, only a tiny number of women would be "entitled" to education and training subsidized by Uncle Sam.[25]

While Congress was turning aside the proposals of the Gold Star Wives, college admissions officers across the United States were turning down record numbers of applications from female high school graduates. Relying on a survey of forty institutions of higher education, Benjamin Fine reported in the *New York Times* that almost every one of them were not meeting the demands of both men and women students—and saw "no sign of immediate relief." Women were becoming "the chief casualty of the post-war educational boom." Women's colleges, Fine noted, were unable—and unwilling—to expand.

Comparatively small, they remained convinced that it was educationally sound for them to stay that way. To accommodate a few more students, for example, Mount Holyoke required 25 percent of its undergraduates to share "temporary doubles." Even so, the enrollment of 1,180, the largest in the institution's history, was only 100 more than peak peacetime registration. Jammed to the rafters, Texas State College for Women rejected 600 applicants in 1946. The board of trustees approved a $4 million expansion program, including three new dormitories, an extension to an existing residence hall, a central dining facility, and two classroom buildings. However, none of these facilities would be available by the fall of 1947.[26]

Some women's colleges, moreover, were granting precious spaces to men. In New York, the presidents of Vassar and Sarah Lawrence complied with Governor Dewey's plea for a "temporary solution" to accommodate World War II veterans. In the spring of 1946, thirty-six males enrolled at Vassar. A year later the number of veterans on campus had tripled. Between 1948 and 1953, 170 veterans took classes at Vassar. Two of them were women. During the same period, 44 veterans matriculated at Sarah Lawrence. At both institutions, the former servicemen hailed from nearby towns—and lived at home while attending classes.[27]

Giving veterans the top priority, coeducational institutions began accepting fewer females as soon as the war ended. Penn State added no women undergraduates to its main campus until applications from GIs peaked and headed downward in 1949. The University of Wisconsin put a cap on enrollment from female applicants who resided outside the state and then rejected virtually all applications from nonresidents. Feeling the strongest pressure, the better schools, public and private, set quotas on the number of women they would admit.[28]

At Cornell, Herbert Williams, director of admissions, reported in 1946 that more than twelve thousand applicants hoped to enter a freshman class of 1,393. At least half of the slots were reserved for veterans. For recent graduates of secondary schools, a quota had been established for women, the number dictated by the accommodations for them in the dormitories. The dozen fraternity houses, leased by the university for use as "cottages" for female undergraduates during the war, were now commandeered and turned into a "Vetsville." This was, of course, bad news for "the flood of fine, well-prepared girls who want to come to Cornell." In the College of Arts and Sciences, Williams indicated, places had been set aside for fifty females (out of two thousand applicants) in an entering class of 350. Throughout the university, the undergraduate population would be no more than 20 percent female, most of them enrolled in the College of Home Economics (today the School of Human Ecology).[29] Lucille Allen, counselor to women at Cornell, pleaded with President Day and Provost Arthur S. Adams to set the quota a bit higher. "The women have accepted their rejection, in most cases, for professional schools," she claimed. "They recognize this gives the veterans the additional needed help." Nonetheless, could not the College of Arts and Sciences for the next few years admit a few more women? "Each time a downward change in numbers is made," Allen warned, "poor public relations with alumnae, with alumni with daughters, and with secondary schools result."[30]

It was not to be. Although the AAUW deemed it "unthinkable that among civilian students, women should suffer discrimination as compared to men," at Cornell and virtually everywhere else in higher education, administrators concluded that, at least for a few years, the number of women students would "inescapably have to be reduced."[31]

Enrollments recovered a bit at the tail end of the 1940s, as new dormitories were completed. In 1950, 104,000 women received undergraduate degrees, about 27,000 more than in 1940, though scarcely enough to keep pace with the increase in high school graduates. At the very moment that higher education had become a ticket to the middle class, women were losing ground. Constituting 40 percent of all college graduates in 1940, women made up a mere 25 percent of degree candidates in 1950. Since veterans received preferential treatment in the most selective private colleges, women often had to choose between a public institution or no institution at all. Nor did gender neutrality return when the World War II GI Bill had run its course. In 1959 women accounted for one-third of the undergraduate degrees in the United States.[32]

Gender disparities were the norm in graduate education as well. Whereas 38 percent of the recipients of a master's or an advanced professional degree in 1940 were women, ten years later the percentage had dropped to 29 percent. Women did not return to prewar levels until 1970. With a large majority of undergraduate degrees awarded to men, a decline in female doctorates was almost inevitable. Women received fewer than 10 percent of the PhDs awarded in 1950.[33]

In colleges and universities, academic and vocational counselors recommended courses of study compatible with marriage. If women wanted or had to work, they suggested teaching, nursing, and secretarial jobs. In a speech to the American Association of University Women in 1947, Lynn White Jr., president of Mills College, called for a distinctly feminine course of study. Since he deemed differences between the sexes, rooted in biology, to be immutable, White supported a curriculum to help young women "foster the intellectual and emotional life of her family and community." Although he granted that women had the freedom to pursue any vocation they chose, White believed they should learn not to compete with men on men's ground.[34]

Though contested, often fiercely, White's attitudes—and self-imposed limitations—kept many women from building on the gains they had made during the war in traditionally male fields. Between 1940 and 1950 the representation of women in professional occupations declined from 42 to 39 percent. During the 1950s, women made up only 20 percent of undergraduate majors in the sciences and mathematics. They made significant gains in journalism but barely inched up in engineering, law, and dentistry. They lost ground in the professoriate in colleges and universities, where their numbers declined from 28 percent of faculty lines in 1940 to 25 percent in 1950 and 22 percent in 1960. In medicine the situation was even worse. In 1949, 12 percent of medical school graduates were women, most of them admitted four years earlier when the men were still at war. However, by the mid-fifties, only 5 percent of newly minted physicians were female. In addition, some hospitals no longer accepted women as interns or residents, and a majority of male medical students believed that only a few women were sufficiently competent to enter the profession.[35]

World War II had held out the promise of educational equity for women. However, as historian Susan Hartmann has concluded, a "desire to compensate those who had defended the nation increased the distance between women's and men's opportunities." In fact if not in form, the GI Bill privileged men. Veterans preference helped sustain the supremacy of men in professions with the highest status and compensation. It did not disturb—and may actually have reinforced—the gendered expectations that governed the public and private lives of so many women in postwar America.[36]

Although women had good reasons to be apprehensive about the gendered implications of the GI Bill, the legislation generated great expectations among the vast majority of the one million black World War II veterans and their families. "Never before in history," wrote Campbell Johnson, an African American army officer, "has such an inclusive program been provided for national heroes of any war." The bill meant that every soldier, black or white, would be an "unforgotten man." Attracted by the whole package of benefits, many African Americans were especially interested in education and training.

"Imagine the excitement of men who could afford higher education under language that called it their right," Johnnetta Cole, president of Spelman College, recalled. Noting that military service provided literacy education, officer training, and extensive experience in an array of skilled and semiskilled jobs, the U.S. Office of Education concluded that blacks would seek further training with only "slight encouragement." The GI Bill "offered an opportunity to lift a whole generation of Negroes onto another rung of the economic ladder."[37]

Title II was a turning point for many black veterans who used education and training to boost themselves into the middle class. As it had for nonblack veterans, use of the benefits sparked participation in civic and political activities, including civil rights. Passed in an era of entrenched racial prejudice, the GI Bill was the most egalitarian and generous initiative blacks had ever experienced. It made no distinctions based on "race, creed, color, or national origin," boasted General Omar Bradley. Nonetheless, because the overwhelming majority of beneficiaries were white—and the legislation did not act affirmatively to overcome Jim Crow institutions and instrumentalities—the GI Bill did not reduce racial disparities in the United States. As journalist Edward Humes has noted, "the rose itself may have been hearty and beautiful, but its roots were planted in poisoned soil."[38]

To begin with, African Americans were underrepresented in the armed forces. A higher percentage of blacks than whites were rejected for enlistment and draft boards on grounds of physical health, literacy, and aptitude. About half of blacks and three-quarters of whites in their twenties and thirties served in the military during World War II. Blacks who served had substantially less education than whites. The average black GI had not completed the eighth grade. About 17 percent (compared to 41 percent of whites) had graduated from high school.[39]

Nonetheless, although most lacked the preparation or credentials to matriculate in a college or university, many black veterans leaped at the chance to return to school. According to a survey conducted by the Veterans Administration in 1950, 49 percent of nonwhites (compared to 43 percent of whites) used education and training benefits at the college or subcollege level. As we would expect from the striking difference in high school completion rates, greater proportions of blacks than whites used their Title II benefit to attend schools and training programs below the college level. Among veterans born between 1923 and 1928, only 12 percent of black GI Bill users (and 28 percent of whites) attended an institution of higher education.[40]

Monte Posey was one of them. His experience illustrates that the GI Bill afforded African Americans greater opportunities than they had ever known—and illuminates the Jim Crow gauntlets they had to run. Born in Chicago in 1927, Posey was descended from slaves who lived on a cotton plantation in Alabama. During the Depression, his mother worked as a seamstress, while his father, a veteran of World War I, passed as white to get his job as a stock clerk for Rockwell Barnes Paper Company. Encouraged by his parents to devote himself to school, Monte graduated from eighth grade at the top of his class. Fibbing about where they lived, the Poseys enrolled their son in an affluent public high school near Northwestern University. Nevertheless, when the white teachers evinced little interest in a black boy, Monte lost his motivation and graduated with mediocre grades.

Fascinated by airplanes, Posey took the army pilot tests and physicals as soon as he turned seventeen in 1944. He was assigned to the University of Wisconsin for training and sailed through courses ranging from cryptography to electrical engineering. He was sent—on a segregated train—to Keesler Air Force Base in Biloxi, Mississippi. Several of his instructors did not hide their anger at orders to teach a "coon" to be a pilot. Unlike white GIs, Posey could not leave the base or frequent clubs on it. As the war ended, he was transferred to Eglin Airfield in Florida and assigned to duty not as a pilot but as an aircraft mechanic. "We were all disillusioned by then," Posey recalled. "My job was okay, I was treated well, but a lot of the other guys were stoking furnaces, sweeping up, doing menial jobs. We couldn't go anywhere in town—when I did, one time, I almost got arrested for sitting in the wrong seat. I was very happy to get out."

Facing the prospect of transfer to the infantry, Posey secured an early discharge and applied to the newly opened Chicago branch of the University of Illinois. With its campus on a navy pier, the institution offered two years of undergraduate instruction, after which students were eligible to transfer to complete their degrees. Seeking VA approval, Posey waited for hours in midtown Chicago before a counselor was ready to see him. Staring at him from a drab, dented desk, the counselor recommended that Posey forego college for on-the-job-training: "Look around. There are no opportunities out there for college-educated Negroes. You'll be wasting your time." Posey had seen it before: white authority figures who were convinced they knew what was best for blacks. This time, though, he persisted. Posey knew that if a college was accredited, the GI Bill decreed that the VA must approve. When he held his ground, the counselor, eager to move on to the white veterans waiting to see him, relented: "Fine. You're wasting your time, but since it's what you want to do, I'll approve it."

Posey did well in his first year. In 1947, however, he decided to marry the young woman he had dated in high school, opted for a full-time job, and took the civil service test. His score placed him as one of twenty-nine cadets (out of four thousand applicants) in the police academy, and he later became one of thirty-one African Americans in the Chicago Police Department. Posey did not receive plum assignments, though he was delighted to stand guard at the homes of blacks who had used GI Bill loans to purchase homes in white neighborhoods. Passed over for promotion, Posey remained a plainclothes officer before relocating to the Los Angeles Police Department in 1953. When the LAPD proved to be even more discriminatory than the police department in Chicago, he completed an undergraduate degree in sociology and criminology and in 1960 took a job as an investigator for the California Fair Employment Practices Commission. By now remarried, he bought a house with a GI Bill loan, remained active in civil rights protests, and in 1965 became an officer in a new federal agency, the Equal Employment Opportunity Commission. Traveling around the country to investigate charges of discrimination in hiring and promotion, Posey worried about his own safety—and that of African Americans who had the courage to file complaints. Although the authorities in many communities were racists, he recalled, "we had subpoena powers...and we brought those people to task." Posey retired in 1975 because of a spinal injury and returned to college to complete a master's degree. After the war, Posey's father began introducing him to his friends as a veteran who was "really somebody."[41]

Robert Eubanks was "really somebody," too. An excellent student, Eubanks graduated from high school in 1942 at age fifteen. He did not have enough money to accept a tuition-only scholarship from Howard University in Washington, D.C.—and could not find anyone who would hire a young black man, so he joined the army. Discharged in 1946, he enrolled at the Illinois Institute of Technology and earned his degree in four years. Confronted again with job discrimination, he stayed at ITT for his master's and doctorate in theoretical and applied mechanical engineering. After a successful career in industry, Eubanks returned to academia and eventually became a tenured professor at the University of Illinois. In the 1940s, he recalled, "restrictions on blacks were rough. The GI Bill gave me my start on being a professional instead of a stock clerk."[42]

Dovey Roundtree was one of thousands of black women who made the most of Title II. Decked out in red, white, and blue clothes, she tried to become a WAAC in 1942, but the recruiting officer in Charlotte, North Carolina, refused to give her an application form. Undaunted, she journeyed to Richmond, Virginia, and talked her way into enlistment. One of the first black women to attend officer candidate school, she left the WAACs as a captain and began working with A. Philip Randolph, the union leader and civil rights activist, to make the Fair Employment Practices Commission into a more permanent and effective federal agency. In time, under the GI Bill, Roundtree entered Howard Law School and opened a practice in Washington, D.C. After completing a second degree, this time at Howard University Divinity School, she became an ordained minister as well.[43]

These stories of success highlight—and hide—the GI Bill's overall impact on African Americans. Provisions for education and training provided hundreds of thousands of black veterans with opportunities for professional advancement and increased earning power. At the same time, many ex-GIs returned home to find that VA administrators and local officials were indifferent or hostile to them. As William Caudill, a scholar affiliated with the Julius Rosenwald Fund, wrote in the waning days of World War II, "the white G.I. will be considered first a veteran, second and incidentally a white man; the Negro G.I. will often be considered first a Negro, second and incidentally a veteran."[44]

The VA instructed its staff members, the vast majority of whom were white, to show no "discrimination whatsoever in the service rendered to either colored or white veterans." Still, the agency did not evince an inclination to counteract the widespread discrimination already in place. When a veterans center opened in Atlanta–Fulton County in Georgia, Lena Sayles was the only black on staff. Although she had a graduate degree in counseling from the School of Social Work at Atlanta University, Sayles worked as a secretary and maid. By the end of 1946 the VA had about twelve black counselors in Georgia and Alabama, all of them housed at Tuskegee and Atlanta University. Claiming that no qualified African Americans had applied, officials in Mississippi had hired no blacks at all.[45]

After a tour of the South, where more than nine out of ten black veterans used their education and training benefits, Joseph Albright, a special assistant to the VA, reported that "whether it will be readily admitted or not," Negro veterans faced "special problems" that required special attention. As of late 1946 the situation was not encouraging: "General morale: Fair. Educational Opportunities: Fair. On the job opportunities: Poor. Treatment by VA: Good. Treatment by veterans' organizations: Fair. Housing: Very Poor. Loans: Poor." Many of the seven thousand black veterans in and around Atlanta, Georgia, Albright reported, were "very reluctant" to talk with a VA counselor because the only guidance center in the entire state was located at all-white Georgia Tech University. Albright urged his superiors to collaborate with the Associated Negro Press to publicize GI Bill benefits; set up counseling offices in every black college; and assign a black contact officer to every deputy administrator of the VA whose area included "an appreciable segment of the Negro population."[46]

Albright, who was black, owed his appointment to pressure from the National Association for the Advancement of Colored People, which also urged the VA to take remedial action to assist black veterans. In January 1945 the NAACP established an Office of Veterans Affairs, headed by Jesse Dedmon, a young lawyer and World War II veteran. In investigating individual complaints, Dedmon walked a tightrope, afraid to antagonize the Veterans Administration. The VA administers the law, he indicated on more than one occasion, "to both Negro and White alike." His reports to his colleagues at the NAACP sugarcoated the truth.[47]

Often VA administrators emphasized that remedies were beyond their jurisdiction. In 1945 newly appointed VA administrator Omar Bradley told civil rights leaders that he could not "issue a blanket order now" to integrate VA hospitals "because it would cause a lot of trouble." Bradley promised to try to "effect integration" by addressing "each problem as it arises." Bradley's VA was not a force for change. It had no mandate to challenge the status quo in race relations. College administrators, one VA official predicted, would "resent such action and it might impair the very pleasant working relationship which exists at the present time." Under pressure from the American Legion (which approved state offices' permission to charter posts for African American servicemen only if they were segregated), the VA refused to accredit the newly formed United Negro and Allied Veterans of America. The agency opposed an NAACP-sponsored bill, introduced into the Eightieth Congress, to prohibit the allocation of GI Bill funds to schools that sponsored segregation. A VA spokesman testified against the initiative, which died in committee.[48]

The VA's unwillingness to enforce or promote African Americans' rights, according to Harold Lett, director of education and training in New Jersey, left "serious gaps in a fair and equitable administration" of the GI Bill. The only commercial school in one area of his state, for example, discriminated against blacks. Through the use of tax funds, Lett pointed out, the federal government was "aiding and abetting" these policies. African Americans had to incur additional expense and leave their communities—or forego training. "In fairness to minority-group veterans, whose depressed status did not relieve them of War sacrifices," Lett recommended that the VA grant "more protection than the regulations you quote seem willing to give." Despite his plea, the agency declined to intervene.[49]

Two structural features of the GI Bill perpetuated existing patterns of racial preference. The legislation gave private institutions, including colleges and universities, exclusive authority over admissions criteria for veterans. Those criteria could—and did—include segregation in the South and racial quotas in the North. Equally important, the bill prohibited any federal agency or department from "exercising supervision or control over any state educational agency." Insisting that "a definite line should be drawn in the schooling on the matter of racial segregation," Representative Rankin beat back a proposal to require the VA to consult the U.S. Office of Education and restrict Title II grants to institutions it approved. "Your bill," the head of a business college in Mississippi informed Rankin, "is particularly desirable for the Southern states."[50]

Although in theory, black veterans could use their vouchers in institutions of higher education in the North, a relatively small number actually did. During the late 1940s, annual black enrollment in colleges and universities outside the South did not exceed five thousand. Without adequate advising, many black veterans could not explore appropriate options. Counselors channeled many bright blacks into agricultural and manual training programs instead of the liberal arts. Including questions about a candidate's race on application forms, northern colleges maintained both formal and informal quotas. At Princeton, a poll conducted during World War II by the campus newspaper revealed that 62.4 percent of students did not want blacks on their campus. Those who supported a limited quota wanted to apply higher academic standards to black than to white applicants—and ban African American undergraduates from Prospect Street, where many juniors and seniors dined. At the University of Pennsylvania, only forty-six of nine thousand students in 1946 were black. In the vast majority of northern institutions, moreover, black students were not allowed to play varsity sports, attend dances, or join fraternities and sororities.[51]

Most Title II black veterans stayed in the segregated South. Although blacks constituted about a quarter of its population, the region contained five white colleges for every black school. Small, overcrowded, and underfunded, historically black colleges, the only game in town for African Americans, were at the bottom of the pyramid in higher education. Their libraries and laboratories were inadequate, and their professors frequently lacked graduate degrees. Student-teacher ratios often exceeded twenty to one. With curricula that promoted "mechanical intelligence to the relative exclusion of both intellectual and social intelligence," more than 95 percent of historically black colleges were not accredited by the Association of American Universities. No historically black college had an accredited engineering department or a doctoral program—and seven southern states offered their black citizens no graduate degree program of any kind. Acclaimed as the best vocational school for blacks in the state, for example, Georgia State Industrial College had inadequate facilities and offered no instruction in advanced skills such as diesel engineering, electrical appliance restoration, and radio repair. The pride of Mississippi, Alcorn Agricultural and Mechanical College, a representative of an accrediting association acknowledged, was "most backward." Limited by the legislature to a "starvation budget," Alcorn provided "makeshift" mechanical courses and agricultural instruction that "would hardly qualify a student to do his own farming."[52]

About half of historically black colleges taught fewer than 250 students. They could not accommodate all of the qualified veterans who applied. According to one survey, about 55 percent of black service men and women were turned away by such institutions, compared to 28 percent at colleges and universities throughout the country. In 1947 about twenty thousand black veterans could not find a place at any institution of higher education. Tens of thousands more in all likelihood did not try.[53]

Southern politicians, moreover, were loath to approve expansion of existing black institutions—or authorize the construction of new ones—even if they confined themselves to training for "black jobs." Taxpayers' money was wasted, they argued, when blacks received an education they could not use. Some states refused to certify new black-run schools. If a city or county superintendent established shop courses for Negroes in Montgomery, Alabama, for example, state officials would not—and federal officials could not—do anything about it. Drawing on private funds, J. T. Saxon, a minister and newspaper editor in Macon, Georgia, opened the Memorial Trade School for Negroes in 1946, offering sixty-five veterans instruction in masonry and auto mechanics. The school building had no windows, doors, ceiling, or rest rooms. In Flora, Mississippi, three hundred whites rallied to protest a state Department of Education plan to convert a war munitions plant into a vocational college for African Americans. Real estate values in the surrounding neighborhood, they insisted, would be ruined. The governor backed down. Not surprisingly, then, Lester Granger, head of the National Urban League, concluded that vocational education in the South in 1947 was worse than it had been two years earlier.[54]

"The G.I. Bill helped blacks go to college," historian John Butler has suggested, "but it helped whites more." The gap in educational attainment (and income) between blacks and whites grew wider in the late '40s and '50s. In a stinging report, *Our Negro Veterans*, Charles Bolté and Louis Harris indicted the nation for failing "to grasp the enormous opportunity which is presented through veterans' benefits for this minority group."[55]

As Ira Katznelson argues, the GI Bill was de facto affirmative action for whites. However, this is not the whole of a more complex story, for the bill also paved the way for an assault on discrimination and legalized racial segregation. Half empty, the glass was also half full. By offering tuition and a living stipend, Title II made it possible for tens of thousands of blacks to get a college degree. A far higher percentage of black than white student-veterans would not have returned to school if they had not had Title II benefits.

Outside of the South, some institutions of higher education began to admit a few African American applicants, some of whom journeyed to the North to study and stayed there. According to Reginald Wilson, a senior scholar at the American Council of Education, about one-third of the students at Wayne State University in Detroit, Michigan, were black. Members of the famed 92nd Infantry Division, an all-black unit that saw action in Italy, attended a wide array of integrated institutions, including Delphi, the University of Iowa, Ohio State, the University of Chicago, Berkeley, the University of Maryland, George Washington University, Georgetown University, San Francisco State, San Jose State, Pasadena Community College, Queens College, City College of New York, and Penn State.[56]

As we have seen, black veterans were not always—or often—welcomed with open arms, but their presence forced some white students to confront prejudice, sometimes for the first time. The City College of New York, suggested Janet Kelley, an instructor in the School of Education, was experiencing a "veritable contortion" in the makeup of the student body because of the GI Bill. With increased awareness of race discrimination, she predicted, public institutions were beginning to resemble "the democracy of the streetcar." In a letter to the editor, a compassionate and concerned, if somewhat condescending, white student at Purdue protested a snack-bar manager's refusal to serve blacks. "Colored students," he noted, were barred from fraternities and sororities. Since whites refused to join them at the dinner table, blacks remained in "secluded corners" in the dining halls. "Are they forever to be ostracized?" he asked. "Is it because of their odor?" Assuring his classmates that blacks used soap and enjoyed good health, the anonymous letter writer opined that God endowed blacks with "very fine sweat pores, finer than yours or mine." He found them "very polite, clean, immaculately dressed, ready to sympathize or help, self-respecting, sociable, intelligent, eager for friendship, ever conscious of their manners, and never boisterous or disrespectful." It was shameful that "while these poor souls are striving to better themselves," Purdue students "show them every discourtesy." To anyone who "feels superior to other races, I suggest that you join Hitler in his grave. He needs friends."[57]

In the South, where most black veterans lived, students could not reach across the color line, but African Americans could—and did—use the GI Bill to get some type of education and training. Enrollments (of veterans and nonveterans) at historically black colleges exploded, growing from 29,000 in 1940 to 73,174 in 1947. The federal government provided some help to accommodate these students. Funds from the Veterans' Education Facilities Program of the Lanham Act were distributed to historically black colleges as well as all-white and integrated institutions. Recognizing the special needs of "Negro colleges," officers of the U.S. Office of Education allocated 33.4 square feet of construction for veterans in black colleges (at a cost of $156 per veteran), as compared with 17.4 square feet in white schools (at $93 per veteran). Black colleges converted temporary structures into permanent buildings and added classrooms, shops, laboratories, and equipment to their campuses. Although the allotment represented only about 75 percent of the need (as estimated by the Office of Education), it generated about a 25-percent increase in capacity. Though Jim Crow was still king, more blacks than ever before could go to college.[58]

When they left college, many black veterans enlisted as foot soldiers or featured players in the civil rights movement. Their education and training had enhanced their economic and professional status and equipped them with the skills and social networks conducive to political organization and action. The GI Bill had proved to them that government could provide equal access to blacks. Among respondents to Suzanne Mettler's veterans survey, black GI Bill users belonged to more national-origins-oriented groups than whites and more organizations dedicated to helping disadvantaged and disenfranchised populations. Between 1950 and 1964, 35 percent of GI Bill users (compared to 8 percent of black nonusers and a mere 2 percent of white users) participated in protests, marches, and demonstrations. They demanded desegregation, open housing, fair employment, better schools, and voting rights. As black veteran Henry Hervey, a graduate of Northwestern, claimed, "you learn that you can fight City Hall, and you have to fight, and there are ways you can bring pressure to make changes."[59]

Among the collegiate black veterans who used the GI Bill to claim "new rights" was Heman Sweatt. Working as a letter carrier, Sweatt applied to the all-white law school at the University of Texas–Austin in February 1946. There were 7,701 white lawyers and 23 black lawyers in the state at the time. Rejected on racial grounds, he went to court, where a judge ordered Texas to establish a law school at Prairie View University, an all-black vocational institution that offered academic credit for mattress and broom making. Complying with the directive, state officials rented rooms in Houston, forty miles from the Prairie View campus, and hired two African American lawyers to teach Sweatt. The district court declared itself satisfied, but the ex-GI refused to go along with the subterfuge, a library-less law school designed for a single student. When Sweatt returned to court, the Texas legislature hastily appropriated $3 million to create a "first-class Texas State University for Negroes," $100,000 of which would be used for a law school. Established in an office building in downtown Austin, the law school consisted of three basement rooms, a trio of part-time instructors, and a library of ten thousand books.

Sweatt stood his ground. The NAACP assigned Thurgood Marshall to represent him—and in deference to majority public opinion in the South, the organization established an all-white branch, the only one of its kind in the United States, on the University of Texas campus. At a giant rally, the white president of the student body, himself a GI, demanded that the democratic values he had fought for in World War II be practiced as well as preached at the university and that no Negro student be mistreated or ostracized.

At his trial Sweatt testified that "I don't believe equality can be given on the basis of segregation." The U.S. Justice Department and 187 law professors formed an ad hoc organization and filed amicus curiae briefs in support of Sweatt. So did the American Veterans Committee, a service association founded in 1944, which argued that African American GIs could not use their benefits freely and fully unless Jim Crow laws were dismantled. In 1950, in *Sweatt v. Painter*, the Supreme Court agreed, though by then the Negro law school had five full-time faculty, twenty-three students, a practice court, and a legal aid association. In a unanimous decision read by Chief Justice Fred Vinson, the justices declared "We cannot find substantial equality in the educational opportunities offered white and Negro law students by the state." The court ordered Texas officials to admit Heman Sweatt to the University of Texas Law School.[60]

For Sweatt, civil rights luminaries Hosea Williams, Aaron Henry, and Medgar Evers, as well as countless other Title II black veterans, the GI Bill was formative and foundational. The legislation, as implemented, did not go beyond its race-neutral language to transform formal freedom into effective freedom. Because so many veterans were white, it did allow racial disparities to grow even greater. At the same time, it empowered and emboldened hundreds of thousands of African Americans. Convinced that government could be a force for racial justice, black veterans were especially likely to become activists. A product of its times, the GI Bill was also visionary: It pointed to and paved the way for a more egalitarian, more inclusive America.

For members of religious and ethnic groups, previously underrepresented in higher education, the GI Bill had an unambiguously positive impact both immediately and in the long term. By providing full tuition and a living stipend to millions of veterans who had earned the gratitude of the American people, the legislation in effect challenged the discriminatory admissions policies of many colleges and universities. Moreover, the GIs' academic achievements provided the context for initiatives in the 1940s and '50s to pressure government and institutions of higher education to remove administrative practices, customs, or quotas that prevented qualified students from matriculating.

Except for women and African Americans, the military in World War II looked more like America than any other organization, public or private. Young men from every state and region and a wide array of religious and ethnic backgrounds were drafted and served in the armed forces. Among nonblack respondents to Suzanne Mettler's survey, 18 percent grew up on farms, 33 percent resided in small municipalities or towns, 18 percent lived in medium-sized urban settings, and 19 percent lived in large cities. Of the nation's service personnel 65 percent had been raised as Protestants, 24 percent were Catholic, and 7 percent were Jewish.[61]

For Daniel Inouye, the war provided an opportunity to demonstrate that "patriotism and love of our great country are not limited to any ethnic group." Born in 1924 in Honolulu, Inouye was a Nisei Japanese American who lived in a neighborhood dominated by Chinese Americans. When he learned of the attack on Pearl Harbor, Inouye rushed to the scene to provide medical assistance. In 1943, when the United States ended its ban on Japanese Americans serving in the military, he dropped his premedical studies at the University of Hawaii and enlisted in the army. Assigned to the fabled "Go for Broke" Nisei 442nd Regimental Combat Team, one of the most highly decorated units in the history of the U.S. Army, Second Lieutenant Inouye lost his arm while taking out machine gun nests near San Terenzo, Italy, on April 21, 1945. In and out of hospitals for almost two years, he was discharged from the army as a captain in 1947, having been awarded the Bronze Star, Purple Heart, and Distinguished Service Cross.

A "quiet revolution" was brewing in the Hawaii to which Inouye returned. It was, he recalled, "a far cry from the bitter 'Speak American' days." Swept up in "the ferment of impending change," Inouye decided to abandon medicine for the law. Using the education benefits provided by the GI Bill, he completed an undergraduate degree in political science at the University of Hawaii in Manoa and then a JD at George Washington Law School in Washington, D.C. His wife, Margaret Awamura Inouye, worked as a file clerk and then an administrative secretary at the Department of the Navy's Bureau of Yards and Docks to supplement the GI Bill living stipend. A member of Phi Delta Phi at George Washington, Inouye spoke out when two Jewish students were blackballed. "You see, I'm not an Anglo-Saxon," he told his fraternity brothers, "and if these men don't belong in this fraternity, neither do I." The decision was reversed.

Once more Inouye returned to Hawaii, now set on a career in politics. In 1954 he was one of several "young hopefuls" elected to the territorial legislature. "Thanks to the GI Bill and the fact that most of us were vets," he has written, "few legislative bodies anywhere in the country could boast the level of professional and educational competence we brought to our task." Following a distinguished career in Hawaii's House of Representatives, where he introduced legislation to replace a permanent Protestant chaplain with a rotating program that engaged Catholic, Jewish, Mormon, and Buddhist clergy as well, Inouye was elected to the U.S. House of Representatives and the U.S. Senate, where he has served for more than four decades.[62]

Like Inouye, Luke LaPorta, the son of an Italian immigrant, learned lessons in "self-worth" and toleration during his service in the military.

After enlisting in the navy, LaPorta was assigned to a minesweeper that never ventured far from the Atlantic coast of the United States. In contrast to his homogeneous Italian neighborhood in Queens, New York, the ship was a veritable melting pot in which Jews and Poles lived and worked shoulder to shoulder with Italians and Irish. "We were all people of the same genre," LaPorta remembered. "It was a great equalizer."[63]

As the war ended, many colleges and universities remained unwilling to serve a similar function. Following the "new immigration" at the turn of the twentieth century, which had brought millions of people from southern and eastern Europe to the United States, college administrators took steps to reserve spaces for the children of their traditional clientele—affluent, white Protestants—and restrict access to the newcomers. They did not need to take action to bar Catholics, who did not apply to selective private colleges in substantial numbers and tended to matriculate at institutions run by the church, but they did adopt quotas to cap the enrollment of Jews. Elite institutions, alas, led the way. Seeking homogeneity, Princeton, according to one influential observer, used its Christian tradition, the exclusiveness of eating clubs, and the prejudices of students to "keep away many Jews." In the mid-1920s, Harvard rejected an admissions policy based on scholarship alone. Using criteria such as athletic ability, family relations to alumni, geographical diversity, and "intangible qualities," Harvard reduced its "Hebrew total" to 15 percent of each class "by simply rejecting without detailed explanation."[64]

Anti-Semitism persisted twenty years later both inside and outside of the academy. Fifty-five percent of Americans told pollsters that Jews had too much power. Another survey revealed that Amherst, Bryn Mawr, Dartmouth, Haverford, Middlebury, Mount Holyoke, Northeastern, Princeton, Swarthmore, Williams, and Yale were among the colleges enrolling "conspicuously small numbers of Jews." Applicants were required to indicate their religious affiliation, and alumni interviewers passed along information about ethnicity and social class characteristics. At Cornell, President Day tried to reassure an anxious alumnus that Jews would not crowd out "legacy" admissions or degrade the campus environment. Because it was not far from New York City and was the land-grant institution for the state, Day acknowledged, Cornell would—and should—"have a reasonable representation of Jewish elements" after the war. Nonetheless, Day understood "the sort of repercussions you have in mind." While he did not believe Cornell could "wisely go as 'pure' as certain of the other Eastern universities," the president pledged to make sure that the presence of Jews on campus was not so large "as to make it unpleasant for first-class Gentile students."[65]

By transforming the market for higher education, the GI Bill struck a blow at exclusion based on social class, religion, and ethnic origin. Among respondents to Mettler's survey, 53 percent of Jewish veterans attended college, followed by 40 percent of Protestants, and 32 percent of Catholics. Many of their parents had been born outside the United States. Since the taxpayers were paying their tuition, a substantial number of these veterans requested admission to the nation's most prestigious and privileged colleges and universities. It was not easy, even for the Ivy League, to turn them down.[66]

Frank O'Hara was one of the GIs who got his foot in the door. Born in 1926, O'Hara grew up in an Irish Catholic community in Grafton, Massachusetts, graduated from St. John's High School in Worcester—an all-boys parochial school run by the Xaverian Brothers—in 1944 and enlisted immediately in the navy. Trained as a sonar operator, O'Hara served on the USS *Nicholas,* a Seventh Fleet destroyer that engaged in several bombardments and sweep-up operations in the Pacific in 1945 and shuttled diplomats to the formal surrender ceremony in Tokyo on September 2. Awarded a Philippine Liberation Campaign ribbon, an American Area Campaign medal, an Asiatic Pacific Campaign medal with an operation and engagement star, and a World War II Victory medal, he received his separation papers in June 1946 and returned home, uncertain about his future.

A gifted pianist, O'Hara considered applying to a music conservatory. His father argued strenuously that Frank apply to his own alma mater, Holy Cross, a good Catholic school, and an aunt hoped that the young man would become a priest. O'Hara compromised. Agreeing to attend a liberal arts college, he took the SAT, received scores of 700 verbal and 483 math, and requested catalogues from Rochester, Cornell, Chicago, and Columbia. He rejected Yale because its quota system was "odious." With his mother's encouragement, he applied to Harvard, which combined preeminence and proximity to home. Fortunately, an alumni interviewer deemed him "a likeable fellow." To O'Hara's surprise, he was accepted.

Asked about his preferences in a roommate, O'Hara declared his indifference to "religion, race, or section," but he felt the pressure of Harvard's elitism and ethnocentrism. "They say it's the death knell of all Catholics," he announced. Despite the number of veterans on campus, he stuck out among those who saw the Yard as part of their family patrimony. One acquaintance described him as "potato Irish, lower class, with pasty skin." A classmate agreed that O'Hara was a "small, thin, angry, sentimental Irish boy from a hick town."

Harvard changed his life. A course on James Joyce, Thomas Mann, and Marcel Proust, taught by the dynamic and daring literary critic Harry Levin, and workshops offered by John Ciardi helped him decide to become a poet instead of a composer. The great poets, young and old—Robert Frost, Wallace Stevens, Dylan Thomas, Richard Wilbur, Violet Lang—visited Cambridge or lived there. He made friends with Harvard undergraduates (and poets) John Ashberry and Donald Hall, and his work began to appear in Harvard's literary publications. Before his graduation in 1950, O'Hara wrote in his journal: "One must hurry, one must avoid impediments, snares, detours; one must not be stifled in a closed social or artistic railway station waiting for the train; I've a long way to go, and I'm late already." O'Hara would become one of the finest poets of his age, a key member of "the New York School," and the author, among other works, of *Lunch Poems*.[67]

For a not inconsequential number of Frank O'Haras and Henry Kissingers, selective schools bent to the prevailing winds. But progress was slow. Jewish enrollments, for example, inched up at elite private colleges. At Harvard in 1946–1947, Jews approached 20 percent of the student body. In 1947–1948, 9.4 percent of Yale's freshmen (most of them veterans) identified themselves as Jews. A year later, as GI enrollment peaked, the proportion had increased to 12.3 percent. At Dartmouth, Princeton, and Williams the percentage of "Hebrew" freshmen rose as well but not much beyond 5 percent of the student population. These relatively modest increases, however, worried administrators, who, like President Day, were convinced that a visible Jewish presence discouraged applicants from boarding schools, their suppliers of choice. When World War II veterans graduated, they hoped, elite institutions would return to their customary practices.[68]

To sustain the momentum for equal access, however, a burgeoning antidiscrimination movement lobbied for legislative reform. The offensive began in 1944, when several Jewish organizations formed the National Community Relations Advisory Council to combat discrimination in education, employment, and housing. With public consciousness raised by the GI Bill and films such as *Gentleman's Agreement* (1947), the council worked with other civil rights organizations to outlaw admissions quotas directed at Jews and blacks. They drew on a spate of studies that identified evidence of bias and denounced discrimination in higher education as "un-American." The most important of these was the six-volume report of the Truman Commission, *Higher Education for American Democracy*. Denying that academic standards had to be diluted in order to expand access, the commissioners rejected the proposition that higher education should be confined to an intellectual elite or, even worse, to the children of affluent parents:

> If the ladder of opportunity rises high at the doors of some youth and scarcely rises at all at the doors of others, while at the same time formal education is made a prerequisite to occupational and social advance, then education may become the means, not of eliminating race and class distinctions, but of deepening and solidifying them. It is obvious then, that free and universal access to education, in terms of interest, ability, and the need of the student, must be a major goal in American education.[69]

In this more favorable cultural and political climate, the American Jewish Committee, the American Jewish Congress, the B'nai B'rith, the Anti-defamation League, and the Jewish War Veterans all launched major efforts to end quotas in college and professional school admissions. Columbia University altered its practices in 1945, after the American Jewish Congress argued that by discriminating against blacks and Jews the institution forfeited its tax-exempt status. The next year, the New York City Mayor's Committee on Unity and a special investigating committee of the city council documented discrimination in private colleges and universities against Jews, Catholics, and African Americans throughout the Empire State, prompting Democratic Party leaders to introduce bills in the state legislature to create a state university at a cost of $50 million. These pressures, combined with the huge number of veterans seeking admission to college, prompted Governor Dewey to establish the Temporary Commission on the Need of a State University, which resulted in the creation of SUNY two years later.[70]

In 1948 the New York State Legislature passed the Quinn-Oliffe Law, which required colleges, universities, and professional schools to admit students "without regard to race, color, creed, or national origin." The law established mechanisms of enforcement as well. An administrative agency in the office of the New York State Commissioner of Education was empowered to investigate admissions practices on its own initiative or following a complaint by an aggrieved applicant. Public and private institutions of higher education throughout the state were required to preserve all data related to admissions for at least three years. The Board of Regents could issue a formal complaint, conduct hearings, and take testimony under oath. Following a finding of guilt, the board could order a college or university to admit an individual and to cease and desist discriminatory practices.[71]

The following year, despite strenuous opposition by Harvard and other private colleges, the Massachusetts legislature passed a Fair Educational Practices Law, modeled on Quinn-Oliffe. Wilbur Bender, the "architect of postwar Harvard," orchestrated the university's response to the bill. A World War II veteran (the first person in ten generations of a pacifist Mennonite family to serve in the armed forces), Bender became counselor to veterans in the '40s and then dean of the college. In 1952 he would become dean of admissions. Working closely with President Conant, Bender (who deemed the GI Bill "a statesmanlike piece of social legislation") moved, albeit under pressure and at a very deliberate pace, to broaden the institution's base.

In public Bender insisted that Harvard had always been in compliance with the law and saw no reason to change "our basic policies." The legislation, he knew, allowed colleges and universities to use any admissions criteria except race, color, religion, or national origin. This loophole gave Harvard the ability to limit the number of Jews by giving extra weight to athletic ability, legacy connection, geographic diversity, and "intangible qualities" such as character and leadership skills. Nonetheless, Bender recognized that the Fair Educational Practices Law was a mandate for change and that the legislation might well be rigorously enforced. A "disgruntled or neurotic" applicant might give Harvard a black eye in the court of public opinion by filing a suit after being rejected.

Consequently, Harvard adjusted its policies, although some of the changes were cosmetic. Alumni interviewers were reminded to ask no questions about the candidate's race, ethnicity, or religion. They were asked to be especially cautious with applicants who appeared to be "touchy" or who belonged to "one of the minority groups that might make trouble." Above all, they were told that written comments such as "This is the finest member of the Negro race I have ever seen" or "This boy is planning to become a Jewish rabbi" were against the law and potentially embarrassing to Harvard. "We must be super careful now," Bender warned.

At the same time, Harvard did admit more Jews. By 1952, 25 percent of the institution's students were Jewish, more even than at Cornell (23 percent), which attracted a large number of applicants from New York City. Harvard continued to maintain what historian Jerome Karabel calls "vigorous affirmative action for the privileged," especially sons of alumni and scions of "upper-crust families." However, by abandoning quotas and increasing financial aid, Harvard was beginning to allow "merit" rather than "accidents of birth" to dictate the distribution of educational opportunity.[72] The pressure of organized and unorganized opinions reached Princeton and Dartmouth as well, where Jewish enrollment in both colleges approached 15 percent of the student body.

Among the Ivies, only Yale stayed the hands of time. Energized by the end of World War II and the experience of student-veterans, individuals and groups mobilized to demand that Yale make admissions decisions based solely on academic and professional considerations. Anti-Semitism and other forms of group discrimination, wrote law professor and Yale alumnus Eugene Rostow, "are no longer merely unattractive social sins" but also potent symbols and signals that universities must neither condone nor spread. "New men and new classes are demanding equal opportunities," he declared. "The fair employment practice statutes are a profound and, as I believe, a healthy sign of the times." Not surprisingly, then, in 1946, when Columbia faced a lawsuit, Yale administrators responded. A new policy repudiated racial and religious quotas by declaring that applicants with "outstanding intellectual capacity" would be given the most favorable consideration. Yale, however, still claimed it would—and should—exercise "discretion" in selecting the freshman class. Administrators, it turned out, were merely pushing discrimination underground.

Throughout the 1940s and '50s, Yale opposed bills introduced in the Connecticut legislature to ban bias in college admissions. In 1949, after a study by the State Interracial Commission declared the record of private nondenominational colleges "dismal," Governor Chester Bowles demanded "vigorous forthright action to eliminate discrimination wherever it exists." Insisting that the state's private colleges and universities had "a proud record" with no evidence of "parochialism and prejudice," Yale's administrators opposed legislation as unnecessary and counterproductive, a blunt instrument for an operation that required "skill, judgment, and experience." Applicants who "could not meet the competition" would sue, thereby doing great damage to the community and to themselves. Despite warnings that Yale "would face serious trouble if she didn't change her homogeneous ways," the institution helped beat back fair educational practices legislation in 1950, 1951, 1953, 1955, and 1957. In the 1961–1962 academic year, Jews accounted for only 12 percent of degree matriculants at Yale, which deserved its reputation as the most gentile college in the Ivy League.[73]

U.S. Pension Building, Washington, DC, constructed between 1882 and 1887 to house the administration of the Civil War pension. (Courtesy National Archives)

Brigadier General Frank T. Hines, Administrator of the Veterans' Bureau and the Department of Veterans Affairs from 1923 to 1945. (Courtesy U.S. Department of Veterans Affairs)

The "Battle of Washington." Bonus army shacks on fire, Washington, July 28, 1932. (Courtesy National Archives)

Francis M. Sullivan, National Legislative Director of the American Legion, surrounded by petitions supporting the Legion's World War II veterans' benefits initiative. (Courtesy American Legion Library)

Harry W. Colmery, a member of the committee sent to Washington by the American Legion in December 1943, drafted the Legion's proposal for a comprehensive benefits bill for World War II veterans. (Courtesy Kansas Historical Society)

Warren Atherton, National Commander of the American Legion (left), shakes hands with Rep. John Rankin (D-Miss.), chairman of the House World War II Veterans Legislative Committee. (Courtesy American Legion Library)

Senator Ernest McFarland (D-Ariz.). Following his proposal to expand eligibility for educational and training benefits to nearly all World War II veterans, McFarland was often referred to as "Father of the GI Bill." (Courtesy McFarland State Historic Park)

"Vetsburg" was specially built housing for veterans and their families near the Cornell University Campus. (Courtesy Rare and Manuscript Collections, Cornell University Library)

Governor Thomas E. Dewey of New York (second from left) visits one of the new ACUNY colleges, built in response to the vastly increased demand for higher education created by the end of the war and Title II of the GI Bill. (Courtesy Cornell University Press)

Instruction in biology at Sampson College in New York State. (Courtesy Cornell University Press)

A student Mr. and Mrs. Club, one of many such organizations formed among veterans and their spouses at American colleges and universities. (Courtesy Cornell University Press)

A dance at Sampson College. It was not all books and babies for some GI Bill students. (Courtesy Cornell University Press)

Abraham Levitt and his sons William (left) and Alfred. William was the driving force behind the building of Levittown, New York, the most legendary of mass-produced post–World War II suburbs. The family firm also built Levittowns in Pennsylvania and New Jersey. (Courtesy Levittown Public Library)

Levittown, New York, sales office. Crowds of prospective homeowners were channeled through a process of selecting, purchasing, and financing that was almost as efficient as the building of the houses themselves. Representatives of the VA and the FHA were present to process loan guarantees. (Courtesy Levittown Public Library)

A four-man crew of African American workers grades the land surrounding a new house in Levittown, New York. African Americans were excluded from the community they helped build. (Courtesy Levittown Public Library)

Levittown, New York, partially completed in 1947 or 1948. Veterans moved from places like "Vetsburg" on the Cornell campus to larger versions of the mass-produced suburban home and community. (Courtesy Levittown Public Library)

Yale was swimming against the tide. In 1949 New Jersey passed a Fair Educational Practices Act, with provisions that went beyond the statutes enacted in New York and Massachusetts. In addition to a ban on discrimination in admissions, the Garden State's Freeman Law also required colleges and universities to grant every student full and unfettered access "to all advantages, facilities, and privileges." Voluntarily or in compliance with government regulations, most institutions of higher education outside of the South adopted more meritocratic standards of admission and promised to recruit students from every walk of life and base no decision on an applicant's race, religion, or national origin.[74]

Discrimination, of course, did not disappear overnight. With a wink and a nod, reliance on "intangible qualities," and/or a strategic use of scholarships and grants of financial aid, administrators limited the numbers of Catholics and Jews, Mexican Americans, Puerto Ricans, and Chinese, Korean, and Japanese Americans. In the '50s, moreover, facilities, including on-campus housing, were not always open to everyone. "Accidents of birth" continued to dictate the assignment of roommates. Moreover, fraternities and sororities remained segregated by social class, race, and religious affiliation.

This is not to say that colleges and universities had not come a long way in a short time. More than anyone, Adolf Hitler ensured that bigotry would be given no official sanction in postwar America. Legislation that outlawed discrimination in employment and housing, as well as in education, stemmed from a dramatic shift in public opinion now shaped by knowledge of Nazi atrocities and new insights about prejudice as a mask for privilege and power. By the early 1950s polls revealed a marked decline in anti-Semitism and somewhat more favorable attitudes toward African Americans. In this context, the GI Bill was a driving force for change. Title II reinforced an emerging consensus on equal access to education. By funding World War II veterans who clearly "deserved" a chance to go to college, it also created a living laboratory in which to test assumptions about whether "average Americans" could make the most of that opportunity. When millions of the former GIs succeeded with a vengeance, there would be no turning back on the democratization of higher education in the United States.

SIX

Overlooked

GI Joe but not Joe College

Cartoon from *The Beacon*, base newspaper of Grenier Field, New Hampshire, November 10, 1945. The sergeant, who wears numerous combat stripes on his sleeve, does not welcome the thought of returning to his civilian job. (Courtesy Edith Bleich)

T HERE CAN BE no doubt that our reverence for the GI Bill is shaped primarily by the college tuition and subsistence program examined in the previous two chapters. To many Americans, the GI Bill *means* the opening of college and the opportunities afforded by a college degree to men and women returning from the Good War. The higher-education provisions of the bill were indeed the keys to a prosperous middle-class life for large numbers of veterans and were a major force in the rapid postwar expansion of higher education that made college part of the life experience of vast numbers of young Americans, veterans and nonveterans alike, in subsequent generations. Nonetheless, it was not the chance to attend college that attracted the attention of most new veterans as they leafed through their VA booklets. Only a minority of them had finished high school before they went to war, and nearly 30 percent had only a pre–high school education.[1] What could college mean to these men and women? And what did it mean to those who wanted to return to their old jobs or open a store or find work of some kind without having to suffer through further schooling?

The GI Bill, in fact, offered a variety of benefits to veterans who did not plan to attend a college or university. Many former GIs received the $20 weekly readjustment allowance while they searched for work, and large numbers who did want to expand their opportunities entered some form of subcollege vocational training. Others availed themselves of government agencies for job counseling and placement, and still others used government loans to open small businesses or operate farms.[2] These are the forgotten beneficiaries of the GI Bill, and they greatly outnumbered the 2.2 million veterans who used the bill's benefits to attend college or graduate school. Of course, some of the nearly 9 million former GIs who received at least one unemployment (or self-employment) readjustment allowance payment also used the GI Bill to attend college, but most did not, and more than a third received no other kind of benefit under the bill.[3] And as we earlier observed, the number of veterans who utilized the college tuition and subsistence program was a good deal smaller than the number who attended subcollege training programs of various kinds: 3.5 million in public and for-profit schools; 1.4 million in nonagricultural on-the-job training; and 700,000 in on-the-farm training—5.6 million veterans in all, more than a third of the men and women who had served in and survived the war and two and a half times the cohort of veterans who marched off to college at government expense in the postwar decade.[4] Even apart from the particular achievements and failures of such programs, the sheer numbers of veterans who undertook subcollege training, accepted readjustment allowance payments, listened to job placement advice, or sought and received business or farm loans suggest the need to look more closely at these largely forgotten components of the GI Bill.

There are, moreover, the rather surprising findings in Suzanne Mettler's survey. We have already seen that three out of every four surveyed veterans who attended college under the GI Bill viewed the experience as a turning point in their lives. This is certainly no surprise. But what of those who, for example, attended subcollege educational programs? Here we might expect a less enthusiastic response. And yet, impressive majorities of Mettler's surveyed veterans who participated in several of the educational and vocational programs below the college level echoed the college attendees in assessing the impact of the GI Bill on their lives. Fully 70 percent of the very large number who attended vocational or trade schools viewed the GI Bill as a personal turning point, as did 56 percent of those who entered apprenticeships and other forms of on-the-job training. Among the smaller numbers who attended subcollege business schools, the percentage who attached deep personal significance to the bill slightly exceeded that of the college attendees.[5] Contemporary appraisals of these and other such programs would have led us to expect a much more qualified or even a negative overall response. Had the aging former GIs who participated in Mettler's survey simply bought into the myth of the bill even in the face of their own contrary experiences? Or had earlier program appraisals missed the meaning of fairly humble and seemingly ineffective courses and training programs to large numbers of young veterans whose lives had been powerfully shaped by the Depression and the war and who had returned from the latter with little or no sense of how to get on with their lives?

Harry Belafonte was one of those young veterans. A native of Harlem, Belafonte, who was a troubled and unruly youth, had been sent as a teenager to live with relatives in Kingston, Jamaica. Returning to New York for a year of high school, he joined the U.S. Navy, where, after scoring high on an IQ test, he was sent first to the navy's

Storekeeper School and then to an all-black company in Northport, Long Island. The "butt of the barracks" because of his West Indian accent, Belafonte nonetheless found in the navy that "there were other things besides poverty and loneliness and the struggle for survival.... There was fellowship and literature and folklore and history and discussion and debate and there was the culture of my people.... And I began to discover that there was Harry Belafonte, an individual who was somebody and who belonged."

After the war and his discharge from the navy, however, Belafonte still faced an uncertain future. He took a job as a maintenance man's helper and found that future only when someone gave him a ticket to the American Negro Theater's production of *Home Is the Hunter*. It was the first play Belafonte had ever seen, and he immediately decided to become an actor. He volunteered as a stagehand at the American Negro Theater and managed to get a few bit parts. However, his ambition was realized only when he discovered the Dramatic Workshop and the possibility of attending it through the GI Bill's subcollege training program. Belafonte attended classes there for two years. These "were the days of the Great Awakening for Harry," according to a friend. Belafonte's first interest was in Shakespeare, but he also appeared in musicals, where he attracted the attention of Monte Kay, a producer who would soon help him launch a brilliant career as a singer and sometime actor. Here is one of the GI Bill's subcollege trainees who would have given a resounding—and accurate—affirmation of the program's potential for changing the lives of young veterans.[6]

The first resort of many of these young men and women was, however, not job training but "52-20"—unemployment payments of $20 per week for up to one year during the two years following discharge from the armed services. This was the provision that had nearly wrecked the GI Bill in John Rankin's House committee early in 1944, and the same fears of government-sponsored idleness and dissipation haunted its implementation after the war. Rankin was worried that payments to black veterans might unsettle the established racial order in his home state of Mississippi, but others expressed broader concerns that had little to do with race. Henry Pringle, for example, began his critical *Ladies' Home Journal* article, "Are We Making a Bum out of G. I. Joe?" with this story:

> The youthful veteran sat across the table at a restaurant in Pontiac, Illinois, and made some rapid calculations on a paper napkin. He had been out of the Army for three months. For the past twelve weeks he

had been drawing, as provided by the G.I. Bill of Rights, readjustment compensation of $20 a week. He intended, he said a little defiantly, to remain on the rolls for weeks to come.

"Look at the figures for yourself, mister," he said and held out the napkin. "I can get a job here for maybe twenty-five dollars. So what? After income tax and Social Security and lunch money, what have I got? Less than the twenty bucks. Do I look like a sucker?"[7]

In September 1946, when Pringle's article was published, the "52-20 Club" was in fact quite large and surely included a number of former GIs who had made the same calculation as the young man from Pontiac. As legislators had expected, Title V of the GI Bill, the readjustment allowance, was at that time by far the largest and most expensive of the bill's benefits, and it would continue to grow for a while longer. During the first year after the war it accounted for nearly 75 percent of benefit payments, and in fiscal 1947, even as veterans rapidly increased their use of other benefits under the bill, it remained the largest. Former GIs received nearly $1.5 billion in readjustment allowance payments during that year, 40 percent of all of the direct payments made under the GI Bill.[8]

The sheer size of the readjustment allowance program focused the fears of some political conservatives in ways that the fledgling college assistance program did not. So, too, did its resemblance to more general unemployment compensation programs that had long been an important part of the liberal political agenda. Less than a month after the end of the war President Truman had revived that agenda by announcing a broad program of domestic reforms that included expansion of the system of federal-state unemployment insurance enacted at the height of the New Deal. The conservative bloc of congressional Republicans and southern Democrats, augmented in the 1946 midterm election by the first Republican majorities in both houses since 1928, had little difficulty in beating back Truman's proposals, including the expansion of unemployment compensation.

The dominance of this conservative bloc continued throughout Truman's entire presidency, even in the face of a new Democratic congressional majority that accompanied the president's miraculous reelection in 1948. The Fair Deal Truman promised in the first State of the Union address following his reelection was almost entirely rejected by a Congress still dominated by conservative interests and voices, and when Truman left office in 1953, he had accomplished very little of his domestic program. Still, the continuing presence of this program on the presidential agenda kept conservatives' fears alive. Republicans and southern Democrats remained on the lookout for any cracks in their wall of resistance, even though, as FDR himself might have assured them, they had nothing to fear but fear itself.

In the first years of the postwar period no part of the GI Bill had yet achieved iconic status among American voters, so conservatives who worried about New Deal-like government expansion could freely attack any part of the bill they felt might leak out beyond its carefully constructed boundaries into the area of general domestic policymaking. Mounting such an attack was not a high priority among conservatives, but the readjustment allowance was, as noted, the likeliest focus of their attention. Of the various GI Bill programs, it could most easily be characterized as a costly government handout to those eager to feed at the public trough. That characterization, in turn, could serve to delegitimize the broader liberal program and reinforce the need to return to limited government in the post–New Deal era. The implications of generous weekly payments to unemployed veterans could be made visible even to those who did not see calculations on restaurant napkins that proved it was more profitable to remain on the public dole rather than to work.

Title V did not in fact make a bum out of GI Joe. Veterans saw the readjustment allowance as a necessary, temporary, and well-deserved hand up rather than a long-term government handout, and most found their way into jobs, schools, and training programs as quickly as they could. Hence, the dropout rate from the "52-20 Club" was quite rapid. If the veteran from Pontiac loafed for an entire year on his $20 per week, he was in a distinct minority. Looking back on the entire experience of the unemployment portion of Title V, the 1956 President's Commission on Veterans' Pensions (the Bradley Commission, after its chairman, Omar Bradley, who now headed the VA) reported that only one of every nine veterans who had received at least one unemployment payment went on to exhaust this benefit, and only 2.5 percent used it up by receiving benefits continuously for an entire year. The average number of payments per recipient was twenty, and the average total payment was $393.24.[9] "The great majority of beneficiaries," the Bradley Commission concluded, "used the benefit for only a limited period of time, and in a manner clearly consistent with the law's objectives."[10]

Closer analysis of the patterns of usage confirmed this judgment. Noting the unexpectedly rapid demobilization that followed the war and the expected difficulty in converting many war-production plants to peacetime production, the Bradley Commission found that unemployment payments in the early days of the program were well above average in states that contained high concentrations of war industries (New York, New Jersey, Pennsylvania, Massachusetts, Michigan). They were also high (and more enduringly so) in a number of rural southern states that had endemic job scarcities. Younger veterans, most of whom lacked good prewar jobs to return to, used the unemployment benefit more frequently than older veterans.[11] All of this made perfect sense if the program were working well, providing needed cash to men and women who confronted difficulties of one kind or another in getting from the armed services into civilian jobs. The Bradley Commission pointed out that some veterans who returned to old jobs or quickly found new work later qualified for unemployment payments under Title V and regretted this use of the program, which was, after all, intended to address only the initial period of readjustment. However, this was a minor problem in a section of the bill that close analysts concluded worked rather well.[12]

Title V of the GI Bill also provided for payments to self-employed veterans who experienced months of very low income or no income at all while awaiting the proceeds of an initial farm harvest or (in far fewer instances) while building or rebuilding a small business or professional practice. For any month in which a farm, business, or practice yielded less than $100 in profit, the government supplied enough to bring the self-employed veteran's income up to that level but with an overall maximum of $1,040, or 10.4 monthly payments irrespective of the total amount received.[13] Fewer than one in twenty veterans received benefits under this provision of Title V, though this by no means insulated the program from the same kind of criticism that was aimed at the unemployment benefit. Recipients of the self-employment readjustment allowance tended to remain in the program longer than the unemployed, and greater numbers received the maximum number of payments. This alone suggests that a program intended to cushion the first few months of operation for a farm or small business had become something quite different, and the Bradley Commission joined a chorus of earlier complaints that this was one GI Bill program that had been misconceived.[14]

A major problem, according to the commission, was that there was no way to prevent the self-employment benefit from evolving into a welfare payment that could be claimed well after the initial period of adjustment, especially among farmers, whose monthly income could be expected to decline or even disappear after a profitable harvest had been brought to market. There was, after all, a naturally sharp seasonal rhythm in the revenue stream to most farms and even some small nonfarm businesses. Furthermore, there was the additional issue of whether it was proper in the first place to fund farmers and small businessmen who were capable of acquiring credit from private sources to tide them over the first difficult months. To illustrate both of these problems the commission pointed to the example of a farmer who applied for and received $100 payments for profitless months both before and after a two-month period in which his first year's harvest netted more than $6,500.[15] Had Congress really intended to support an operation of this sort before and even after it had yielded such a large profit? The Bradley Commission clearly did not think so, yet this is how the self-employment readjustment benefit had worked in many instances.

This relatively small component of the bill provided an opportunity for more aggressive contemporary attacks on Title V and in some instances on the bill as a whole. Among all of the print media in the United States in the postwar era, none provided a more influential voice for Main Street political conservatism than the *Reader's Digest*. In May 1949, even as readjustment allowance payments were rapidly winding down (and college assistance was under full sail), the *Digest* published an article under the defiant title "Keep Your Money, Uncle Sam." In it a fledgling author named Arthur Gordon recounts and reflects on his brief flirtation with the self-employment readjustment allowance. At the urging of a friend, Gordon had gone to the VA to ask about his eligibility and was told that, as the book he was writing would produce no income for several months ("If ever," Gordon gloomily replied), he was eligible for the $100 monthly self-employment readjustment benefit even though he had found and then left a well-paying job after leaving the army. Gordon expressed astonishment at this and at the other GI Bill benefits the VA official went on to explain. He then describes the inner demons that urged him to accept them:

> Don't be a sucker, spoke up a small voice in my ear. The money's already appropriated. Everybody else will get his share; why not you?...How much income tax did you pay last year, the voice went on. A lot more than the thousand dollars you can get now. So you'll really be getting your own money back, don't you see?...Come on, don't be a fool—be practical![16]

Then comes the gratifying resurgence of Gordon's true-American inner voice:

> But I guess I am a fool—and not very practical. I don't want your money, Uncle Sam, even if it is really my money. I'm afraid of it. I'm afraid of what it might do to my backbone—that it might rob me of the very slim margin of *something* that makes me face this grinning typewriter day after day when I'd rather go hunting and fishing.[17]

Gordon continues in this vein, lecturing his readers about the threat of government-provided security to American initiative and freedom, the consequences of that $100 per month readjustment allowance growing ever greater in his mind: "If waiting for the check from Washington ever becomes the favorite American pastime, we are lost—and if we are lost, the Western World is lost, too."[18]

This little political morality tale may have been a complete fiction, though this would not have mattered to the *Reader's Digest*'s editors and readers. As with attacks on readjustment allowance payments to the unemployed, it expressed conservatives' concerns that the GI Bill might contribute after all to the perpetuation of the New Deal in the postwar era. (Gordon's recitation of fears includes voting out of spineless self-interest for the administration that provided him with his freedom-sapping security).[19] This indictment might seem rather disingenuous given the fact that Title V was anything but permanent, but it was the habit of dependency, apparently quickly formed, that worried Arthur Gordon, the *Digest*, and many congressional Republicans. Acceptance of benefits under the self-liquidating provisions of the bill might whet the appetite for more permanent public-sector programs and alter political expectations even among Americans who had never tasted the addictive lotus blossoms offered first to veterans of this latter-day Trojan War.

It was, naturally, more difficult to mount this kind of attack on programs that seemed to increase rather than threaten individual initiative—the college tuition and subsistence benefit above all, though also the various veterans' training programs developed at the subcollege level. Criticisms abounded here as well, but, if at times only for strategic reasons, they tended to be operational rather than philosophical; that is, they focused on the way the programs worked, not on their very existence as a threat to American values. As we examine the subcollege training programs established by Title II of the GI Bill, we take note of some of these criticisms and direct them not so much toward postwar ideological battles as toward their practical underlying premise: that, for operational reasons, this very large and complex component of the bill may or may not have served its recipients' legitimate aspirations, and may or may not have helped meet the labor needs of the postwar economy.

Mettler's survey of World War II veterans offers the best evidence pertaining to the first of these issues, and the question arises again whether the positive responses to Mettler's questions about subcollege training were colored by nostalgia and the general sanctification of the GI Bill in contemporary America. A survey conducted much earlier in the veterans' lives suggests that this might have been the case. In 1955 former GIs were asked: "In your present job or business, how much do you use the skills, education, or training received under VA programs?" Nearly two-thirds of those who had attended college responded either that the training was "indispensable" or that they "use it a great deal," while only 20 percent dismissed it as mostly or entirely irrelevant to their work. The responses of those who had participated in various subcollege training programs, however, were significantly different and more at variance from Mettler's later results. Fewer than a third of veterans who had attended schools below college level found their training indispensable or very useful in 1955—Harry Belafonte, had he been asked, would surely have been one of these—while a majority (55 percent) considered it mostly or largely irrelevant. On-the-job and on-the-farm training produced somewhat more positive results, but the numbers who reported that their training was indispensable or very useful still amounted to a minority of all of the respondents (49 percent and 41 percent, respectively).[20]

We should be quick to note that the question asked of veterans in 1955 was different from Mettler's question nearly a half-century later. The earlier survey referred to the respondents' present work, which for some might not have been the occupation for which they had been trained—indeed, among these were surely some who had moved up the occupational ladder after having done quite well at the work for which subcollege training had fitted them. These were men and women who would have found that their training was now largely irrelevant, even while considering (and long remembering) that initial training as a turning point in their lives. Still, for subcollege school attendees particularly, the disparity between the two surveys, conducted near the beginning and end of veterans' careers, is too large to be explained entirely in this way. A significant if unspecifiable number of these former GIs had consciously or unconsciously reinvented history when Mettler asked them to assess the impact of the GI Bill on their lives.

The second issue offers difficulties of its own. What exactly were the labor needs of this era, and how shall we measure the contribution of the GI Bill's subcollege training programs toward meeting them? The civilian labor force of the United States grew from 54 million to 66 million during the decade following the war; hence, the 5.6 million veterans who participated in some form of subcollege training under the GI Bill constituted a significant portion of the men and women who took up jobs in the peacetime economy.[21] What was the nature of their contribution to that economy? Was it concentrated within specific sectors, and were these the sectors most critical to economic conversion and growth? The major part of the conversion from wartime to peacetime production occurred before very many former GIs had completed their vocational training, so this cannot be a story of the bill's rescue of the American economy in the face of this dangerous moment of fundamental restructuring. However, questions about the role of GI Bill trainees remain significant with reference to the next phases of postwar economic development. How did they participate in and contribute to the economic miracle that followed more than fifteen years of depression, war, and reconversion? The first step toward an answer, surely, is to examine the training programs themselves with an eye toward their apparent outcomes—their operational successes and failures and the men and women they trained or failed to train to perform specific roles in the peacetime economy.

The largest and no doubt the most significant component of GI Bill–sponsored subcollege training involved schooling within a vast array of for-profit and nonprofit institutions. The latter were mostly public elementary, secondary, and vocational schools that faced the return of former students (and dropouts) two, three, and four years after they had gone off to war. Quite unlike the colleges and universities, public school administrators did not simply insert these older and service-hardened veterans into ordinary classes alongside children proceeding through school in the usual way. Typically, the schools created separate programs for veterans (often scheduled in the evening) and usually focused on vocational or accelerated academic courses. This separation of veterans from ordinary students helped reduce the physical pressure on schools, and in any case the number of former GIs who sought training in this way was not very large.

In October 1949, with subcollege schooling of veterans at a near-peak level of 800,000, only 212,000 were enrolled in nonprofit institutions, and most of these attended vocational and trade schools. The number attending ordinary elementary and secondary schools was only

83,000.[22] It is likely that most of the nonprofit school attendees went directly into the labor market after completing (or failing to complete) their schooling; hence, it is reasonable to conclude that the small number of veterans who received high school diplomas in academic programs created little additional pressure on America's colleges and universities. As for pressure to expand the public schools themselves, this would come not from veterans returning to school but, within a very few years, from the vast new "army" of baby boomers produced by these and other young Americans after years of interrupted marriage and childbearing.

Most subcollege schooling under the education provisions of the GI Bill took place in for-profit institutions, attendance at which was handled in the same manner as the universities, colleges, and other schools; that is, the VA was directed to pay for veterans' tuitions of up to $500 per annum at institutions approved by state authorities, while the veterans themselves received their monthly subsistence allowance. That this was a business opportunity to which entrepreneurs of all stripes would readily respond was understood even before the bill was passed. Here is the Bradley Commission's citation of Representative William R. Poage's "remarkable prediction" on the floor of the House in May 1944:

> There is not a man or woman on this floor who does not know that if we establish a system whereby 6 or 7 million young people come back from military or naval service and receive training at the Government's expense…and then get $50 or $75 a month for going to school in addition to having that tuition paid for at the rate of $500, which is terribly high and far in excess of what most institutions charge, that there is going to be a racket established all over this country of so-called institutions of learning that are simply going to spring up here, there, and yonder to get the kids' money. Do not think that easy money is not going to be taken care of; there are going to be plenty of people to profit financially. You and I could make money by quitting Congress and going into the school business.[23]

There is no record of anyone quitting Congress to go into the school business, but few of Poage's colleagues could have been surprised to see for-profit schools increase rapidly in number as veterans returned from Europe and the Pacific. By the autumn of 1949 there were more than 8,800 institutions on the approved list of for-profit schools offering training below the college level. Of these, 5,600—five of every eight—had come into existence after the GI Bill was enacted, and to this number we should add at least another 5,000 schools that had been placed on and then removed from the approved list. The newly founded institutions that remained on the list were mainly vocational and trade schools, which tripled from one thousand to three thousand, and flight schools (the particular focus of much criticism of this program), which multiplied amazingly, from 351 to 3,134. Business schools (which, according to Mettler's survey, produced the highest percentage of grateful former enrollees) expanded only modestly in number, from just over a thousand to just under twelve hundred.[24]

These striking numbers do not in themselves confirm Congressman Poage's cynical prediction of widespread fraud in schools created in response to Title II of the GI Bill. The postwar increase in demand for training was real, and if at the college level it was accommodated mainly by expanding existing institutions, at the subcollege level it was met by creating new ones—smaller, simpler in structure, and less heavily capitalized. Subcollege schools could be brought into existence just to serve the veterans and then, unlike the colleges and universities, simply disappear when the market for veterans' training declined, the capital that brought them to life moving on to exploit other opportunities. There is nothing inherently fraudulent in this alternative response to the heightened postwar demand for training; indeed, one might point here to institutional flexibility and capital mobility even while wondering whether this very quality—meeting a temporary need with temporary institutions—has not been at least partly responsible for the disappearance of subcollege training from popular memory of the GI Bill.

Nonetheless, there was undeniably a good deal of scamming of the system of subcollege training established under Title II. Many schools were founded to "take care" of the "easy money" described by Congressman Poage and offered very little training in return, knowing that there would be few complaints from veterans who signed up primarily to get the monthly subsistence allowance. A number of veterans, moreover, collected the allowance while taking courses that had nothing to do with their vocational ambitions—dancing classes (a good place to meet members of the opposite sex), horseback riding lessons, photography classes, and flight training, among others. Postwar America might well have needed newly trained dancing instructors, horsemen, and photographers, and a rapidly growing commercial aviation industry surely needed quite a few pilots and navigators. However, the number of enrollees was disproportionate to the demand in these and other areas, and the conviction quickly spread that many former GIs were abusing the subcollege training provisions of Title II, taking government money for courses that were recreational rather than vocational. Indeed, this conviction soon led to specific congressional action. In February 1948 the director of the Bureau of the Budget estimated that training for "avocational and recreational purposes" was costing the government more than $200 million per annum, and in June of that year Congress responded with a law that prohibited the funding of such training while granting the VA broad powers of investigation.[25] The focus of reports leading up to the new law was flight training, much of which was found to be in light recreational aircraft rather than in the larger planes flown by commercial carriers. Whether the VA was able to sort out fully the potential weekend flyers from real vocational trainees cannot be stated with certainty, but in the period following the new regulations the number of veterans in flight training declined dramatically—from nearly 125,000 in November of 1947 to 30,000 in October of 1949.[26]

Criticisms of the subcollege training program were by no means restricted to this kind of abuse. For-profit schools offering courses that could be only vocational were accused of inflating tuitions, extending the length of courses, enrolling too many students, and keeping on students who did little more than collect their subsistence payments. When in May of 1948 *Collier's* asked "What's Wrong with Veterans' Schools?" it noted, along with the coming oversupply of dancing instructors, the great pains being taken to train veterans in the decidedly nonrecreational practice of chicken sexing. "Before the war," wrote Albert Q. Maisel for *Collier's*, "a fewscore Japanese-Americans made a not-too-splendid living by separating male baby chicks from the females. If one Nisei wanted to learn the trade he worked beside another, and that was all there was to it."[27] But the promise of up to $500 a year in government money for each enrolled trainee had given birth after the war to "a chain of chicken-sexing colleges," of which the National Chicken Sexing School of Chicago was the unfortunate recipient of Maisel's close attention. The school, located on the premises of the Sagano Brothers—distributors of eggs—and operated by George Sagano, offered a $500 course in chicken sexing that lasted fully seven months. The school's assets, according to its report to the state of Illinois, consisted of two tables, eight chairs, eight lamps, a blackboard with "accessories" (presumably chalk and an eraser), and an unspecified number of boxes of newly hatched chicks. Remarkably, after seven months of peering at the bottoms of little chicks—and collecting all the while the monthly subsistence allowance—the trainee, according to Mr. Sagano, was not yet fully qualified. A year or two of on-the-job training at employers such as the Sagano Brothers might well cost the government still more. All of this money and effort, noted Maisel, was devoted to learning a skill that was not taught as a separate course in a single accredited agricultural college and was taught in the for-profit schools of other states for as little as $40 in courses that lasted less than a month.[28]

Maisel's example is at once amusing and outrageous, and the author no doubt deliberately added a little extra fuel for the latter feeling by focusing on a school operated by a Japanese American. Even so, was subcollege training under Title II of the GI Bill "in many instances...the greatest boondoggle of all time"?[29] Many of the abuses of the program were uncovered by government investigators as part of the process of weeding out fraud and excessive costs, and the VA was often able to eliminate these abuses, as even Maisel admitted.[30] Furthermore, if the federal government was unable to control the process of approval of for-profit schools, it was because of the administrative decentralization built into the bill by the same conservatives who were loudest in their denunciations of the program's excesses.

A more significant rejoinder, however, is that successful and honestly run schools, which perhaps made for less dramatic reporting in national magazines, were also part of the history of subcollege training under the GI Bill. A good example, as spectacular in its affirmation of Title II as the National Chicken Sexing School may have been of its misuse, is New York's School of the Visual Arts, founded in 1947 as the Cartoonists' and Illustrators' School by Silas H. Rhodes and the aptly named Burne Hogarth. Rhodes, who was himself a veteran of World War II, had worked for the VA after the war, and it was there that he, with Hogarth's collaboration, conceived of the idea of an art school designed for veterans and financed by the GI Bill. This was no scam; rather, the school was an immediate and enduring success, training a number of prominent artists and illustrators and evolving by the 1970s into a highly respected degree-granting college of art that now enrolls more than three thousand students.[31]

A vocational or trade school could succeed without transforming itself into a degree-granting college, and there were no doubt many such successes among the thousands of schools wholly or partially underwritten by Title II of the GI Bill. Weighing successes against the scams and failures is extremely difficult, however, given the size, obscurity, and ephemerality of many of these institutions—the substantial and well-recorded contributions to Title II of, say, the University of

Michigan are not difficult to assess, but what of those of a backstairs Ann Arbor electricians' school that went out of business soon after the market of returning veterans had dried up? Investigative journalists paid little attention to such institutions, particularly if they were honestly and effectively run, and neither did government officials charged with ferreting out fraudulent use of public funds.

The most thorough contemporary analysis of subcollege training under the GI Bill was conducted by the VA in late 1949 and resulted in a report to John Rankin's House Committee on Veterans' Affairs in January of 1950. Its purpose was not to assess the program as a whole but to identify the nature and extent of abuses. Hence, the report says nothing at all about good schools and effective training while detailing an impressive array of dishonest practices on the part of both school operators and enrolled veterans. An appendix lists 258 examples of schools that overcharged the government through schemes ranging in complexity from dummy corporations that charged the school high prices for goods and rental space that could then be passed along to the government in the form of inflated tuition, to simple scams such as inflating enrollments and putting one's nonworking spouse on the school's payroll. Even very small sums' are recorded: a bartending school that charged the VA for maximum rather than actual hours of instruction for a total overcharge of $500; a similar overcharge by a hair-styling school for trainees' supplies; a flight school that charged a little more tuition for veteran than for nonveteran trainees, which resulted in an overcharge to the VA of exactly $628.26.[32]

The 1956 Bradley Commission Report takes a larger view, but its acknowledgment of honest and effective schooling at the subcollege level is as brief as it is grudging. Considering the difficulties that faced school operators, the commission writes, "it may be said that some profit schools did render a great service to many veterans." Just *how many* schools and veterans dispensed and received this "great service" the commission does not venture to say. In any case, this fleeting acknowledgment is hastily qualified by the kinds of criticisms that we find in the 1950 VA report. The commission's final word is very blunt: "The greatest amount of waste, inefficiency, and fraud occurred in schools below the college level. The great influx of new trade schools catering to the veteran student caused the greatest single problem in the administration of the program."[33]

Official judgments of this sort must be considered seriously, but they were not flawless. Even apart from the natural tendency for guardians of the public purse to focus on examples of fraud and waste rather than efficiency, there is the question of how immune these investigations were from ideological currents and, in the case of manual training schools, even from class prejudice. Errors of judgment could indeed arise in many ways. Consider the case of the Restaurant Institute of Connecticut, founded in 1946 in New Haven as a school for veterans who sought careers in cooking or baking. This school is listed in the 1950 VA report as one of the 258 examples of institutional malpractice in subcollege training; indeed, it appears among the worst offenders, overcharging the VA in several different ways, including some $37,000 in excess tuitions.[34] Not surprisingly, the director of the institute, Frances L. Roth, was among those subcollege school officials asked to testify in December of 1950 before a House Select Committee investigating GI Bill educational and training programs. Her testimony, however, was anything but a chronicle of abuse of the public trust, and it provided little opportunity for outraged congressmen to get out their own chef's knives to carve up a conveniently hapless witness. In great detail, Roth described the founding of the school as a nonprofit institution responding to the needs of both veterans and the restaurant and hotel industry; its backing by Katherine Angell, a wealthy New Haven resident who saw the school as a memorial to the son she lost in the war; the excellent relations the school enjoyed with both the VA and the Connecticut Department of Education until a new VA contract officer began to level charges of improper practices; the unfounded nature of these charges; the flow of revenues, charges, and reimbursements, indicating that the VA owed money to the school rather than the reverse; and surely most important of all, the school's great success in training and placing its students—of the six hundred and fifty enrollees to date, more than five hundred had finished the program, and every one of the graduates had been placed in a good job.[35]

Long before the end of her testimony Roth had convinced the Select Committee that her school was honestly run and successful, and much of the questioning by the humbled committee members solicited her advice about improving subcollege training for future veterans. One congressman wistfully asked her whether the Capitol Restaurant had inquired about her students. The question was not foolish. As with the Cartoonists' and Illustrators' School in New York, the Restaurant Institute of Connecticut was the seed of a much larger and consequential institution. Two generations later it still thrives, with campuses in Hyde Park, New York, and the Napa Valley of California, as the Culinary Institute of America, widely acclaimed as the nation's premier school for the training of professional cooks and bakers.

Frances Roth's testimony before the Select Committee includes an interesting statement about the kind of social prejudice that might well have influenced contemporary evaluations of subcollege training institutions:

> The feeling I have gotten is that it is kind of a little off-color to be connected with anything in the trade-school level. We are always designated as the lower level of training. Everything that comes out in the press from the top officers down seems to have a little paragraph on the bottom of it that makes it something a little below normal to want to go to a trade school under the GI bill of rights. I have had boys come with their parents to our school to inspect and be absolutely astonished to find it the way it is pictured in the brochure. They simply have no faith in it until they come and actually see it....
>
> I am white collar myself [Roth was a prominent attorney in New Haven as well as director of the school]. I have taught many white-collar students. I feel the way Dr. Conant said he felt in the *New York Times* article and very much the way Dr. Angell said he felt—that we have gone white-collar haywire in this country of ours.[36]

The VA investigators, who wore the white collar, may well have more readily criticized subcollege training programs because of such a prejudice. This is understandably difficult to pinpoint in investigative reports that maintain the language and air of objectivity, and it is especially difficult to associate with criticisms of the large number of subcollege programs that, as we will see, did train veterans for white-collar jobs. One gains a somewhat clearer sense of a different kind of prejudice at work in the seemingly straightforward observation in the 1950 report that a number of schools were enticing veterans "to enroll in order to profit from subsistence payments, tools, and equipment furnished or other advantages not associated with the actual training to be received."[37] This claim points for evidence to an appendix that reproduces some three dozen newspaper ads, handbills, and form letters that mention such inducements along with descriptions of the training offered. About half of the ads and handbills appeared in African American newspapers or were addressed specifically to "colored veterans." What is striking here is not merely the disproportion but also the interpretation by the VA. Most of the ads and handbills do mention subsistence benefits or free tools, but several note only that the school is "state approved for GI training," and none appears to induce enrollment falsely or primarily for purposes other than training. The VA, it would appear, was bolstering a poor argument by associating the purported abuse with black schools.

Whatever may have tilted government investigators against institutions of subcollege training, we can regret the paucity of information in their reports about schools that provided effective instruction and honest administration. We can regret, too, that the responsibility of documenting and correcting abuses in Title II programs deflected the attention of public officials and other critics from the broader questions we raised earlier about the contributions of GI Bill trainees to the postwar economy. Admittedly, such questions were not easily answered. They required, at the very least, labor benchmarks for the assessment of specific training programs, and we note that the analysis and advice from economists and planners of the 1940s appear not to have been especially helpful, in that they focused mainly on the need to maintain full employment without specifying the industries or even the broader economic sectors where this employment should be deployed. On the other hand, there is little doubt that most postwar analysts would have agreed with the assessment made by the Council of Economic Advisers a few months after the passage of the Employment Act of 1946 that "the outstanding factor in the present situation is that we are working under a strong domestic urge and foreign demand to catch up on durable (producer and consumer) goods.... Everybody without a house or a car wants one this year."[38] Here was one economic sector that clearly needed a good deal of help from whatever job training programs the postwar economy might offer.

The demand for homes, cars, and other durable goods continued to grow into and well beyond the period in which subcollege schooling under Title II grew, peaked, and declined, maintaining a steady need for workers at all levels in America's factories, mills, and mines, in the offices and sales forces of its industrial corporations, and on hundreds of thousands of domestic and commercial building sites. And yet, this, the largest of the GI Bill's educational and training programs, fed surprisingly few veterans into the production sectors of the economy. By far the largest numbers of manual workers were trained for repair work rather than manufacturing.

In October 1949 approximately 730,000 veterans were enrolled in courses leading to specific kinds of nonagricultural jobs (another 70,000 or so were enrollees in "elementary and secondary" courses). Of these, fully 140,000 pursued courses in automobile and radio and television "mechanics" (80,000 in automobiles, 60,000 in radios and televisions), and it is clear from the longer list of courses that this term is meant to refer to repair work rather than production. Another 60,000 or so were enrolled in other "mechanical" courses or in still others that suggest training for repair and maintenance. Approximately 45,000 veterans were enrolled in engineering courses of various kinds, but the more specific categorization of these courses raises questions about whether their graduates were headed toward factories or repair shops. Only 1,687 of these students were enrolled in industrial engineering, 210 were in mining engineering, and 4,305 studied mechanical engineering. By far the largest category of "engineering" courses, with more than 30,000 enrollees, was labeled "electrical (including radio and television)." Surely some of these were repair and maintenance courses offered under a more imposing name. In sum, at least 20 percent and perhaps as many as 30 percent of veterans in schools below the college level were being trained for repair and maintenance jobs that constituted only about 3 percent of the total array of jobs in the U.S. economy in 1950.[39]

Significant numbers of subcollege trainees attended courses that led to jobs in the white-collar sectors of the economy, and it does not appear that many of them would have found their way into the offices of industrial corporations. The largest number among the October 1949 enrollees (nearly 42,000) studied accounting, and some of these students, perhaps most, would have found work in professional firms and nonindustrial offices. The same could be said of the 18,000 veterans enrolled in various kinds of secretarial and clerical courses and of the 7,000 who pursued courses labeled "all other business." A number of other veterans were clearly being trained for a wide variety of jobs in the service sector of the economy (white- and blue-collar alike); among them were teachers, musicians, entertainers, barbers and hairdressers, cooks, domestic and personal service workers, undertakers, commercial artists, architects and decorators, policemen and firemen, and, yes, commercial pilots, navigators, and flight instructors (still 30,000, a significant number in relation to the broader array of training programs). As with the repair and maintenance courses, many of these white-collar and service courses trained disproportionately large numbers of veterans for jobs that had very little to do with beating swords into plowshares.[40]

The most substantial contribution made by subcollege schooling to the durable-goods sector was in construction. Approximately 90,000 veterans on the October 1949 list were enrolled in courses that taught carpentry, bricklaying, painting, plumbing, and other construction-related occupations. The 12 percent of nonagricultural trainees attending these courses should be compared with the 6 percent that construction tradesmen bore to the total workforce in 1950. However, even here there are ambiguities. For example, among the 37,000 students of carpentry in the autumn of 1949, only 426 are listed under the title "construction carpentry." More than 12,000 were being trained as cabinetmakers (durable-goods producers but of a different sort), while nearly 25,000 are listed, rather unhelpfully, under "all other carpentry courses." Still, it is clear enough that subcollege schools were turning out at least their share of construction tradesmen. On the other hand, when these tradesmen are added to the repairmen, accountants, pilots, and others we have noted, they nearly exhaust the list of GI Bill trainees. Very few among the subcollege school attendees, we must conclude, were being prepared for production or supervisory work in America's industries.[41]

These patterns are not entirely surprising. Veterans would not ordinarily have thought of schools as the training grounds for factory work. What, then, of the on-the-job training provisions of Title II? In the first few years following the war, on-the-job training enrolled greater numbers of veterans than did the subcollege schools. In 1947, for example, the average number of veterans enrolled in each was 566,000 and 403,000, respectively.[42] However, these two programs were headed in opposite directions. During the next two years, as subcollege schools doubled their enrollments, on-the-job-training declined by half—to only 285,000 in October of 1949.[43] Still, some 1.4 million former GIs received nonagricultural on-the-job training in the decade following the war. Was this, then, a significant source of labor for American industry? In fact, some 21 percent of on-the-job trainees worked in manufacturing jobs in both 1947 and 1949. This is a much higher proportion than we find among enrollees in subcollege schools, and it exceeds the proportion (around 15 percent) of industrial workers in the workforce as a whole. However, it is still a minority of a significantly smaller program, and we cannot make too much of the 300,000 or so production workers supplied to U.S. industry between 1945 and 1955 by this provision of Title II. The same can be said of the 10 percent of on-the-job trainees who worked in construction. In addition, as with the subcollege schools, we observe the large numbers being trained for repair work (21 percent, equaling those in manufacturing) and the still larger numbers in retail management, sales, and a wide variety of jobs in the service sector.[44]

In tracing these patterns we must make allowances for distortions caused by dishonest practices, which even defenders of specific programs, such as Frances Roth, admitted were widespread. Both in subcollege vocational schooling and in on-the-job training, the official enrollment figures obscure some numbers of veterans who used these programs primarily or entirely to get the monthly subsistence allowance, as well as others who, despite honest efforts to attend and to learn, received little training from unscrupulous school operators or employers. Still, whatever the effects of such abuses on the overall contribution of nonfarm subcollege schooling and training to the postwar economy and to the careers of former GIs, certain conclusions about the pattern of that contribution seem reasonable. First, large numbers of veterans who lacked the qualifications or desire to attend college nonetheless sought training for jobs in the white-collar sector as accountants, retail managers, salespersons, office workers, and a wide variety of other such positions. Second, among those who were trained in manual work, a disproportionate number sought jobs in repair shops and to a lesser extent on construction sites rather than in factories. The Council of Economic Advisers may have stressed the importance of durable-goods production in the postwar economy, but the former GIs in these programs saw their own careers rather differently and in doing so anticipated and made their own contributions to what would later be called the postindustrial economy.

Few if any would have explained themselves this way. They were taking care of their own business, not the nation's (they had already seen to that), which could mean anything from a lucrative and satisfying career to a few extra months of payments from Uncle Sam. Still, in the aggregate they voted with their feet, and in the result we see no single-file march to the factory gate but a wide dispersal across the job sites of a diversifying and increasingly service-oriented economy.

Some, of course, marched back to the land and to the most traditional of livelihoods. On-the-farm training was a smaller component of the subcollege training provisions of Title II, but it was significant in relation to the agricultural sector. In 1950 there were some 4.4 million farm owners and managers in the United States and another 2.5 million men and women who worked on farms, including nearly a million who were unpaid members of farm families.[45] Even if we exclude the latter, these are not small numbers. On the other hand, agriculture was the only major sector of the U.S. economy that was declining in both the relative and the absolute numbers of proprietors and workers, so a program that enrolled a total of only 700,000 trainees could be seen as quite significant in helping to preserve a venerable American institution, the family farm. How well, then, did the GI Bill help train America's next generation of farmers? As with the other forms of subcollege instruction, contemporary analysts were quicker to point to the defects than to the contributions. The program itself combined coursework with practical advice and instruction on the farm, but investigators concluded that the courses were often useless, and many veterans admitted that they continued to take them and to suffer the on-farm visits of course instructors only to get the monthly subsistence benefit.[46]

The geographic pattern of participation reinforces the charge that on-the-farm training was yet another unintended GI Bill welfare payment. By far the greatest numbers were in southern states, where agricultural incomes were very low. In the autumn of 1949 slightly more than two-thirds of the nation's on-the-farm trainees resided in fourteen southern states (the eleven states of the former Confederacy plus Kentucky, Oklahoma, and Missouri). North Carolina led the nation with 25,246, while Tennessee enrolled 22,628. By contrast, California, with a large and prospering agricultural sector, enrolled only 3,897, while New York, still the most populous state, had 2,840. The wheat-belt state of South Dakota enrolled only 408.[47] Although there were many trainees in the upper south, the greatest concentration was in the Cotton Belt, a region in which large numbers of sharecroppers, cash tenants, and other small farmers struggled to gain a livelihood from a crop that seemed to yield less and less income with the passing years. No doubt many of the Cotton-Belt trainees, black and white alike, had come from families that had experienced years of debt, and some may have experienced it themselves. In this connection, the nation's on-the-farm trainees as a whole were, on average, older by several years than the veterans enrolled in other forms of subcollege training: Their median age in the autumn of 1947 was 28.5; a year later it was 29.7; and in the autumn of 1952 it was over 33. They were also less well educated. More than half of the trainees enrolled in October of 1949 had had only elementary-level schooling, and on average they had attended 3.2 fewer years of school than other Title II trainees.[48] These national figures undoubtedly would have been even more striking in the Cotton-Belt South. We can well understand, therefore, why on-the-farm training in this region may have been a different kind of veterans' reward than the one intended by the legislators of the GI Bill.

While taking note of various defects, the 1956 Bradley Commission Report includes the results of several state surveys that suggest that on-the-farm training, with all its faults, may have helped preserve the family farm as a viable institution. In Arkansas, a state with more than its share of struggling sharecroppers, a 1954 survey found that 72 percent of former trainees were farm proprietors and that all but about 5 percent of these were working and living above the margin. About half of the farm proprietors in the survey were described as "firmly established as substantial citizens and farmers." North Carolina and California also found large numbers of their former trainees working in agriculture, albeit with somewhat lower rates of farm proprietorship, and Texas issued a positive assessment of the role of the program in that state.[49] Nonetheless, the question remains as to what role on-the-farm training actually played in preserving or enhancing farming as a good way for veterans to make a living. Most of the participants in the program were already farm proprietors or operators of one sort or another, and it is by no means clear how much their hold on the land was improved by GI Bill training. The Bradley Commission gave it a qualified endorsement, concluding that this smallest of Title II programs did help young farm operators at least in some states, while it failed to improve the lives of farmworkers. It criticized the program even with respect to farm proprietors for including too many farmers who were too marginal to succeed even with good training and too many who did not need the government's help in the first place.[50]

The Bradley Commission's overall assessment of subcollege education and training was similarly mixed. On one hand, the commission validated, in soaring language, the educational provisions of the GI Bill:

> We have produced hundreds of thousands of technicians, doctors, lawyers, engineers, craftsmen, farmers, and business workers. These trained men and women represent a great national asset. Furthermore, as a readjustment device, the educational programs helped to prevent any serious national problems of unemployment, unrest, and dissatisfaction among veterans.... The veterans' educational program was a major contribution to the national welfare, and the country would be weaker educationally, economically, and in terms of national defense, if educators, veterans' organizations, the President, and the Congress had not seen fit to embark on this new and momentous educational enterprise.[51]

On the other hand, it is clear that most of this praise was intended for the college-level component of Title II, which by 1956 was already imparting iconic status to the GI Bill and which the commission described as "more successful than any of the other types of education and training provided for veterans."[52] The latter, subcollege training of all three types, is described in the commission's summary remarks almost entirely in terms of the array of problems already reviewed, and we can already sense here the diverging paths of college and subcollege training in the longer history of the GI Bill's role in America's political discourse.[53] To some extent, the divergence apparent in the commission's 1956 report was grounded in realities that ought not be disputed—college training under Title II did accumulate fewer frauds, administrative headaches, and poorly educated program participants than did subcollege training, and the most salient facts were the extraordinary success of Title II at the college level and the more qualified successes of each of its other programs. However, the Bradley Commission's conclusions about subcollege training, much like those of earlier investigations, focused too heavily on problems and too readily pushed successes to the periphery of attention. In this most complete of contemporary appraisals of the GI Bill we simply do not see much evidence of schools, nonfarm employers, or on-the-farm programs that effectively trained former GIs for satisfying careers.

If the Bradley Commission was generally too critical of subcollege training under Title II, in one sense it was not critical enough. Although there was ample opportunity for administrators and instructors to favor men over women or whites over blacks, the several volumes of the 1956 report contain hardly a word that addresses personal or categorical discrimination in any of the GI Bill subcollege programs. Gender was simply not a category of analysis for the commission or any of its predecessors, and race is mentioned only to note, without reference to supporting data, that, among African American veterans, participation in various GI Bill programs was as high or higher as it was among whites.[54] Presumably it was at least partly for this reason that the commission did not pursue race any further, even while it carefully analyzed participation according to variables such as geographical location, age group, and level of previous education attainment. Gender may have been excluded because of numbers—only 2 percent of America's World War II veterans were women, and the commission no doubt assumed that most women veterans would not seek subcollege training.

The most basic explanations for the exclusion of both gender and race, however, reside in the purposes of such studies and in prevailing social and political values. The Bradley Commission and other investigatory public bodies were interested in the effectiveness of training programs, not in justice or injustice in the distribution of their benefits, and one can only guess whether they would have framed the latter kind of analysis around concerns that would only later press significantly upon the political consciousness of white male public officials. There had been much talk of GI Jane as Americans contemplated the reintegration of soldiers and sailors into civilian life, and by the mid-1950s the black-led civil rights movement was compelling white Americans to take heed of racial injustice as a fundamental fact of life in the United States. The Servicemen's Readjustment Act, moreover, had been loudly trumpeted as a bill of *rights*. Nonetheless, even in the aftermath of the Supreme Court's historic decision in *Brown v. Board of Education* (a decision that involved most immediately the education of an African American girl), neither race nor gender—more specifically, the rights of African Americans and of women—had as yet become issues to which the leaders and staff members of Washington's various investigatory bodies had to pay much heed. Interpreting their responsibilities through the filter of prevailing values, those bodies that took on the weighty task of examining the GI Bill's successes and failures simply focused their attention on other matters.

There is very little information outside the official reports to tell us whether women encountered more obstacles than men in entering or completing subcollege training. The evidence of discrimination against black male veterans, though often anecdotal, is more substantial, particularly in relation to the way these programs functioned in southern states. The decentralization of program administration gave officials, schools, and employers in the South a good deal of latitude in maintaining an essentially segregated system in subcollege training no less than in higher education. Joseph Albright, who toured southern states as a special assistant to the VA administrator, reported from Port Jackson, South Carolina, that white employers simply did not accept black trainees for better-paying jobs and warned that VA policies sensitive to "local customs" were reducing "the already limited number of institutions offering training to Negro veterans."[55] Throughout the South and no doubt in other regions as well, black applicants were steered to black schools and employers, many of which lacked the resources to provide effective training, or to prepare their trainees for any but the least remunerative jobs.[56]

Black veterans, nonetheless, participated at higher rates than white veterans in the South, and the effects of their efforts may have been more transforming than early surveys of discriminatory practices would lead us to believe. In Suzanne Mettler's survey, an astonishing 89 percent of African American veterans who had experienced subcollege training under Title II reported it as a turning point in their lives.[57] We can question a portion of this response, as we did with white respondents, but so strong an affirmation cannot be explained away. However one might measure gains by black men in postwar America, most black subcollege trainees saw their own as substantial, even in the face of continuing patterns of racial discrimination.

To arrive at a more complete assessment of this largely forgotten component of the GI Bill we must broaden the context to include the very large number of veterans—about half of those who returned from the war—who did not seek any kind of training. Many, as we have seen, received readjustment allowances for a time, but many others simply returned to work at old jobs or found new ones without any help from the bill. The bill did assist many of these men and women through provisions relating to the U.S. Employment Service (USES); Title IV of the bill provided for a Veterans' Employment Service that would place a veterans' employment representative in each of the USES offices throughout the country. Guidelines were created for counseling job-seeking veterans and for establishing priorities for veterans over nonveterans and, among the veterans themselves, for those with disabilities over the able bodied. Although its costs were minimal, this was actually a very large and significant program that overcame the early poor performance we noted in chapter 3. In the decade following the war some 17.7 million applications were made by veterans to the USES (some of these were by World War I veterans and, toward the end of the decade, by veterans of the Korean conflict), and more than 13.6 million of these requests resulted in employment, an overall placement rate of 77 percent. The peak year was 1947, during which jobs for nearly two million veterans were found.[58] This was yet another overlooked component of the GI Bill, though we must emphasize that Title IV did little more than carry forward a program that had existed for many years. A veterans' placement service had been formed by the federal government shortly after World War I. Largely dormant during much of the 1920s, it was revived as the job market deteriorated at the end of the decade and was then incorporated into the new U.S. Employment Service, founded by the Wagner-Peyser Act of 1933. The USES was to be a nationwide job placement service administered by each state and available to both veterans and nonveterans, and it did function that way, recognizing veterans as a separate and special category of job seekers both before and after the GI Bill created the Veterans' Employment Service. The GI Bill's guidelines for evaluating veterans' applications may have altered USES procedures somewhat, at least with respect to white veterans, but the new guidelines were far from revolutionary. They certainly did nothing to create new procedures for protecting the rights of black veterans, who, in the South at least, were channeled almost exclusively by the USES to unskilled jobs even though many had been trained to do skilled work before or during the war.[59] Title IV's greatest contribution was in publicizing this established public job placement service to millions of veterans who otherwise might never have known of its existence.[60]

The most controversial public intervention into the process by which former GIs entered civilian employment takes us even further from the innovative provisions of the GI Bill. The Selective Training and Service Act of 1940—that is, the initial World War II draft—had stipulated that regularly employed men conscripted into the armed services would, upon reentering civilian life, be entitled to their old jobs or to similar ones with the same employer without loss of seniority or any other job benefit, provided that they were still able to perform the work and applied for reemployment in a timely way. This entitlement, which was intended in part to make the draft more palatable, was further expanded before the war's end by General Lewis B. Hershey, then in the early days of his long tenure as Selective Service director. General Hershey ruled that veterans were entitled to "superseniority" over even those civilian workers with longer standing in the workplace. It can easily be imagined how controversial such a measure was among existing workers, labor unions, and even some businesses. Superseniority was overruled by the Supreme Court in May of 1946, but in the meantime controversy raged over the entire issue of how veterans' rights compared with those of civilian workers and with negotiated agreements between unions and businesses regarding closed shops and seniority.[61]

None of this resulted from any of the terms of the GI Bill, and in that sense the entire matter lies beyond our scope. However, we introduce it in order to establish an important point: With respect to the issue of postwar workforce reintegration, the various GI Bill programs we have reviewed here were not always at the center of public attention in the middle and late 1940s; indeed, in recalling these programs we run the risk of losing sight of a larger world in which some veterans sought the training, advice, and temporary financial assistance provided by the bill while others found new jobs for themselves or returned to old ones under terms established not by the bill but by the congressional act that put them in the military in the first place. The GI Bill contributed significantly to the reintegration of veterans into the civilian workforce, but to recount its contributions—and its failures—is to tell only part of a larger story.

Thus far, this story has been, for the most part, about the preparation and search for jobs with paychecks written by other people. What about that part of the American dream that looks toward the day when one can be one's own boss? Among the GI Bill programs were loan guarantees under Title III for the purchase and operation of farms and small businesses by veterans who wanted to work for themselves. As chapter 3 points out, the initial limit on loan guarantees (50 percent of the loan with a maximum guarantee of $2,000) was dismissed by critics of the bill as wholly inadequate for the purchase of even very marginal businesses and farms. Bankers and the VA, moreover, were very circumspect about approving loans to young veterans who had little or no business or farming experience for the purchase of enterprises that had only slim chances of success: Frank Gervasi's complaint that veterans sought loans for "juke joints, hamburger heavens and tourist camps and other impractical ventures" reflected the thinking of those who controlled the purse strings.

In the early days of the program, therefore, the number of approved business loans under Title III of the GI Bill was tiny—only 500 in the second quarter of 1945, for example, and 900 during the following three months. The raising of the guarantee limit to $4,000 on the realty portion of loans in December of 1945, along with a dramatic increase in military discharges, seemed to inject new life into the loan program. In 1946 44,000 business loans and 18,000 farm loans were closed, and 1947 added another 59,000 in both programs. However, the numbers were already falling in 1947, and they would continue a rapid decline that reversed briefly in 1951 and the first half of 1952 with a temporary revival in the number of business loans. By the end of 1955, after ten years of active operations, the business loan program totaled only some 224,000 loans with a total value of $609 million. Farm loans totaled only 69,000 with a total value of $270 million.[62]

As low as these figures are in relation to the vast numbers who returned from the war—only about two of every one hundred veterans received a business or farm loan—the numbers that relate to the opening or purchase of a business or farm are smaller still. About half of the farm loans were used to purchase equipment, livestock, and seed for existing farms, and a substantial share of business loans financed equipment and fixtures.[63] Observing that veterans lagged significantly behind nonveterans of similar ages in the ownership of businesses or farms (14 percent as compared with 25 percent in 1955), the Bradley Commission concluded that "the business and farm loans have done little to encourage the veteran to become self-employed."[64]

A different kind of loan guarantee authorized under Title III of the GI Bill was not so easily dismissed. It related neither to businesses nor farms nor any other aspect of the gainful employment of returning GIs. Veterans needed homes as much as livelihoods, and here the loan program was of an entirely different dimension. If fewer than 300,000 veterans obtained government-guaranteed business and farm loans in the decade following the war, the number who secured loans for the purchase of nonfarm homes approached four million. If the total value of business and farm loans remained under $1 billion during that period, the value of home loans exceeded $30 billion.[65] A program of such size and significance, touching for the first time upon the domestic lives of the men and women who had fought their country's battles, could not have been forgotten over the years, as were the various programs, large and small, discussed in this chapter. And it has not been forgotten. Second only to the college tuition and subsistence program, the VA mortgage remains in the popular mind as the GI Bill's substantial reward to veterans of the Good War. We turn to it in the next chapter.

SEVEN

Finding a Home

The VA Mortgage

Levittown, New York, late 1940s. Millions of former GIs used VA-backed loans to buy homes, many of them in suburbs like this one. (Courtesy Levittown Public Library)

B UYING A HOME was not the first priority of most veterans
of World War II. Finding work or getting into college or
some kind of job training—and in the meantime picking up
mustering-out pay and perhaps that weekly or monthly readjustment
allowance—came first even for large numbers of veterans eager to
marry long-missed sweethearts or to return to brides and the "good-
bye babies" many of the newlyweds of 1941 and 1942 had produced
before the long and dangerous separation of war. College-bound
veterans settled into dormitory rooms or makeshift married students'
housing for periods as long as four years and did not begin to look
for a private home until a postcollege job was secured. Other former
GIs, many of them still quite young, headed for parental homes, some
bringing new wives or husbands with them, some joining wives and
babies already living there throughout the war years. The war—and
the Depression before it—had taught many American families how to
share small living spaces in this way, and for large numbers of immigrant families, only now ready to produce their second generation of
American-born children, this was a lesson that did not need learning.
With some exceptions, returning veterans squeezed into living spaces
not their own while they began to sort out a future that suddenly was.

Two external conditions contributed to the continuation of this
space squeeze beyond the immediate postwar period. The most important was an acute housing shortage that would take a number of years
to alleviate. As we noted earlier, the numbers of new homes built in
the United States declined precipitously during the early years of the
Great Depression and fell off again during the war. Housing starts
had actually started to drop as early as 1926; indeed, economic historians point to the reduction from 937,000 new homes in 1925 to only
509,000 in 1929 as a harbinger and even a significant cause of the misery to come. It hardly needs stating that the Depression itself witnessed
an even steeper decline that all but wrecked the home-construction
industry. The worst year was 1933, when, astonishingly, only 93,000
new homes were built for the nation's nearly 31 million households.

The new Roosevelt administration responded quickly to restore the badly damaged banking system and to encourage investment in new construction. At least partly as a consequence of New Deal initiatives, including the first federal civilian public-housing programs, housing starts climbed gradually after that dismal year and reached 706,000 in 1941. However, the war's insatiable demands on both labor and materials reduced them again, such that by 1944 only 142,000 new homes were built in the United States, less than a sixth of the number built at the high point of home construction nearly twenty years earlier.[1]

Except for the few productive years just before the war, those two decades had seen the nation's housing stock slip further and further behind the normal demand for homes. When, not long after the return of peace, that demand was pushed beyond normal by millions of veterans and their newly formed families—and by newly unfettered wartime savings by veteran and nonveteran families alike—the long-accumulating housing shortage became a personally painful and politically dangerous reality.

The second external condition that contributed to the housing squeeze in the immediate postwar period was the inadequacy of public programs supporting home finance and in particular the new loan guarantee program written into the GI Bill. In its first formulation within Title III of the Servicemen's Readjustment Act, the VA mortgage was virtually useless to most veterans. As chapter 3 observes, Title III provided for a government guarantee of 50 percent of qualifying home loans negotiated with lenders by veterans and housing developers selling to veterans but with a cap on the guarantee of only $2,000. Included within the language of the GI Bill, moreover, was the stipulation that any home purchased with a VA mortgage must be priced within a formally appraised "reasonable normal value," with the term *normal* understood to refer to the price such a home would fetch in the absence of unusually rapid inflation.[2] Given the severe shortage of houses even before many GIs had mustered out or begun looking for homes, rapid inflation was anything but absent—housing analysts and journalists from all over the country were reporting increases at rates that had not been seen for decades.[3]

This meant that a provision of the GI Bill intended to protect veterans from price gouging by builders and other home sellers was, in practice, making it all but impossible to find a home that qualified for a VA mortgage. Moreover, given the prices to which houses had so quickly risen, the $2,000 guarantee limit was itself obsolete as an inducement to lenders. Nor could the veteran simply wait for home prices to return to "normal" or for $4,000 homes magically to appear: The bill required application within two years of one's military discharge or of the official end of the war. Title III limited the interest rate on loans to 4 percent and directed the VA to pay the first year's interest, but by setting the loan amortization period at a maximum of twenty years it also guaranteed that monthly payments would be too high for most veterans who somehow found qualifying homes within that period. A little-known provision of the GI Bill did make Title III useful to certain potential homeowners who qualified for mortgages guaranteed by other federal agencies (principally the Federal Housing Administration). A secondary loan guarantee limited to $2,000 and 20 percent of the total purchase price could be used to extend the government's guarantee to 100 percent of an FHA loan, effectively eliminating the need for a down payment.[4] Theoretically, this secondary loan guarantee opened the door to homeownership to all veterans who could prove themselves to be a reasonable credit risk. Still, where were the homes these veterans could actually buy under conditions set by both the GI Bill and the FHA? Only some 43,000 of the 8.3 million veterans mustered out by the end of 1945 found a satisfactory answer to this question.[5]

Congress quickly responded to complaints about the VA mortgage program and by December of 1945 had enacted several significant changes. Market realities compelled lawmakers to increase the guarantee level to $4,000 and—as noted earlier—to eliminate the word *normal* from the program's pricing standard, thereby leaving the much more flexible, inflation-sensitive criterion of "reasonable value" to guide VA officials. The loan amortization period was extended from 20 to 25 years, thus reducing monthly payments, and the period of veterans' eligibility for submitting applications was extended to 10 years. The program's red tape, another widely noted problem, was attacked by granting automatic VA approval of loans to qualified veterans by lenders subject to federal or state regulation, in this way replacing the more cumbersome and time-consuming process of case-by-case review.[6]

These and other more modest changes helped to jump-start the loan guarantee program. In 1946 and 1947 veterans turned to the VA in numbers that far exceeded those of 1944 and 1945. Nearly a million VA-backed home loans were closed in those two years, increasing the total monetary amount from $192 million to more than $5.5 billion. Borrowing slowed somewhat during 1948 and 1949 because of a new surge in inflation and interest rates, but the 600,000 new VA mortgages, totaling $3.3 billion, were by no means insignificant.[7] By the end of 1949 nearly 7 percent of World War II veterans—many now with growing families—had moved from their parents' and in-laws' homes, from rented apartments, and from college housing into homes purchased with VA-guaranteed loans. This was still a much lower proportion than the 51 percent who had received unemployment or self-employment readjustment allowances or the 31 percent who had attended or completed college or subcollege training, but it was on the rise and would continue to increase when the proportions of veterans using these other GI Bill benefits leveled off or declined.[8] The VA mortgage program, after an unpromising start, was becoming a success.

The more rapid construction of new houses was one reason for the continuing growth of the program, and the remarkable increase in marriages and births—the legendary postwar baby boom—was obviously another, the one pulling, the other pushing young veterans and their families into the private housing market. A third influence was a new round of changes to the program itself. The Housing Act of 1950 raised the maximum guarantee on VA mortgage loans from 50 percent to 60 percent and increased the maximum amount of the guarantee from $4,000 to $7,500. These higher limits permitted the discontinuation of the secondary loan program, which, because of heavy FHA participation, resulted in overall interest rates on FHA-VA packages that exceeded the 4 percent VA limit. Now all VA-backed loans could be limited to 4 percent.[9] The maximum loan period was again extended, this time from 25 to 30 years, which for many veterans resulted in monthly mortgage payments that were actually lower than the rents these new homeowners had been paying on apartments. The 1950 revisions also made unremarried war widows eligible for VA mortgages and instituted a direct government loan program in those (mostly rural) areas of the country where private mortgage loans were not readily available.[10]

The direct loan program would remain small (fewer than 73,000 direct loans were made through 1955), but the other provisions of the 1950 Housing Act opened the gates to a new surge in VA-backed borrowing.[11] In 1950 and 1951 nearly a million veterans purchased homes with VA mortgages, securing loans that totaled more than $3.7 billion. These numbers declined during the next two years, as they did after the initial surge of 1946 and 1947, and then increased again, rising by 1955 to a record 650,000 loans totaling more than $7 billion.[12] We must note that this latter figure includes a number of loans obtained by veterans of the Korean conflict (the VA estimates that 268,000 veterans of Korea used VA home mortgages during the first half of the 1950s), but we can estimate, as did the VA, that during the decade 1945–1955 nearly 4 million World War II veterans used this GI Bill benefit and that the total value of their VA-backed mortgage loans exceeded $30 billion.[13]

These are very large numbers, and their significance is magnified by the fact that so many of these veterans were making the initial transition to homeownership. Among veterans who in 1955 owned their own homes for longer than five years, fully 88 percent were first-time homeowners. The equivalent proportion among nonveterans was only 55 percent.[14] Not all veterans' homes were purchased with VA-backed loans, but we have more than a whiff here of a social revolution spurred in no small part by the GI Bill.

Was it of the sort that gave nightmares to conservatives determined to roll back the New Deal? Perhaps surprisingly, it does not appear that anyone—in Washington or elsewhere—thought of the VA mortgage in these terms or even anticipated its significance. Interestingly, when the American Legion proposed and publicized an omnibus benefits bill for World War II veterans, including loan guarantees among a variety of other measures, the organization's publicists did not emphasize this part of the benefits package. In an undated typescript in the American Legion's archives titled "Omnibus Bill Introduced into House and Senate Affecting World War II Veterans," a long discussion of VA hospital construction, demobilization, and various proposals for veterans' benefits includes only one sentence on government-backed loans.[15] And in the January 1944 edition of the *National Legionnaire*, the headline story, "Legion's Bill for Veterans in Congress," entirely omits loan guarantees from its rundown of proposed benefits.[16]

It is clear from still other documents that both Congress and the American Legion thought of a VA-based loan-guarantee program mostly in terms of the convenience to veterans of having various benefits located in a single government agency and much less of the program's substance as an innovative (and government-aggrandizing) way of compensating veterans and reintegrating them into civilian life. Veterans' benefits had never before included such a program, but after ten years of Americans' experience with government-guaranteed mortgage loans through the FHA, it could hardly be said that the VA mortgage was an innovation. In Title III of the GI Bill Congress did little more than replicate a well-established federal program within the purview of the VA in accordance with the idea that veterans ought to be able to get all of their benefits, whatever they might be, in one place.

Nor was the FHA itself, though a product of the New Deal, a particular problem for conservatives in Congress, the American Legion, or elsewhere. In the shorthand of American politics and political history, "New Deal" too often stands for centralized and expensive federal programs with regulatory or redistributional effects. However, this shorthand misses the many New Deal programs that utilized and reinforced existing institutions outside government in order to revitalize specific sectors of the economy. The FHA was one of these initiatives. As Kenneth T. Jackson has written in his classic history of American suburbanization, the FHA was designed "to meet President Roosevelt's desire for at least one program that could stimulate building without government spending and that would rely on private enterprise."[17]

A federal agency that offers the U.S. Treasury as a loan guarantor to banks and other private lending institutions is a long way from the creeping socialism that Roosevelt's opponents found in various other New Deal programs, and the National Housing Act of 1934, which created the FHA, was in fact vigorously supported by the National Association of Real Estate Boards and other industry groups that stood to benefit from this public support of private business. The Home Owners' Loan Corporation (HOLC), created the previous year, injected federal cash and bonds directly into the system of home finance by refinancing defaulted mortgage loans, and it is telling that it was the business-backed FHA, not the HOLC, that survived as a permanent presence in the home-finance sector once the immediate crisis had passed.[18] The future of public participation in this sector would be defined mostly by guarantees that protected the loan portfolios of banks and other private lenders, not by loans from the government to private borrowers. The rest of that future was provided by a quite different form of direct public financing, the secondary mortgage market established by Roosevelt in 1938 through the Federal National Mortgage Association (FNMA or, more affectionately, Fannie Mae). Fannie Mae's initial purpose was to purchase FHA mortgages from private lenders, thereby enabling and encouraging these lenders to make new loans whenever they saw profit in doing so.[19] No less than the FHA, Fannie Mae was the kind of New Deal program pro-business conservatives could readily support.

Thus, when the VA mortgage was created on the model of the FHA (and when, a few years later, VA mortgage lenders were given access to Fannie Mae), there was little fear among conservatives that Congress had brought the New Deal into the postwar period in a way that threatened their political values. Conservatives' opposition to Title III may have been made more difficult, too, by the curious embrace by their philosophical leader, Senator Robert A. Taft of Ohio, of solutions to the postwar housing shortage that were far more government centered than those in the GI Bill. Taft was the Republican Party's most insistent and respected opponent of the New Deal. He spoke endlessly of the need to reverse New Deal programs that he felt produced little more than meddlesome bureaucracy and high taxes, and his prominent opposition to what seemed to be everything the Democrats had done or wished to do earned him the sobriquet "Mr. Republican." His best-remembered achievement as a senator is surely the Taft-Hartley Act, which nullified or offset many of the pro-labor provisions of a New Deal bill long known as the American labor movement's "Magna Carta," Senator Robert F. Wagner's National Labor Relations Act of 1935.

And yet Taft did not in fact oppose every New Deal initiative, and in the years following the war he worked closely with Wagner, as well as with Southern Democrat Allen J. Ellender, on a bill that called for large-scale federal support for low-rent public housing. This had been a New Deal program of only modest proportions, enacted in 1937 but unable to accomplish much before the war foreclosed most construction unrelated to war production. After the war Taft called for public housing expansion, starting with hearings of the Senate Subcommittee on Housing and Urban Development, which he chaired in the summer of 1945, and ending after a long struggle with the real estate lobby and conservative opponents in the House of Representatives with the passage of the Housing Act of 1949. The public housing program, as Wagner himself had described it as early as 1935, was intended to inject the federal government into the housing market only insofar as the latter failed to find on its own a profitable way of building living spaces for the poor, and this is probably what enabled so thoroughgoing a conservative as Taft to support it. However, the Taft-Ellender-Wagner Act, as the 1949 law is generally known, was nonetheless a good deal further to the left on the political spectrum than Title III of the GI Bill. Its coauthorship by "Mr. Republican" reduced the impulse on the part of congressional conservatives to object on philosophical grounds to the GI Bill's market-driven system of public loan guarantees.

This is not to say that no criticism of Title III was voiced, but as was the case with subcollege training, the VA mortgage program was criticized mainly on operational grounds both before and after its obvious early defects were corrected. Wartime congressional hearings led to the significant reforms of 1945. These inquiries continued long after that year and responded to veterans' complaints of shoddy construction in

VA-financed housing developments, as well as rumors of and objections to dishonest practices by lenders, developers, and VA officials. In one hearing of a House Select Committee held in San Diego late in 1951, committee members listened to a group of local bankers, attorneys, real estate agents, property developers, and VA loan officers, a number of them related by blood or marriage, defend their actions, deny allegations, or refuse to answer questions about a number of suspicious practices investigated by committee staffers, including an apparently widespread practice of purchasing veterans' VA mortgage-eligibility certificates. One journeyman plumber who had sold his certificate for $500 informed the committee that an advertisement offering at least three times that sum had appeared in the local paper. The plumber was annoyed that he had sold for so much lower a price, while the committee was outraged at so blatant a violation of VA regulations.[20] A local contractor, one Carlos Tavares, was asked about the policy of sending gifts of whisky to VA officials. "Did you give whisky in case lots?" asked committee chairman Olin E. Teague. Tavares responded, "If we liked a fellow, we might send them a case." "There has been enough whisky sent to the Veterans' Administration," Congressman Teague concluded, "to keep them drunk for a year."[21]

Cases of whisky flew back and forth between many of the players, sober or drunk, in this business of building houses for veterans (or for nonveterans, using illegally purchased certificates of eligibility) in San Diego, but the extent of improper gains they might have wrung from the VA mortgage program is difficult to discern from the recorded testimony. The goings-on in San Diego, moreover, do not seem to have characterized the program's operations in the nation at large. Faults were uncovered elsewhere, though neither Teague's committee nor any other found cause to make a general indictment. With all of its red tape and all of the opportunities it provided for gaming the system, the VA mortgage guarantee program appeared to work rather well.

But with what effects? We have already alluded to the magnitude of the transition to homeownership among former GIs in the postwar period, a movement that contributed mightily to the transition from rent to ownership in the nation as a whole. Before the war, only 44 percent of the nation's 35 million dwellings were owner occupied. By 1956, with the postwar housing shortage largely overcome by the addition of 15 million new houses and apartments, the proportion of owner-occupied dwellings had risen to 60 percent.[22] For the first time since the United States had been a nation of farms and small towns—perhaps for the first time ever—a significant majority of American families had realized the dream of homeownership. This was a dream of no small consequence, especially in an age of proliferating consumerism, in which the house was the principal consumer good and, no less, the principal receptacle of many others—furniture, appliances, and all the other things people bought to maintain and embellish their domestic lives.

The VA mortgage played a significant role in enabling one component of the American population, young veterans, to make the move from renters (or dependents) to owners. We must nonetheless be careful not to overstate its influence. For one thing, the major portion of the nation's shift toward ownership—from 44 percent to 53 percent— occurred *during* the war—before the VA mortgage program established its presence in the financial marketplace. Obviously, this phase of the movement toward homeownership was dominated by nonmilitary families, significant numbers of whom managed to find new houses to buy despite the wartime decline in home construction. Increased wartime savings, which increased from less than $15 billion to more than $54 billion between 1940 and 1944,[23] was an important factor, as was the pent-up demand for homeownership caused by the depression and released by high and steady wartime wages, at least for families not separated by war. During the war years FHA mortgages increased gradually, turning savings into down payments and wages into monthly mortgage payments on large numbers of privately owned homes.

After the war and after the legislative refinements of the VA mortgage program, veterans contributed to the shift to homeownership in a big way. To what extent did they rely on the VA-backed financing established by the GI Bill? A special survey of veterans conducted by the Bureau of the Census in October of 1955 tabulated more than 10.7 million veteran homeowners, of whom all but a small proportion were veterans of World War II. Just under 4 million, nearly 37 percent, had purchased their homes with VA-backed mortgages. This is a large number, yet it fails to account for even a majority of veterans who financed their homes during the decade following the war. Approximately 7.7 percent turned to the FHA instead of the VA, and a much larger number, more than 55 percent, purchased their homes with loans that were not guaranteed by any government agency.[24]

These proportions may seem surprising, especially in light of the somewhat lower interest rates and overall costs mandated by Title III for VA-backed loans. However, the veteran was not always in the driver's seat when it came to securing a home loan. Many bought homes from developers who arranged financing for sales within large-scale projects even before the individual buyer appeared on the scene. Others relied on lenders who passed up the VA guarantee in favor of higher interest rates and the absence of red tape, and some veterans may themselves have had little patience with the latter. The VA mortgage was not expected to absorb the entire market in home finance for veterans, and it never came close to doing so. Most veterans simply did not use it. Its contribution, by no means inconsiderable, was in enabling a significant number of GIs to buy private homes they otherwise would not have been able to afford and to increase the already substantial flow of veterans from renting and dependency to homeownership.

At first, most of the houses purchased by veterans with VA mortgages had been lived in by others—some 84 percent before 1947[25]— and though it is impossible to locate these homes with precision, it is likely that most of them were in cities and towns, in neighborhoods that would not be regarded today as suburbs.[26] This, however, would change quickly and dramatically, to a point where the vast majority of VA-backed home purchases were of brand-new houses built in equally new and distinctly suburban communities. It is a tale that has been told many times before as part of a larger story of massive postwar American suburbanization—a story so striking in its sweep and significance and so important in the way that it has shaped our understanding of the postwar physical and social landscape that it may be said to rise to the status of legend. At the very least, it is a central part of the still-larger legend of postwar America as the place and time "when dreams came true" (to borrow the title of one fairly recent history of the purported effects of the GI Bill), specifically, dreams of suburban peace and plenty, realized by millions of young Americans, safe at last from the horrors of both war and the heterogeneous turmoil of the inner city.

Among these millions was Bill Thomas, whose story is told by Edward Humes in his recent book celebrating the achievements of the GI Bill. Thomas, the son of a Greek-born barber in Detroit (the original family name was Thomaides), had dropped out of high school to help his family get through the Depression and soon found himself a twenty-year-old U.S. Army artilleryman bound for combat duty in Anzio, the Ardennes, and far across the Rhine. Facing an uncertain future after the war, Thomas worked at a number of jobs back in Detroit before setting out for California. At a VA office in Long Beach, where he had hoped to find advice about work, he was instead encouraged to enter college and was soon enrolled in business classes at Long Beach City College. He took to his courses with enthusiasm and, after completing his studies, became manager of the school's bookstore. His future now a bit more settled, Thomas drove back across the country, well beyond Detroit to Durham, North Carolina, where he proposed to Soula, a Greek American girl he had met before he moved west. The marriage would not be immediate, so Thomas returned to his job and to the boarding-house room he was renting in Long Beach for $30 a week. The room, of course, would not do for his future bride, so Thomas bought a house—or rather the promise of a house—to be built in the proposed suburban development of Lakewood, located between Long Beach and Los Angeles. The house was to have three bedrooms, and with his VA mortgage Thomas would pay nothing down and only $64 a month—about half the cost of his room at the Long Beach boarding house. The house was built according to schedule, and Bill and Soula Thomas moved into it in 1951. They raised their three children there and in a larger house in another suburban community nearby after selling the Lakewood house for twice its original price. According to Humes, the Thomases have always loved their life in the suburbs, and Bill remembers the GI Bill's education and home-loan benefits with gratitude: "'No doubt about it,' Bill Thomas says. 'I was very lucky. Still am.'"[27]

To multiply the story of Bill and Soula Thomas by millions is to recognize the very rapid deconcentration of urban populations in the postwar period and the vast new expanse of primarily residential communities beyond the previously understood boundaries of the nation's cities. This was a general phenomenon, but it was at first most dramatic in the largest metropolitan areas. In 1940 some 37 percent of the nation's large-scale metropolitan population lived outside the central cities of metropolitan areas. During the 1940s and in particular the half-decade following the war, the rapid movement of big-city dwellers to new homes outside the central city increased that proportion to 41 percent, and in the 1950s it grew again to 49 percent. Major cities did increase in population during these critical decades, but the areas just beyond them grew significantly faster—by 36 percent compared to 15 percent in the central cities during the 1940s and by 49 percent compared to only 11 percent during the 1950s.[28]

Sometime during the early 1960s, the areas outside the nation's largest cities surpassed these cities in population, and the balance has continued to shift from the center to the periphery ever since, both in these largest metropolitan areas and in smaller urban areas as well. By the 1970s, moreover, an accelerating regional movement from the "Rust Belt" to "Sun Belt" suburbs surrounding large and small cities of the Southeast, Southwest, Mountain West, and Pacific West (Bill and

Soula Thomas were in the vanguard here) gave metropolitan deconcentration another new boost. By the end of the century, the suburban
residents of the United States outnumbered all the people who lived
in cities and towns of all sizes, as well as those who lived on all of
the farms and in all of the villages of rural America. Remarkably, the
majority of Americans had come to live in a form of community that
did not even exist when the nation was founded and that would have
been incomprehensible to the residents of the farms, villages, small
towns, and port cities of the early republic.

In truth, this tracing of people from central city to metropolitan
periphery oversimplifies the story of suburbanization. It suggests
that the entire population increase in the areas beyond the central
city consisted of people moving outward from the city and that all
the localities that existed or developed on the periphery were residential suburbs that were tied to the central city by daily travel to and
from urban workplaces. The suburbs were, of course, more complicated than that, even during the earliest postwar years, when residential deconcentration did outweigh any other type and when residential
developments grew faster than corn on the fields they had replaced.
Some suburbs were old rural villages or small towns that retained a
nonmetropolitan character and daily round, upon which suburban
life and urban commutation were only partly overlaid.[29] Others were
more substantial places, including some that grew to become cities in
their own right—"edge cities," surrounded by their own suburbs even
while they formed part of the physical and human periphery of still
larger places.[30] The outward migration of department stores, corporate offices, and other institutions once found only in the heart of great
cities further complicated (and still complicate today) the geographical space that is so often called—too simply—"the suburbs." And yet,
"suburbanization" is a good term to describe the dramatic reshaping
of the American metropolis in the years immediately following World
War II. The outward trek of millions of young American families to a
new "crabgrass frontier" of domestic fulfillment is a legend grounded
in real experience.[31]

Like most legends, this one has a hero. His name was not Cuchulain
or Siegfried, King Arthur or Robin Hood but, unlikely as it may seem,
William J. Levitt. Levitt was the man who is generally credited with
inventing both the huge new suburban development, built almost
overnight in the form of standardized, single-family houses arrayed
endlessly across a bulldozed landscape of gently curving roads, and
the organizational techniques for building, financing, and selling new

houses on so large a scale. And his is the name that dominates nearly every narrative of postwar suburbanization. As Sam Bass Warner Jr. long ago pointed out, the "streetcar suburbs" of the late nineteenth century had been built by very large numbers of small-scale builders—in three suburbs of Boston, some 22,000 new houses had been put up between 1870 and 1900 by nine thousand different builders.[32] Small-scale suburban building of this sort remained the norm up to and throughout the war years, although the Levitt family was itself one of a small number of builders engaged in larger projects during the 1930s, including one Long Island subdivision of 200 houses.

During the war the Levitts built homes and barracks for war production workers, and this experience helped prepare them for still-larger projects with the return of peace. Their operations did grow after the war, but nothing they or anyone else had done anticipated the scale of the first Levittown, conceived and carried out by William Levitt between 1947 and 1951 on four thousand acres of former Long Island farmland about twenty-five miles east of New York City. Levitt, who had been a navy Seabee during the war, created a plan for the mass production of what eventually amounted to more than seventeen thousand houses (they were not, as some believe, all built according to the same design). His plan refined the process of delivering materials, organizing the sequence of assembly, and finishing tasks to such an extent that as many as thirty houses could be completed in a single day. One result of such scale and efficiency was the lowering of prices, and the houses of Levittown were snapped up by eager young families, including many headed by veterans. Another was a significant and portentous transformation of the landscape. This was the largest single housing development in U.S. history, but within a few years it had established a new norm in suburban home construction.

The Levitts built two more Levittowns, one in Pennsylvania and another New Jersey, and they were soon copied by large-scale developers all over the country, including the builders of Lakewood, California. By 1955, according to Kenneth Jackson, such subdivisions accounted for more than three-quarters of all of the homes being built in metropolitan America.[33] The home-building industry, as well as significant parts of the American landscape, had been transformed. Of nearly equal importance, moreover, was the transformation of Americans' understanding of what their homes and communities would and should look like. The suburban legend—and its hero—were in place.

Levitt and the other home builders were not the only creators of the new suburban landscape. Developers of shopping malls, designers

Levittown, New York, in 1961. As new suburbs matured, growing trees and home modifications by individual owners made them appear less uniform and barren. By this time many of the original veteran owners had moved on to other places. (Courtesy Levittown Public Library)

of limited-access commuter highways, and builders of new kinds of manufactured homes were also influential in varying ways and to varying degrees. The latter included several ventures that are as interesting in their failure as Levitt is in his success. One of these was the Lustron Home, announced to the public in the spring of 1948 through large advertisements in *Life* and other mass-circulation magazines as "the house America has been waiting for."[34] The brainchild of businessman Carl G. Strandlund, the Lustron Home was a factory-made house composed almost entirely of steel, with baked-on porcelain enamel finishes on both the exterior and interior walls. It was designed to be comfortable, efficient, and nearly maintenance free, "a home of cheerful convenience" that would also be affordable because of the efficiencies of both its design and its mass production, which Strandlund predicted would reach forty-five thousand annually once the business was fully established. The design of the Lustron Home was devoid of any of the clutter of historical domestic styles, but it was not bizarre or threateningly innovative; hence, it could fit comfortably within the fabric of any suburban community of more conventionally built homes. That it was made in a plant recently converted from the manufacture of warplanes made it a perfect symbol of the transition from war to the suburban dream.

Unfortunately for Strandlund, Americans did not buy symbols or at least not those whose costs spun out of control and wound up on the market at too high a price. Only some twenty-six hundred Lustron Homes were sold and assembled before the company went bankrupt and ceased production in 1950.[35] Strandlund was right about the durability of the Lustron—the steel walls and roofs of the ones he sold have weathered quite well after more than half a century. He was also right about the need to supply large numbers of affordable houses built with modern techniques of mass production. However, it would be mass production on the ground, not in factories, that would prevail in America's new suburbs. Like any legendary hero worth his salt, William Levitt easily slew any competitive dragons that happened along.

What was the GI Bill's contribution to the creation of this new American landscape of sprawling suburban homes? Authors of popular books have eagerly joined the legend of postwar suburbanization and familial domestication to the equally powerful legend of the GI Bill as the just reward to "the Greatest Generation," finding in it the prime (or even the sole) cause of metropolitan deconcentration. When the war ended, writes Michael J. Bennett in *When Dreams Came True*, "the GI Bill brought a total relandscaping of America with the growth of the suburbs."[36] As bold as this claim is, it is more than matched by Edward Humes. Expanding on the story of Bill and Soula Thomas, Humes observes: "The American suburban exodus of the 1950s did not simply spring into existence on its own: It is no exaggeration to say that the creation of suburbia and the resulting extension of homeownership to a majority of families in America was launched, underwritten, and paid for by the G.I. Bill."[37]

This is in fact a very great exaggeration, as is Bennett's similar assessment of the GI Bill as the unique source of postwar suburbanization. As previously noted, only a minority of those veterans who purchased homes during the decade after the war used the VA mortgage-guarantee program created by Title III of the GI Bill. To this somewhat sobering observation we should add that the story of postwar suburbanization includes large numbers of nonveterans who were not even eligible for VA-guaranteed loans, so that when we look specifically at the financing of new homes, so many of which were built in suburbs, we find that the role of the VA mortgage shrinks even further. During the eleven years from 1945 through 1955, only some 17 percent of the nation's nonfarm housing starts were financed through VA-guaranteed mortgage loans. Nearly 27 percent were financed with FHA backing, while a majority, 55 percent, used conventional loans with no government guarantees.[38] In 1954 and 1955, with increasing numbers of Korean-conflict veterans added to the VA pool, VA-backed housing starts did increase significantly, to the point where they actually outnumbered FHA starts. Nonetheless, even during those years neither program came close to the numbers of conventional mortgage loans on new houses.[39]

Veterans were somewhat overrepresented in metropolitan areas, and it is possible that the proportion of VA-backed housing starts in suburbs was somewhat higher than in the nation as a whole.[40] Still, the difference could not have been so great as to make the VA mortgage a dominant force in the financing of postwar suburbanization. Once again, we must be content with the more modest claim that the importance of the VA mortgage lay in the opportunity it gave to a significant number of ex-GIs to find their way to suburban homeownership, alongside the much larger numbers who got there by other means. The American suburb was certainly not "launched, underwritten, and paid for by the G.I. Bill."[41]

It is possible to exaggerate, too, the relative importance of the FHA and VA mortgage programs within the broader array of public policies that shaped suburban development. Other public-sector programs may have been just as influential or even more so in promoting homeownership and the peculiarly American form of suburban sprawl. The federal income tax code, for example, favors homeowners over tenants through the deductibility of home mortgage interest and local property taxes and promotes automobile usage in various ways, as do state tax laws that undercharge motorists for their use of public roads.[42] Transportation policy at all levels of government has favored the automobile over mass transit systems to a very great extent and did so increasingly in the aftermath of the war. While postwar European governments built clustered "new towns" beyond the peripheries of large cities and linked these towns to the cities with impressive rail networks (connecting these in turn to well-financed intraurban networks of subways, trolleys, and buses), U.S. governments built roads for cars and invested massively in highways that carried suburbanites to and from central cities, as well as in local suburban roads that served and promoted the spread of detached houses across the land.[43]

To these various public-sector programs and policies we must add the cultural predilections that underlie them all. The central argument of Kenneth Jackson's history of American suburbanization is that the nation's cities began to deconcentrate almost as soon as they became large enough to do so—long before World War II (indeed, even before the Civil War)—and that suburbanization expresses a long-established primacy in American culture of individualism and private life over communalism and the public welfare.[44] In essence, Jackson offers two correctives to the linked legends of postwar suburbanization and the GI Bill. One is that the postwar American suburb was revolutionary in its scale and many of its particular forms but not in its existence. The other is that the bill was but part of a larger package of public programs that gave shape to this latest phase of a much longer and more gradual transformation in the nation's social geography, and that the package itself was but the surface expression of deeper forces in American culture.

Other forces, too, were at work to give particular shape to the distribution of benefits under Title III. We refer here not to the overall incidence of homeownership or the physical landscapes the GI Bill helped to refashion but to the manner in which attitudes toward race and gender created patterns of exclusion in the implementation of a bill in which the only distinctions were supposed to be between the veteran and the nonveteran. The GI Bill, as the previous chapters show, was in practice neither colorblind nor gender neutral. John Rankin and his allies in Congress built a good deal of decentralization into the administration of veterans' benefits so that local officials could make sure that federal funds for unemployment payments or school tuitions were not used to upset the racial order of southern states. Women were not targeted with such legislative care and skill. However, when they stood in the way of male veterans eager to use the GI Bill's educational and training benefits or to return to the jobs those men had left to go to war, women became the largely unintended—but generally unmourned—victims of the concept and practice of veterans' preference. Title III of the GI Bill, which established the VA mortgage, worked in similar ways. Formally, it did not discriminate, or at least it did not do so for the stated purpose of upholding the privileges of whites and males. However, in practice it was a component of the bill that was particularly unresponsive to the legitimate claims and aspirations of women and African Americans.

The key to understanding this aspect of the VA mortgage program is its roots in the FHA's system of support for private credit institutions and their customary practices in assessing the credit worthiness of loan applicants. Banks and other mortgage lenders typically require assurances on three counts before they release funds to a potential borrower: first, that the property offered as security is worth more than the amount of the loan; second, that the value of the property is not likely to decline over the term of the loan; and third, that the borrower is likely to pay back the loan and the interest it bears, according to the terms of the loan agreement. The FHA accepted these risk-minimizing criteria as the foundation of the credit industry and adopted its own version of them to guide its own support of mortgage lenders: As a public agency that offered these lenders the backing of the U.S. Treasury, it was acutely aware of the need to find specific guidelines and procedures for minimizing risk to American taxpayers. The VA, in its turn, accepted the principles and many of the procedures that the FHA had developed over the previous decade, as it assessed the credit worthiness of veterans who applied for guaranteed home loans.[45]

Women veterans who applied for such a loan typically encountered the assumption, shared by lenders and VA loan officers alike, that women's incomes were merely supplemental to their husbands' and were likely to be temporary as well. Therefore, even if a woman veteran had a high-paying job that she intended to keep at least as long as the mortgage amortization period, she had very little chance of getting a VA-guaranteed home loan in her own name. Moreover, when lenders and VA officers examined her husband's income for credit worthiness, they disregarded hers as only a temporary contribution, which they expected to end not long after the house was purchased and the babies began to arrive. It is not clear how many married or single women veterans were denied VA mortgages in this way (or simply demeaned in the process of being granted one on the basis of a well-paid husband's income), but the policy continued throughout and well past the period when most World War II veterans sought their first home loans. Only in 1968 did the VA recognize the possibility of considering a wife's income in assessing credit worthiness, and only in 1973 did it issue a gender policy statement—and even then it was only to grant latitude to regional offices for deciding when the wife's income is "a definite characteristic of the family life."[46]

Some women encountered a different obstacle that had nothing to do with VA policy. After the Women's Army Auxiliary Corps (WAAC) was created in 1942, the women who joined were not officially enlisted in the army. Even though WAACs wore uniforms, they were regarded by the army as civilians and were not made eligible for veterans' benefits. This was changed a year later, when the term "auxiliary" was dropped, and the WAAC was replaced by the Women's Army Corps (WAC). Although WACs were now enlisted in the U.S. Army, approximately one-fourth of the original WAACs, according to June Willenz, elected not to make the transition to the military and, therefore, remained ineligible for veterans' benefits at the end of the war. The Women's Air Force Service Pilots (WASP), who performed the valuable and dangerous service of flying new military planes from factories to domestic air bases, were also left out. Again, policy was changed long after the war. In 1977 Congress awarded veteran status to WAACs and WASPs—years after many GI Bill benefit programs, including college tuition and subsistence, had expired.[47] As it happened, the VA mortgage was still an active benefit for World War II veterans, as the eligibility deadline had been extended and then, in 1970, entirely removed. Former WAACs and WASPs finally became eligible for VA-backed mortgage loans, but for most it came far too late to be of any use in finding the path to homeownership.

Discrimination against women in the VA mortgage program was in many cases less consequential than discrimination against African Americans—in the former case it often meant only that the loan guarantee would be granted on the husband's credit worthiness; in the latter it generally meant there would be no loan at all. In some instances black veterans came up against individual racism, as when a white banker or VA loan officer refused to offer or approve of a loan to black applicants simply because of their race. Again, it is impossible to know how often this happened, but it is clear that it was not exceptional and was not confined to the South. Historian David Onkst's examination of the administration of GI Bill benefits in three southern states in the years immediately following the war reveals an extensive pattern of racial discrimination among private lenders and local VA officials. According to Onkst, in Mississippi, where half the population was black, only 1 of every 36 VA loans went to African American veterans in the second half of 1946. A survey by *Ebony* magazine in 1947 turned up far more lopsided numbers: Of 3,229 loans guaranteed by that summer in Mississippi, only 2 went to blacks. Whatever the more accurate ratio, it is clear that Rankin's decentralization of VA administration was working to preserve white supremacy in the South. Onkst quotes Southern Regional Council agent Henry Wright: "To Negro veterans in Mississippi getting a GI loan is similar to seeking the Holy Grail."[48] The search, moreover, may have been just as difficult in northern states. Lizabeth Cohen reports that in the New York–New Jersey metropolitan area in 1950, nonwhites owned 2.1 percent of properties financed with conventional mortgages, 0.9 percent of those financed with FHA mortgages, and 0.1 percent of those purchased with loans backed by the VA.[49]

Not all of this disparity resulted simply from the racial prejudices of specific bankers and local VA loan officers. A good deal of it reflected the much broader and longer-standing effects of racial discrimination on incomes, employment rates, and wealth levels among African Americans (effects made somewhat worse in the postwar period by the administration of other GI Bill benefits, such as the channeling of black veterans to unskilled jobs and to segregated and less-effective job training programs). Proportionately fewer black veterans must have applied for VA mortgages, and even the least prejudiced of lenders and loan officers must have rejected black loan applicants who, because of low and unstable incomes, were not good credit risks. What is perhaps most important to recognize here, however, are the ways racial discrimination was built into the very structure of the mortgage guarantee program—not merely in the decentralized administration that allowed bigotry to thrive behind the closed doors of a local bank or VA office but also in the way those at the highest levels of the VA understood their responsibilities as guardians of the public purse. Again, it was an understanding developed by and inherited from the FHA and reflected the concept imbedded in both programs that a loan must be secured by an asset of stable value, no less than by the income and character of the loan applicant. Well before the war, the FHA developed operating procedures for directing the agency's guarantees toward properties with stable or increasing value and away from those likely to decline. Racial distinctions were central to these procedures and, even in the face of protestations by the VA that veterans' benefits were distributed without reference to race, the VA mortgage program followed the FHA's lead. Until Supreme Court rulings and civil rights legislation charted a new course for all government agencies, the FHA and the VA did a great deal to deprive African Americans of fair access to home mortgage loans and to promote the racial segregation of neighborhoods in both the suburbs and the city.

The first of these was the product of what has become widely known as "redlining." In 1933 the new HOLC initiated an intensive study of property appraisal methods and of the economic and social geography of every U.S. city. The latter exercise resulted in the agency's Residential Security Maps, which placed each city's neighborhoods within four zones defined according to selected socioeconomic conditions and prospects. The first zone, outlined on the map in green (perhaps not coincidentally, the color of money, of trees and grass, of traffic lights signifying "go"—even of the light at the end of Daisy Buchanan's dock), consisted of the new and prosperous neighborhoods "in demand as residential locations in good times and bad" and those of "American [that is, nonimmigrant] business and professional men." The second zone, outlined in blue (like green, a cool color), outlined "still desirable" neighborhoods that had "reached their peak." The third—and (perilously) yellow—zone defined areas that were declining but were not (or not yet) among the worst in the city. The fourth zone, outlined in red (the hot color of danger, of Satan and Stalin, of sexual promiscuity, of "stop") indicated areas of the city that had reached the bottom and were defined as "hazardous"—slums, tenderloins, and, most to the point, the places where black people lived, irrespective of their wealth, their prospects, or the attractiveness and condition of their homes.

It does not appear that the HOLC used these maps in a way that deprived the third or fourth zones of mortgage capital. On the contrary, as an agency charged with the refinancing of foreclosed and distressed loans, it directed more mortgage money to the bottom than to the top and with very good results. Kenneth Jackson calculates that more than 60 percent of HOLC loans in two selected cities (Newark, New Jersey, and Memphis, Tennessee) were granted to people in the lower two zones, and he observes that the payback rate from these zones in the nation as a whole was better than it was from the upper two.[50] However, the simple use of race on the HOLC maps—the equation of black with bad—portended other, less happy outcomes.

It was the FHA and the private bankers it supported in the home mortgage market that turned the HOLC Residential Security Maps into instruments for directing mortgage lending away from the older and poorer neighborhoods of the city and toward the newer and wealthier neighborhoods and developments of the suburbs. Redlining became a way of defining where not to risk a bank's capital or the nation's treasury, and since every African American urban family lived, virtually by definition, in a red zone, it became extremely difficult for black residents of the city to obtain a home loan. The FHA did guarantee loans inside the city but not in black neighborhoods, and private lenders who followed the Residential Security Maps generally followed the same exclusionary practice, whether or not they sought FHA (or, after the war, VA) backing. As time went on and the postwar suburbs began to boom, the FHA and VA, as we have seen, directed most of their activity to and beyond the urban periphery.

But what of blacks—and black veterans in particular—who left the "red zones" for the suburbs? Here they encountered another race-based restrictive policy, again justified by the need to minimize risk. The current value of a suburban home was not difficult to appraise, but its future depended on what kinds of people would come to occupy it and other houses in its vicinity. Lenders, government loan officers, and many white homeowners simply assumed that the value of a house would decline sharply if any black family succeeded in moving into its neighborhood, for this was an event that foretold the arrival of others (and still others), driving home prices and physical conditions down as it drove frightened white families away—a self-fulfilling prophecy of decline, nearly as convincing among the racially tolerant as among the intolerant, and of the utmost importance to families whose most important financial investment was in their homes.[51]

The FHA and VA answer was essentially to forbid government backing for any loan that would result in a black family's moving into a white neighborhood. Before 1950 the National Association of Real Estate Boards prohibited brokers from selling homes "to members of any race" whose presence in a neighborhood would cause values to decline, and the FHA, which, as Mark Gelfand has written, "had no social purpose beyond the mortgage," built the same prohibition into its own operating code.[52] "If a neighborhood is to retain stability," reads the agency's *Underwriting Manual* from this period, "it is necessary that properties shall continue to be occupied by the same social and racial classes," and to realize this goal the FHA firmly embraced restrictive covenants governing the future sale of houses in ways that preserved racial segregation far into the future.[53] Restrictive covenants were struck down by the Supreme Court in 1948, but the FHA (and the VA) complied only slowly and reluctantly and continued to permit and encourage segregation until civil rights laws forced a policy reversal a decade and more later.

For the first fifteen years or so of postwar suburban development, therefore, the federal government denied mortgage loan guarantees to most African Americans and actively promoted the continuing segregation of all-white neighborhoods. All of this was promulgated as sound financial practice designed to protect the U.S. Treasury from the costs of defaults on loans to perceived high-risk borrowers and of foreclosures on properties no longer worth the value of the loan. With respect to World War II veterans and to this purely fiscal objective, the policy may be said to have worked quite well. Defaults on VA mortgages were rare, amounting to only about 0.5 percent of the total number of loans, and the entire VA mortgage program cost the federal government less than $600 million over the first postwar decade.[54] Critics of other components of the GI Bill pointed to this with considerable approval, rarely if ever taking note of a high human cost that only later generations would recognize.

Perhaps that oversight was more willful than neglectful, and in any case we can point to one important setting in which even the logic of FHA and VA segregationist policy seems to fail. Preserving the character—and by extension the asset value—of an existing neighborhood was one thing, but excluding black families from a brand-new suburban development was quite another. And yet, even where there was no preexisting neighborhood character to be preserved, government agencies enforced or supported the exclusion of African Americans who would have qualified on economic grounds. The first Levittown, the epicenter of the postwar suburban legend, is an excellent case in point. William Levitt refused to sell homes to black families, and as late as 1960, with the Levittown population standing at 82,000, there was not a single black resident in the entire development. Levitt was at least aware of the issue. "We can solve a housing problem," he explained, "or we can try to solve a racial problem. But we cannot combine the two."[55]

Nonetheless, here was the best opportunity to do just that. The armed services had begun to grapple with the issue of racial segregation even before the end of the war, and in July of 1948 President Truman issued Executive Order 9981, which called for the integration of the U.S. military. It took another six years to achieve full racial integration in all of the armed services, but the process was well under way when the first Levittown homes appeared on the market. If the military could grapple with race, civilian agencies overseeing and enabling the building of these postwar veterans' "barracks" could have done so as well. Instead, they exerted their considerable influence in the opposite direction, and an opportunity to help reshape one portion of the postwar suburban boom was lost. Title III of the GI Bill helped many young Americans to become homeowners and to enter the suburban world that most of them preferred as the best place to live and to raise their families. Still, its benefits did not extend to everyone. Black veterans were locked out when the VA mortgage handed some 4 million veterans the keys to a kingdom of peace and plenty.

The GI Bill was in this sense of and not ahead of its time. To find fault with its promotion of racial exclusion in Title III and elsewhere is to find fault with the long history of racial injustice in the United

States and with the continuation of this history into the postwar period. When white America, goaded by the civil rights movement, began to recognize and adjust to the aspirations of black citizens, and when the feminist movement made similar demands on American men, government agencies such as the VA adjusted their policies. And if one can argue that the government moved somewhat ahead of the curve of public sentiment during the rights revolution of the 1960s, leading rather than lagging, one can make the same argument about the various veterans' benefits programs created by the GI Bill. With respect to the long history of veterans' benefits in the United States and to the aspirations of millions of men and women who returned to civilian life after World War II, the GI Bill was an innovative force not merely for readjustment but also for the realization of richer and more satisfying lives. The limits of the bill's achievements, including those in the VA mortgage program, were those of a society still struggling, as it struggles today, against intolerance.

Epilogue

Soldiers from 1st Squadron, 33rd Cavalry Regiment, 3rd Brigade Combat Team, 101st Airborne Division, in Iraq. (Courtesy U.S. Army)

A LITTLE LESS than five years after V-J Day the United States was at war again. More than 5.7 million Americans participated in the United Nations' "police action" in Korea between 1950 and 1953, and by the end of the decade some 5.5 million had returned to civilian life as a new veteran cohort. How would the nation respond to this latest batch of former GIs, injected so soon into the veteran population that they included a number who were also veterans of World War II?[1] Veterans' programs following the previous two wars had been shaped in sharp reaction to the policies that preceded them: Whereas the excesses of the Civil War pension system limited the rewards offered to veterans of World War I, the stinginess of post–World War I policies led to the far more generous GI Bill after World War II. Would the historical pendulum swing again? Or had the GI Bill stopped it, ending time and motion by creating the model for all future veterans' programs?

There is, of course, no "end of history," not as long as there are humans to make and to write it. Furthermore, even though the swing of the pendulum may not be the best metaphor for expressing how human affairs move through time, it works here. The "Korean GI Bill"—formally, the Veterans' Readjustment Assistance Act of 1952— was enacted not long after various congressional committee hearings and Veterans Administration studies had revealed numerous frauds and inefficiencies in the implementation of the amended Servicemen's Readjustment Act of 1944, particularly in the subcollege training portion of Title II but also in other GI Bill programs. Even apart from these critical studies of the still-current World War II GI Bill, the law itself did not yet glow with the historical patina that would later make it an icon of federal wisdom and national goodwill. And in one other sense the Korean GI Bill arrived too soon. If World War II veterans benefited from the specific lapse of time between the two world wars— the twenty-three years between the 1918 armistice and the attack on Pearl Harbor, which left large numbers of disgruntled World War I veterans in their prime years of political influence—veterans of the

Korean conflict were hurt by the very brief interlude of peace that followed World War II and the original GI Bill. Veterans of the Good War were still young and were continuing to make their own way into civilian life; indeed, many were still claiming the benefits of their own GI Bill. Very few, it seems, were either able or inclined to exert significant political influence on behalf of the new (and in some respects *competing*) veterans of Korea. Among the still-active veterans of World War I, meanwhile, were many who considered their work complete after the enactment of the 1944 GI Bill and a number of others who were disaffected by the bill's recently publicized excesses.

These circumstances help us understand why the Korean GI Bill of 1952 provided benefits that were significantly less generous than those created by the post–World War II bill. We must recognize, too, the effects of the continuing concern on the part of congressional conservatives that the original GI Bill might be paving the road toward more general social welfare policies. This concern is expressed in both the title and the text of the Korean bill. The Veterans' Readjustment Assistance Act reiterates in its title the original concept of veterans' readjustment—indeed, it ratchets down even that modest goal by introducing the word "assistance," thereby emphasizing the government's role as secondary to the veterans' own efforts to reestablish themselves in civilian society. That this semantic choice was intentional is made clear by language incorporated into the bill itself:

> The Congress of the United States hereby declares that the veterans' education and training program created by this act is for the purpose of providing vocational readjustment and restoring lost educational opportunities to those service men and women whose educational or vocational ambitions have been interrupted or impeded by reason of active service...and for the purpose of aiding such persons in attaining the educational and training status which they might normally have aspired to and obtained had they not served their country; and that the home, farm, and business-loan benefits, the mustering-out payments, and the employment assistance provided for by this act are for the purpose of assisting in the readjustment of such persons from military to civilian life.[2]

This emphasis on readjustment, wars' interruption, and the restoration of the veterans to a place in society *not lower* than they were likely to have attained had they not served in the military—the original goal of the 1944 GI Bill before it evolved into a program for enhancing veterans' opportunities—was just as clearly expressed in the 1952 bill's more modest provisions. The loan programs for veterans of the Korean conflict were essentially the same as those for veterans of World War II. Other programs, however, were scaled back significantly. The readjustment allowance for unemployed veterans was raised from $20 to $26 to compensate for inflation, but the maximum number of payments was reduced from 52 to 26, and allowances for the self-employed were eliminated entirely.

Education benefits were dramatically different. Under the Korean GI Bill, tuition payments were not paid directly to schools. Rather, veterans were given a monthly education or training allowance that ranged from $110 to $160 according to the number of dependents (or lesser amounts for part-time schooling or training) and were expected to make their own arrangements for tuition and other costs. Eligibility was reduced from 48 months to 36 months and was linked more decisively to length of service. Veterans earned 1.5 months of the education allowance for each month in service, which meant that the full allowance was paid only to those who had served for at least two years. Veterans of Korea, in short, received government scholarships under the new GI Bill that may have covered most of the tuition and other costs of attending public universities, colleges, and community colleges but that left most private institutions well out of reach. In no case did the scholarship amount to a free four-year college education.[3]

The 1944 GI Bill did remain the model for the Korean-era veterans' law, and in this sense the metaphor of the swinging pendulum is not entirely apt. There was no attempt to rework the entire system of benefits inherited from the previous war. The next law, too, modified rather than rejected the basic structures established after World War II, even while reducing still further the real value of veterans' benefits.

The Veterans' Readjustment Benefits Act of 1966, passed in the midst of the Vietnam War, was much like the Korean GI Bill, differing from it mainly in the higher qualification threshold for the education and training allowance (Korean veterans qualified after 90 days of active service; Vietnam veterans had to serve at least 180 days) and in the somewhat smaller initial allowance ($100 for single veterans rather than $110). This allowance was increased fairly regularly after 1966, but college costs were rising as well, particularly at private institutions, so the Vietnam-era bill, no less than the Korean bill, fell well short of the original GI Bill in the financing of veterans' education.[4] Interestingly, the proportions of veterans attending college under these two later GI Bills were significantly higher than the proportion attending under the original bill, and the overall cost of the higher education benefit was greater as well. To some extent this reflects restrictive provisions that related to subcollege training in the Korean and Vietnam-era GI Bills. However, mostly it reflects changes in the veteran population and in the changing role of higher education in the United States—larger proportions of Korea and Vietnam veterans were high school graduates, and the colleges and universities that had grown to accommodate the post–World War II veterans were becoming the customary destinations of millions of young Americans who before would have gone directly from school to work. If more than 6 million veterans attended college with support provided by latter-day GI Bills, it was not because these measures provided more generous benefits than the original; rather, it was in no small part because the original GI Bill had widened the college gates.

The Veterans' Readjustment Benefits Act of 1966 differed in one important respect from preceding veterans' legislation: Benefits were extended retroactively to veterans who had served during the interlude of peace between Korea and Vietnam, as well as to servicemen and servicewomen still on active duty. This was an important step toward the separation of veterans' legislation from a specific war and even from war itself. Benefits established by the 1944 bill and its 1945 amendments and modified in the Korean bill of 1952 were routinized by this provision of the 1966 law, which pointed toward the establishment of a continuing system of benefits to replace episodic and more politically charged legislative responses to the aftermath of specific wars.

By 1966 the political context was quite different from that of 1944, 1945, or 1952. Amid the flurry of new domestic initiatives pushed through a liberal-dominated Congress by President Lyndon Johnson, an FDR protégé, conservatives could hardly be expected to focus on the dangers of a new GI Bill. The New Deal revival they had so long feared and so successfully beaten back during Harry Truman's presidency was happening all around them, as was a civil rights revolution. This is not to say that either liberals or conservatives turned their backs on veterans' legislation while they fought more important battles but that the new laws for veterans and service members they did write were no longer so suffused by the hidden racial and socioeconomic agendas of the immediate post–World War II period.

By extending benefits to peacetime veterans and active service personnel, the Vietnam-era GI Bill also reintroduced a long-absent motive into veterans' legislation. As a study commissioned by the Senate Committee on Veterans' Affairs observed in comparing the three GI Bills, veterans' benefits were now being offered at least in part as an inducement to join the armed services.[5] This motive would be significantly enhanced after 1973, when the draft was ended and the nation began to rely on an all-volunteer military. Benefit laws enacted after that date were designed primarily as permanent tools for military recruitment rather than as public assistance for the readjustment of veterans. Laws of the 1970s and 1980s, focusing on the regularization of educational benefits for military recruits, bring us full circle to the nation's earliest military benefit provisions, the cash and land bounties of the Revolutionary War, which were also measures of recruitment rather than reward. These earliest and latest of veterans' benefit laws differ fundamentally from the original GI Bill, that extracontractual bounty offered by a grateful (and somewhat nervous) nation to its "Greatest Generation."

Although the loan provisions of the Servicemen's Readjustment Act of 1944 survive for all veterans, the GI Bill of which it was a part no longer serves as either a legislative model or as a potential wedge for larger domestic agendas to be promoted or resisted. It is now more a memory than a model. One deep irony is that it was during the same years that Congress regularized veterans' benefits as an ongoing tool of military recruitment that Americans began to sanctify the original document. The GI Bill was placed in the historical display case when it was no longer an active political force.

That memory can itself generate political force is evident in the still more recent history of veterans' benefits. The new laws of the 1970s and beyond may have been geared to military recruitment, but their provisions were not as generous as those of the original GI Bill and of course proved no match for the rapidly rising costs of a college education. The Veterans Educational Assistance Program created in the mid-1970s established a postservice training fund for recruits, who contributed to it from their monthly paychecks, with the government contributing two dollars for every dollar paid in by the recruit. The Montgomery GI Bill of 1985, named after its congressional sponsor, G. V. Montgomery—a Mississippi Democrat who was a veteran of both World War II and the Korean conflict[6]—reduced the self-contribution of participating service men and women while raising the eventual education or training benefit. However, as Dan Ephron writes in a *Newsweek* article published late in 2007, the story of post–World War II veterans' benefits in the United States, up to and including the Montgomery GI Bill program, "is best illustrated by two crisscrossing lines on a graph: one marks the decline in GI benefits, the other the rising cost of college tuition." Ephron offers the examples of Charles

Schelberg, a World War II veteran whose college costs were entirely covered by the original GI Bill, and his grandson Matthew Schelberg, a veteran of the Iraq invasion, whose educational benefits amount to less than a tenth of his tuition and housing at Bucknell University.[7]

There have been several responses to this decay in the real value of veterans' benefits, and these, like Ephron's, invariably draw on the original GI Bill as the long-lost standard. Some of these responses are in the private sector—the Fund for Veterans' Education, set up by financier and World War II veteran Jerome Kohlberg; gifts from two donors to Wesleyan University for veterans' scholarships; the Hodson Trust's scholarship program for veterans at four private colleges in Maryland—and in describing them late in 2007 USA Today's Mary Beth Marklein makes the clear distinction between the original GI Bill, which obviated the need for such efforts, and the prevailing law, which stimulated them.[8] Similarly, a new bill introduced by Senator Jim Webb of Virginia, which called for a substantial increase in benefits, was justified by Webb and by journalists who supported him, by referring to the Servicemen's Readjustment Act of 1944. Ephron quotes Webb: "All I'm saying is, let's give them the same educational chance that the Greatest Generation had."[9] Anna Quindlen, writing in support of Webb's bill, expands somewhat on that enshrined historical moment without losing Webb's directness: "The original GI Bill set the standard for innovative and audacious legislation. It was right in both senses of that word: the sensible thing to do, and the moral thing as well."[10]

Webb's new GI Bill was rather less "audacious" than the original in that it provided for tuition payments only up to the cost of the most expensive in-state public university, plus stipends for books and housing, and only to service members who enlisted after September 11, 2001 and served three years or more on active duty. Still, it did promise a significant increase in benefits from prevailing levels, at a projected ten-year cost of $63 billion. Initially opposed by the Bush administration and by Republican senators such as John McCain and Ted Stevens (the latter a beneficiary of the 1944 GI Bill) because of fears that it would stimulate departures from the country's already overstressed military forces, it was given little chance of passage until Webb lined up support from fellow veterans Chuck Hagel, Frank Lautenberg, and John Warner. Ultimately, the bill attracted 58 cosponsors in the Senate and 302 in the House of Representatives and was enacted as part of a larger bill extending funding for the war in Iraq. It was signed by President Bush on June 30, 2008, with yet another reference to the original GI Bill's "historic legacy of ensuring brighter futures for service members and families."[11]

So the GI Bill of 1944—the New Deal for veterans—has not, after all, been removed entirely from the historical present. Like the New Deal itself but with a much broader consensus, it survives as a remarkable response to a critical moment in the nation's history and as a standard against which to measure the present. More than with the New Deal, which even political liberals feel free to criticize, Americans overlook the limits and faults of the GI Bill and ignore political differences belied by its bipartisan enactment so that the standard will remain intact—a guide not only to the treatment of those who return from war but also to the larger democratic imperative of rising, when the occasion requires, to do the right thing.

Acknowledgments

Historians cannot do their work without the assistance of skilled professionals in libraries and other scholarly institutions. We benefited immensely from the expertise of staff members at the American Legion Library, Indianapolis, Indiana; the Department of Veterans Affairs, Washington, D.C.; the Franklin D. Roosevelt Presidential Library and Museum, Hyde Park, New York; the Kansas State Historical Society, Topeka, Kansas; and the Department of Manuscripts and Archives, Olin Library, Cornell University, Ithaca, New York.

Several scholars shared with us ideas for and reactions to our work. Conversations with our Cornell colleague Suzanne Mettler, whose work is cited prominently in these pages, helped us identify key sources and explore significant themes related to the GI Bill. James McPherson and David Hackett Fischer read the manuscript with great care, attending to matters of both style and substance. We are especially grateful to David Fischer for his detailed commentary and insightful suggestions for revision.

Timothy Bent, our editor at Oxford University Press, has been extraordinarily supportive in all phases of the preparation of the manuscript, including a skillful line-by-line edit that greatly improved the text. His assistant, Dayne Poshusta, along with Esther Tzivanis and Beth Howard at Cornell, have helped in numerous ways, ranging from what used to be called typing to the processing of illustrations.

Able research assistance was provided by Rob Summers, Cornell Class of 1998, who now teaches high school in Arlington, Virginia;

Cornell undergraduate Lindsay MacKaye; and Natalie Carver, who is now an undergraduate at the University of British Columbia.

Finally, we wish to thank each other, as well as the superb institution that brought us together—and that made our friendship and our collaboration possible. We are pleased to dedicate this book to Cornell University.

TO CORNELL UNIVERSITY

A miracle, really, this place
    where growing things must thrust
    through hard clay under slate gray skies;
where ivy learned to thrive against new stone
    not so long ago,
    perilously near a silent track.

There are no idlers here, nor futile weaving
    and unraveling;
Odysseus, your adventure's here, improbably,
    a gathered greatness far from Troy,
    making in central isolation
    a splendid thing.

SMB

Notes

Introduction

1. Quoted in Ira Katznelson, *When Affirmative Action Was White: An Untold History of Racial Inequality in Twentieth-century America* (New York: Norton, 2005), 114. Katznelson himself cites Theda Skocpol, "The G.I. Bill and U.S. Social Policy, Past and Future," *Social Philosophy and Policy* 14 (Summer 1997): 95–96.

2. Tom Brokaw, *The Greatest Generation* (New York: Random House, 1998).

3. Bob Michel, telephone interview by Glenn C. Altschuler, July 10, 2008.

4. Peter F. Drucker, *Post-capitalist Society* (New York: HarperBusiness, 1993), 3. Cited in Michael J. Bennett, *When Dreams Came True: The GI Bill and the Making of Modern America* (Washington, D.C.: Brassey's, 1996), 7.

5. Charles Lane, "Head of the Class," *Stanford Magazine* (July/August 2005); National Public Radio, "Weekend Edition," Sept. 24, 2005.

6. Edward Humes, *Over Here: How the G.I. Bill Transformed the American Dream* (Orlando: Harcourt, 2006).

7. Lizabeth Cohen, *A Consumers' Republic: The Politics of Mass Consumption in Postwar America* (New York: Knopf, 2003); Katznelson, *When Affirmative Action Was White*. See also David Onkst, "Black World War II Veterans and the G.I. Bill in Georgia, Alabama, and Mississippi, 1944–1947," (MA thesis, University of Georgia, 1990).

8. Suzanne Mettler, *Soldiers to Citizens: The G.I. Bill and the Making of the Greatest Generation* (New York: Oxford University Press, 2005). See also Kathleen Frydl, "The G.I. Bill" (PhD diss., University of Chicago, 2000).

9. John Higham, "Is This Education? Subsidy, or Sympathy?" *American Scholar Forum* (July 1947).

10. Harold M. Hyman, *American Singularity: The 1787 Northwest Ordinance, the 1862 Homestead and Morrill Acts, and the 1944 GI Bill* (Athens: University of Georgia Press, 1986), 65.

11. Cited in Bennett, *When Dreams Came True*, 121.

12. President's Commission on Veterans' Pensions, *Readjustment Benefits: General Survey and Appraisal*, Staff Report No. IX, Part A (Washington, D.C.: U.S. Government Printing Office, 1956), 50. A note to this tabulation suggests that the "sample data slightly understate the extent of participation in each program." Other data

suggest that readjustment benefits were received by 8.9 million veterans but that the other two estimates are closer to the true number.

13. The story of Albert Bleich is based on interviews with Edith Bleich (by Stuart M. Blumin) and on the extensive military personnel file in her possession.

14. The GI Bill did direct the U.S. Employment Service to follow new rules granting priority in job counseling to veterans and, among the latter, to those with disabilities. Similar priorities within the federal civil service were continued from World War I. Chapter 6 discusses these components of the bill.

Chapter 1

1. William Henry Glasson, *History of Military Pension Legislation in the United States*. Vol. 12, no. 3, of *Studies in History, Economics, and Public Law* (New York: Columbia University Press, 1900), 12.

2. Ibid., 12–52.

3. Lloyd DeWitt Bockstruck, *Revolutionary War Bounty Land Grants Awarded by State Governments* (Baltimore: Genealogical Publishing, 1996), v. The exceptions among the original thirteen states were Delaware, New Jersey, New Hampshire, and Rhode Island. The Massachusetts land bounty was not enacted until 1801 (see xvi); hence, it cannot be regarded as a tool for military recruitment. The new nation's fourteenth state, Vermont, did not offer a land bounty even though it had significant amounts of frontier land to develop.

4. Nearly all histories of the Revolutionary era include some discussion of soldiers' land bounties. More focused studies, in addition to Bockstruck (1996), include Jean H. Vivian, "Military Land Bounties during the Revolutionary and Confederation Periods," *Maryland Historical Magazine* 61 (1966): 231–56; and Paul V. Lutz, "Land Grants for Service in the Revolution," *New-York Historical Society Quarterly* 48 (1964): 221–35. The issue of the success or failure of the land bounties appears to be one of those long-settled historical issues that could benefit from a fresh look.

5. Glasson, *History of Military Pension Legislation*, 15–22.

6. John Resch, *Suffering Soldiers: Revolutionary War Veterans, Moral Sentiment, and Political Culture in the Early Republic* (Amherst: University of Massachusetts Press, 1999), 2.

7. U.S. Bureau of the Census, *Historical Statistics of the United States, Colonial Times to 1970* (Washington, D.C.: U.S. Government Printing Office, 1975), 1106, 1115.

8. Glasson, *History of Military Pension Legislation*, 33–36; Resch, *Suffering Soldiers*, 99–118.

9. *Historical Statistics*, 1106, 1115; Glasson, *History of Military Pension Legislation*, 37; Resch, *Suffering Soldiers*, 142–43.

10. The politics behind the pension law of 1832 were actually somewhat more complicated than this brief account suggests. For example, the proposal for a new pension law came originally from President Andrew Jackson, leader of the emerging Democrats but also a former military commander. See Glasson, *History of Military Pension Legislation*, 41.

11. Ibid., 41–48; William H. Glasson, *Federal Military Pensions in the United States* (New York: Oxford University Press, 1918), 77–85. The quotation from Adams is on p. 85 of this book by Glasson.

12. A pension for able-bodied veterans of the War of 1812 was enacted in 1871, fifty-six years after the signing of the Treaty of Ghent. Mexican War veterans received a pension in 1887, while veterans of Indian wars concluded before 1843 received a pension in 1892. See Glasson, *History of Military Pension Legislation*, 60–69.

13. Patrick J. Kelly, *Creating a National Home: Building the Veterans' Welfare State, 1860–1900* (Cambridge, Mass.: Harvard University Press, 1997). The 1884 law is

quoted on p. 207n18. A majority of the states also established veterans' homes, which after 1888 were subsidized by the federal government. Theda Skocpol estimates that in 1910 about 5 percent of surviving Union veterans were being cared for in federal and state homes. See Skocpol, *Protecting Soldiers and Mothers: The Political Origins of Social Policy in the United States* (Cambridge, Mass.: Harvard University Press, 1992), 141. Residents of the homes continued to receive their federal pensions.

14. Glasson, *History of Military Pension Legislation*, 114–15.

15. Glasson, *Federal Military Pensions*, 246–50.

16. *Historical Statistics*, 1140.

17. Ibid., 1114. On the 1862 Pension Act see Glasson, *History of Military Pension Legislation*, 73–75.

18. Skocpol, *Protecting Soldiers and Mothers*, 108–109.

19. *Historical Statistics*, 1114; Glasson, *History of Military Pension Legislation*, 88–95, 104; Glasson, *Federal Military Pensions*, 123, 145–46; Skocpol, *Protecting Soldiers and Mothers*, 115–19, 128.

20. Stephen Skowronek, *Building a New American State: The Expansion of National Administrative Capacities, 1877–1920* (New York: Cambridge University Press, 1982). See also Richard Franklin Bensel, *Yankee Leviathan: The Origins of Central State Authority in America, 1859–1877* (New York: Cambridge University Press, 1990), which focuses more on legislation than on administration while arguing that the Civil War transformed the American state.

21. *Historical Statistics*, 1102–1103.

22. Glasson, *Federal Military Pensions*, 266; Richard Franklin Bensel, *Sectionalism and American Political Development, 1880–1980* (Madison: University of Wisconsin Press, 1984), chap. 3.

23. Skocpol, *Protecting Soldiers and Mothers*, 113.

24. Ibid., 117.

25. Ibid., esp. 1–11, 130–35, 148–51.

26. Glasson, *History of Military Pension Legislation*, 117.

27. Skocpol, *Protecting Soldiers and Mothers*, esp. 1–11, 30–38, part III.

28. *Historical Statistics*, 1140.

29. Glasson, *History of Military Pension Legislation*, 121. Glasson notes that the 1890 law applied specifically to Civil War veterans; hence, able-bodied Spanish-American War veterans would have required subsequent legislation to qualify for a military pension. By the time it might have been proposed, such pension laws were no longer on anyone's political agenda. See also Glasson, *Federal Military Pensions*, 145, which notes that in 1916 there were 24,101 Spanish-American War veterans with disabilities and 4,371 widows and dependents of men killed in that war on federal pension roles and that the total cost of Spanish-American War pensions through that year amounted to more than $53 million.

30. Glasson, *Federal Military Pensions*, 283–94; William Pyle Dillingham, *Federal Aid to Veterans, 1917–1941* (Gainesville: University of Florida Press, 1952), 11, 21–40.

31. Dillingham, *Federal Aid to Veterans*, 147–48; Roger Daniels, *The Bonus March: An Episode of the Great Depression* (Westport, Conn.: Greenwood, 1971), 20–22; Bill G. Reid, "Franklin K. Lane's Idea for Veterans' Colonization, 1918–1921," *Pacific Historical Review* 33(4) (November 1964): 447–61.

32. Dillingham, *Federal Aid to Veterans*, 145–50; Daniels, *Bonus March*, 24–26; William Pencak, *For God and Country: The American Legion, 1919–1941* (Boston: Northeastern University Press, 1989), 60–61, 74–75, 83, 197–99.

33. Dillingham, *Federal Aid to Veterans*, 150–55; Pencak, *For God and Country*, 199–200; Daniels, *Bonus March*, 25–40; Jennifer D. Keene, *Doughboys, the Great War, and the Remaking of America* (Baltimore: Johns Hopkins University Press, 2001),

171–74. The insurance policies created by the 1924 bonus bill should not be confused with those that remained from the 1917 War Risk Insurance Act. The crucial difference was that the government, not the policyholder, paid the premiums of the policies generated by the 1924 bonus; hence, the latter was just the kind of expensive program the earlier plan was designed to avoid.

34. Much has been written about the 1932 bonus march; indeed, it is a staple of depression-era political history. Two book-length accounts are Daniels, *Bonus March*, and Paul Dickson and Thomas B. Allen, *The Bonus Army: An American Epic* (New York: Walker, 2004).

35. Daniels, *Bonus March*, 219–26; Dickson and Allen, *Bonus Army*, 207–23.

36. Samuel I. Rosenman, comp., *The Public Papers and Addresses of Franklin D. Roosevelt*, vol. 4 (New York: Random House, 1938), 190–93.

37. Dillingham, *Federal Aid to Veterans*, 166–69. A portion of the $1.4 billion took the form of direct cash payments to make up the difference between amounts owed on the bonus certificates and the $50 denominated savings bonds.

38. Ibid., 51–53. The provision that related to the payment of income tax was an attempt to define need, but the threshold for incomes liable to taxation was then relatively high. More than half a million claims were filed during the year following the act, of which only 2 percent were disqualified because of the income tax provision (ibid., 53).

39. *Historical Statistics*, 1115.

40. Ibid.

41. Dillingham, *Federal Aid to Veterans*, 78–79.

42. Committee on Veterans Affairs, House of Representatives, Eighty-first Congress, *State Veterans' Laws: Indices and Digests of State Laws Granting Rights, Benefits, and Privileges to Veterans, Their Dependents, and Their Organizations*, comp. and ed. Carrie E. Hunter (Washington, D.C.: U.S. Government Printing Office, 1950), 30, 272; Daniels, *Bonus March*, 73, 288.

43. Keith W. Olson, *The GI Bill, the Veterans, and the Colleges* (Lexington: University Press of Kentucky, 1974), 7.

Chapter 2

1. Alan Brinkley, *The End of Reform: New Deal Liberalism in Recession and War* (New York: Knopf, 1995), 154, 139.

2. David M. Kennedy, *Freedom from Fear: The American People in Depression and War, 1929–1945* (New York: Oxford University Press, 1999), 111; Jean Edward Smith, *FDR* (New York: Random House, 2007), xiii.

3. Kennedy, *Freedom from Fear*, 113.

4. Smith, *FDR*, xiv.

5. For a history of the NRPB see Philip W. Warken, *A History of the National Resources Planning Board, 1933–1943* (New York: Garland, 1979).

6. National Resources Planning Board, *National Resources Development Report for 1943*. Part 1, *Post-War Plan and Program* (Washington, D.C.: U.S. Government Printing Office, 1943), 3.

7. Ibid., 9–10.

8. National Resources Planning Board, *Security, Work, and Relief Policies* (Washington, D.C.: U.S. Government Printing Office, 1942). This report had been delivered to the president in December 1941, three days before Pearl Harbor. It was released to the public along with the two-part *National Resources Development Report for 1943*. The subtitle of Part 2 of the latter is *Wartime Planning for War and Post War*.

9. NRPB, *Security, Work, and Relief Policies*, 545.

10. Ibid., 546–49. The quotation is from p. 548.

11. Brinkley, *End of Reform*, 251.

12. Paul Addison, *The Road to 1945: British Politics and the Second World War* (London: Jonathan Cape, 1975).

13. The events of 1942–1943 are recounted in Brinkley, *End of Reform*, 245–58, and in Warken, *History of the National Resources Planning Board*, 182–250.

14. National Resources Planning Board, *Demobilization and Readjustment: Report of the Conference on Postwar Readjustment of Civilian and Military Personnel* (Washington, D.C.: U.S. Government Printing Office, 1943). For discussions of this report see Davis R. B. Ross, *Preparing for Ulysses: Politics and Veterans during World War II* (New York: Columbia University Press, 1969), 55–63; Warken, *History of the National Resources Planning Board*, 194–96.

15. Quoted in Keith W. Olson, *The GI Bill, the Veterans, and the Colleges* (Lexington: University Press of Kentucky, 1974), 11–12.

16. Suzanne Mettler, *Soldiers to Citizens: The G.I. Bill and the Making of the Greatest Generation* (New York: Oxford University Press), 19.

17. Quoted in Ross, *Preparing for Ulysses*, 54.

18. Samuel I. Rosenman, *Working with Roosevelt* (New York: Harper and Brothers, 1952), 394–95.

19. Samuel I. Rosenman, comp., *The Public Papers and Addresses of Franklin D. Roosevelt*, 4 vols. (New York: Harper and Brothers, 1950), 1943 vol., 122.

20. Ibid., 334.

21. Ibid., 343.

22. Rosenman, *Working with Roosevelt*, 414–16. Roosevelt's specification of government-fostered economic expansion as the engine of social well-being is more in accord with domestic ideas characteristic of the post–New Deal years than of the New Deal itself. This is Alan Brinkley's argument, cited above.

23. For a full discussion see Cass R. Sunstein, *The Second Bill of Rights: FDR's Unfinished Revolution and Why We Need It More than Ever* (New York: Basic Books, 2004).

24. Rosenman, comp., *Public Papers and Addresses*, 1943 vol., 333–44.

25. *Newsweek* (Aug. 9, 1943), 36–40.

26. Rosenman, comp., *Public Papers and Addresses*, 1943 vol., 449–55.

27. Ibid., 522–28.

Chapter 3

1. Warren Atherton, "American Legion Demands Elimination of Delays in Handling Claims of Disabled World War II Veterans," American Legion Archives, Indianapolis, Indiana.

2. David Camelon, "I Saw the G.I. Bill Written, Part One," *American Legion Magazine* (September 1949). Although 300,000 civilians had been injured in defense-related work, the American Legion, Hearst, and their allies supported legislation directed exclusively at rehabilitation for soldiers, about 500,000 of whom had been disabled. "The disabled veterans are in a different class from civilians taken care of by social security," declared John Rankin, congressman from Mississippi. "These veterans faced the firing line. They must be looked upon differently from persons whose destitute conditions are due to their own incapacities or to their own indolence." Quoted in Kathleen Frydl, "The G.I. Bill" (PhD diss., University of Chicago, 2000), 70.

3. Davis R. B. Ross, *Preparing for Ulysses: Politics and Veterans during World War II* (New York: Columbia University Press, 1969), 80–81.

4. "Chronology of Legion G.I. Bill 1943–1944," American Legion Archives, Indianapolis, Indiana; Frydl, "G.I. Bill," 146.

5. A biographical sketch of Colmery introduces the Harry W. Colmery Papers, housed at the Kansas Historical Society, Topeka, Kansas.

6. Quoted in "Chronology of Legion G.I. Bill 1943–1944," 147.

7. Ross, *Preparing for Ulysses*, 99; "Address of Warren Atherton over Mutual Network Station WOL, Washington, D.C., May 2, 1944," American Legion Archives, Indianapolis, Indiana.

8. Ross, *Preparing for Ulysses*, 82–87, 100–102; "Address of Mrs. Edith Jones, President of the National Education Association," *Summary of Proceedings of the Twenty-fifth Annual National Convention of the American Legion*, Omaha, Nebraska, Sept. 21–23, 1943; Donald Glascoff to Leon Humphreyville, May 31, 1944, American Legion Archives, Indianapolis, Indiana.

9. Donald Glascoff, "G.I. Joe's New Horizon," *American Legion Magazine* (August 1944); "Address of Warren Atherton over Mutual Network Station WOL, Washington, D.C., May 2, 1944."

10. Suzanne Mettler, *Soldiers to Citizens: The G.I. Bill and the Making of the Greatest Generation* (New York: Oxford University Press, 2005), 16–18; Michael J. Bennett, *When Dreams Came True: The GI Bill and the Making of Modern America* (Washington, D.C.: Brassey's, 1996), 88.

11. Edward Bennett to National Adjutant of the American Legion, July 18, 1984, American Legion Archives, Indianapolis, Indiana; David Camelon, "I Saw the G.I. Bill Written, Part Two," *American Legion Magazine* (October 1949); Bennett, *When Dreams Came True*, 194; Ross, *Preparing for Ulysses*, 59.

12. Quoted in Ross, *Preparing for Ulysses*, 43.

13. Quoted in Bennett, *When Dreams Came True*, 84.

14. Stanley Rector to All State Administrative Agencies, Mar. 3, 1944; Stanley Rector to Robert M. LaFollette, Mar. 3, 1944, both in American Legion Archives, Indianapolis, Indiana.

15. Bernard DeVoto, "The Easy Chair," *Harper's Magazine* (May 1943).

16. Frydl, "G.I. Bill," 176; *Reports to the Twenty-fifth Annual Convention of the American Legion*, Omaha, Nebraska, Sept. 21–23, 1943, American Legion Archives, Indianapolis, Indiana; "Publicity Release," American Legion, May 18, 1944, American Legion Archives, Indianapolis, Indiana. Ironically, although Colmery boasted that his organization "has stood in the heat of the noonday sun when others clamored for large federal appropriations through which education in the states might be controlled" and refused to yield, the American Council on Education (ACE) and the National Education Association initially opposed the American Legion bill because it possessed "a very strong color of federalization through the Veterans Administration." "It seems rather ironical to me," an ACE official opined, "that the American Legion, which has opposed on some occasions federal control and the extension of federal power, is blind to this break in the dike." Quoted in Frydl, "G.I. Bill," 167–69.

17. Frydl, "G.I. Bill," 134; Ross, *Preparing for Ulysses*, 28, 31–32, 70–71, 75; "Human Demobilizer," *Newsweek* (Apr. 3, 1944). Nonetheless, between December 1945 and February 1947 the staff of the VA expanded from 72,607 to 226,131 employees. See Mettler, *Soldiers to Citizens*, 62–63.

18. Frydl, "G.I. Bill," 154; Camelon, "I Saw The G.I. Bill Written, Part Two."

19. "Press Release," n.d., National Publicity Division, American Legion Archives, Indianapolis, Indiana.

20. "Chronology of Legion G.I. Bill, 1943–1944," American Legion Archives, Indianapolis, Indiana; Donald Glascoff, "Pattern for Law-making: The Dramatic Story of the G.I. Bill of Rights," n.d., American Legion Archives, Indianapolis, Indiana; Jack Cejnar to Commander Wagner, Nov. 22, 1955, American Legion Archives, Indianapolis, Indiana.

21. John Stelle, "Omnibus Bill of Rights for World War II Veterans," Feb. 6, 1944, American Legion Archives, Indianapolis, Indiana.

22. "Suggested 7-Minute Talk"; "Suggested Interview"; "Suggested Radio Interview (10 Minutes)"; n.d., American Legion Archives, Indianapolis, Indiana.

23. Ross, *Preparing for Ulysses*, 82–88.

24. Ibid., 73–78.

25. "John Elliott Rankin," *Dictionary of American Biography*, suppl. 6, 1956–1960, ed. John A. Garraty (New York: Scribner, 1980), 525–26.

26. Dorothy M. Brown, "Edith Nourse Rogers," *American National Biography* (New York: Oxford University Press, 1999), 752–53.

27. "Bennett Champ Clark," *Dictionary of American Biography*, suppl. 5, 1951–1955, ed. John A. Garraty (New York: Scribner, 1977), 113–15. Clark's role in the adoption of the GI bill did not save his political career, however. In the fall of 1944 he was defeated in the Democratic primary.

28. *Hearings before a Subcommittee of the Committee on Finance, United States Senate, Seventy-eighth Congress, Second Session on S. 1617, a Bill to Provide Federal Government Aid for the Readjustment in Civilian Life of Returning World War II Veterans*, January 14, 15, 21, 24; February 11, 14, 23; March 8 and 10, 1944 (Washington, D.C.: U.S. Government Printing Office, 1944), 27.

29. Omar B. Ketchum, Frank Haley, Millard W. Rice, and W. M. Floyd to John E. Rankin, Feb. 16, 1944, House Committee on World War Veterans Legislation Records, Record Group 233, National Archives, Washington, D.C.

30. Millard W. Rice to John E. Rankin, Feb. 22, 1944, House Committee on World War Veterans Legislation Records; Ross, *Preparing for Ulysses*, 104.

31. *Senate Subcommittee of the Committee on Finance*, 172; as late as May 15, Rice declared that the GI Bill "would overload the Veterans Administration with new responsibilities." See "Urges Amending G.I. Bill: Official of Disabled Veterans Asks Spread of Responsibility," *New York Times* (May 15, 1944).

32. *Hearings before the Committee on World War Veterans Legislation, House of Representatives, Seventy-eighth Congress, Second Session on H.R. 3917 and S. 1767 to Provide Federal Government Aid for the Readjustment in Civilian Life of Returning World War II Veterans*, January 11, 12, 13, 17, 18; February 24; March 9, 10, 27, 28, 29, 30, 31, 1944 (Washington, D.C.: U.S. Government Printing Office, 1944), 159, 161, 377, 387.

33. Ibid., 252–54.

34. Ibid., 449.

35. Ibid.

36. Ibid., 445–47.

37. Ibid., 15–16; Frydl, "G.I. Bill," 158.

38. Keith W. Olson, *The GI Bill, the Veterans, and the Colleges* (Lexington: University Press of Kentucky, 1974), 30–31; Earl McGrath, "The Education of the Veteran," *Annals of the American Academy* (March 1945): 85.

39. *Hearings before the Committee on World War Veterans Legislation*, 160–63, 313, 431.

40. *Senate Subcommittee of the Committee on Finance*, 139.

41. James E. McMillan, "Father of the GI Bill: Ernest W. McFarland and Veterans Legislation," *Journal of Arizona History* (Winter 1994): 357–76; James E. McMillan, ed., *The Ernest W. McFarland Papers: The United States Senate Years, 1940–1952* (Prescott, Ariz.: Sharlot Hall Museum Press, 1995), 81–82, 85–86, 90–91); *Mac: The Autobiography of Ernest W. McFarland* (privately published, 1979), 86–89. As U.S. senator, governor, and chief justice of the Arizona Supreme Court, McFarland would become one of the few Americans to attain the highest offices in the executive, legislative, and judicial branches of his state.

42. *Senate Subcommittee of the Committee on Finance*, 253; "Senate Subcommittee Completes Action on Education Bill: Reaches Agreement on Billion-dollar Program on Post-war Education," *New York Times* (Jan. 14, 1944).

43. *Senate Subcommittee of the Committee on Finance*, 253. McFarland made several joint appearances with Colmery on radio to promote the package.

44. "House by 387 to 0 Approves G.I. Bill," *New York Times* (May 19, 1944); Ross, *Preparing for Ulysses*, 111–16.

45. Donald Glascoff to Roy McMillan, Apr. 7, 1944, American Legion Archives, Indianapolis, Indiana; "Statement of Representative Rankin," Washington, D.C., Apr. 27, 1944, American Legion Archives, Indianapolis, Indiana; John Rankin to David W. Knepper, Apr. 26, 1944, House Committee on World War Veterans Legislation Records, Record Group 233, National Archives, Washington, D.C. Rankin's sensibility to union opposition was well grounded. A resolution that passed unanimously on June 6, 1944, by the Chicago District Council of the United Electrical, Radio, and Machine Workers of America urged adoption of the Senate version of the GI Bill and condemned Rankin "for his anti-labor record" and "his stand on the G.I. Bill of Rights," characterizing him as "an open spokesman of race superiority and anti-Semitism in the House of Representatives." Franklin D. Roosevelt Papers as president, Official File 4675, Container 29, "GI Bill of Rights (World War II)," Franklin D. Roosevelt Presidential Library, Hyde Park, New York.

46. David Camelon, "I Saw the G.I. Bill Written, Part Three," *American Legion Magazine* (November 1947); Ross, *Preparing for Ulysses*, 117; "G.I. Bill Goes to the White House," *New York Times* (June 14, 1944).

47. Camelon, "I Saw The G.I. Bill Written, Part Three"; Ross, *Preparing for Ulysses*, 116–18; "Conferees Accept G.I. Bill of Rights," *New York Times* (June 11, 1944). The episode was featured on a "March of Time" newsreel produced by Time, Inc., on Aug. 3, 1944. The text is available in the American Legion Archives, Indianapolis, Indiana. After the newsreel appeared, Gibson asked Atherton for help in persuading Hollywood to make a feature film about his role in the GI Bill: "It is thought by many who are well informed that, all things considered, it would go over as big as did *Gone with the Wind*." Apparently Darryl Zanuck expressed some interest, envisioning a 16-mm, nonprofit film suitable for use overseas. However, the War Department would not give clearance for a movie "made as an exclusive for the American Legion only." See John Gibson to Warren Atherton, Aug. 10, 1944, and Eugene Biscailuz to Warren Atherton, July 21, 1944, American Legion Archives, Indianapolis, Indiana.

48. "Roosevelt Signs G.I. Bill of Rights," *New York Times* (June 23, 1944).

49. Roosevelt's address appears to have been drafted by Samuel Rosenman, who, nearly two months earlier, had sent Eleanor Roosevelt a copy of the pending GI bill, to which he had appended a note observing that the bill "carries out with a few exceptions the program announced by the President last Summer for the benefit of veterans." Samuel I. Rosenman Papers, Container 8, "G.I. Bill," Franklin D. Roosevelt Presidential Library, Hyde Park, New York.

50. "Roosevelt on Rights Bill," *New York Times* (June 23, 1944).

51. Olson, *GI Bill*, 27; "The G.I. Bill of Rights," *New Republic* (Oct. 23, 1944). The *New York Times* did, however, report that, with the passage of the bill, politicians were predicting "that the American Legion will become the greatest political force in the country, even greater than labor, as its membership expands with veterans of this war." "Legion Is Pictured Mighty in Politics," *New York Times* (Apr. 22, 1944).

52. C. W. Wilson to John Stelle, Apr. 3, 1945, American Legion Archives, Indianapolis, Indiana; "Justice for All," *Life Magazine* (June 1995).

53. "The Vets' Best Bet," *Collier's* (Apr. 27, 1946); Boris Shishkin, "Organized Labor and the Veteran," *American Academy of Political and Social Science* (March 1945);

Ross, *Preparing for Ulysses*, 235–36; "Digest of Minutes," National Executive Committee Meeting, American Legion, Nov. 18–20, 1944, American Legion Archives, Indianapolis, Indiana.

54. Henry Pringle, "Are We Making a Bum out of G.I. Joe?" *Ladies' Home Journal* (September 1946).

55. Ross, *Preparing for Ulysses*, 237.

56. *Historical Statistics*, 639–40; President's Commission on Veterans' Pensions, *Veterans' Loan Guaranty and Direct Loan Benefits: A Report on Veterans' Benefits in the United States*, Staff Report no. IX, Part C (Washington, D.C.: U.S. Government Printing Office, 1956), 102. Michael J. Bennett claims that forty-three thousand VA-guaranteed mortgage loans were issued on 324,900 new homes in 1945, a proportion of 7.5 percent. However, Bennett fails to differentiate between private and public housing units and between loans on new and preexisting homes. His discussion of the growth of VA mortgage activity after 1945 is similarly flawed. See Bennett, *When Dreams Came True*, 287.

57. Ross, *Preparing for Ulysses*, 242; Frank Gervasi, "No Place to Live," *Collier's* (February 1946).

58. Ross, *Preparing for Ulysses*, 248; Henry Schubart, "The Housing Crisis," *Public Affairs* (March 1946); Mrs. Samuel Rosenman, "The Racket in Veterans' Housing," *American Magazine* (September 1946).

59. John D. Black and Charles D. Hyson, "Postwar Soldier Settlement," *Quarterly Journal of Economics* (November 1944).

60. "Veterans Loans," *Business Week* (Jan. 6, 1945); Frank Gervasi, "Cradle of Free Enterprise," *Collier's* (Mar. 16, 1946).

61. Stephen Thompson, "Free Education for Our Veterans," *Science Digest* (February 1945); Edith Efron, "Veterans Storm the Academic Beachhead," *New York Times* (Aug. 12, 1945).

62. Robert M. Hutchins, "The Threat to American Education," *Collier's* (Dec. 30, 1944); "Bursars Rub Hands over G.I. Bill but College Standards May Suffer," *Newsweek* (Jan. 8, 1945); Frydl, "G.I. Bill," 388, 390, 392.

63. "President Conant Urges a Revision of the G.I. Bill of Rights," *School and Society* (Feb. 10, 1945).

64. Major S. H. Kraines, "The Veteran and Post-war Education," *Journal of Higher Education* (June 1945); Willard Waller, "Which Veterans Should Go to College?" *Ladies Home Journal* (May 1945).

65. Stanley Frank, "The GI's Reject Education," *Saturday Evening Post* (Aug. 18, 1945).

66. Charles Hurd, "The Veteran," *New York Times* (Feb. 18, 1945).

67. Ibid., Mar. 11, 1945, and May 13, 1945. Three American Legion committees studied the implementation of the bill, went "right to work on the bug hunt," and by April 1945 had recommended amendments to liberalize certain provisions. See Mettler, *Soldiers to Citizens*, 60–61.

68. *Hearings before the Committee on World War Veterans Legislation, House of Representatives, Seventy-ninth Congress, First Session on H.R. 3749 and Related Bills to Amend the Servicemen's Readjustment Act of 1944*, June 19, 20, 21, 28 and July 5, 1945 (Washington, D.C.: U.S. Government Printing Office, 1945), 54–55.

69. Ibid., 6, 194.

70. Ibid., 148–49; *Hearings before a Subcommittee of the Committee on Finance, United States Senate, Seventy-ninth Congress, First Session on H.R. 3749, an Act to Amend the Servicemen's Readjustment Act of 1944 to Provide for a Readjustment Allowance for All Veterans of World War II*, October 8–12, 1945 (Washington, D.C.: U.S. Government Printing Office, 1945), 275.

71. *Hearings of the Committee on World War Veterans Legislation, House of Representatives*, 50, 52; *Hearings before a Subcommittee of the Committee on Finance, United States Senate*, 164.

72. *Hearings before a Subcommittee of the Committee on Finance, United States Senate*, 166; *Hearings of the Committee on World War Veterans Legislation, House of Representatives*, 131, 166.

73. *Hearings before a Subcommittee of the Committee on Finance, United States Senate*, 294.

74. *Hearings of the Committee on World War Veterans Legislation, House of Representatives*, 187; *Hearings before a Subcommittee of the Committee on Finance, United States Senate*, 120.

75. *Hearings of the Committee on World War Veterans Legislation, House of Representatives*, 108, 111.

76. "Veterans: More Rights," *Time* (Nov. 19, 1945); Mettler, *Soldiers to Citizens*, 61–62; Olson, *GI Bill*, 37, 123–24.

77. Mettler, *Soldiers to Citizens*, 6–7; Keith W. Olson, "The G.I. Bill and Higher Education: Success and Surprise," *American Quarterly* (December 1973).

Chapter 4

1. "S.R.O." *Time Magazine* (Mar. 18, 1946); Milton MacKaye, "Crisis at the Colleges," *Saturday Evening Post* (Aug. 3, 1946).

2. Keith W. Olson, *The GI Bill, the Veterans, and the Colleges* (Lexington: University Press of Kentucky, 1974), 109.

3. Harold W. Stoke, "The Veterans Educate the Nation," *Association of American Colleges Bulletin* (October 1947).

4. Gary L. Hylander, "The Educational Features of the G.I. Bill and Its Impact on Selected Boston Area Universities" (PhD diss., Boston College, 1985), 203; John Norberg, *A Force for Change: The Class of 1950* (West Lafayette, Ind.: Purdue University Press, 1995), 7; J. Robert Greene with Karrie A. Baron, *Syracuse University*, vol. 4, *The Tolley Years, 1942–1969* (Syracuse, N.Y.: Syracuse University Press, 1996), 39–40; Kathleen Frydl, "The G.I. Bill" (PhD diss., University of Chicago, 2000), 350; "A Follow-up on Plans for the Education of Veterans," *School and Society* (Aug. 26, 1944).

5. "Summary and Interpretation of Data on Veterans' Education, Supplied by 100 Colleges and Universities and Amendments to Federal Legislation," *Higher Education and National Affairs* (Washington, D.C.: American Council on Education, Nov. 26, 1945); Olson, *GI Bill*, 66.

6. Olson, *GI Bill*, 67; Frydl, "G.I. Bill," 347–48.

7. "Growing Pains," *Cornell Daily Sun* (Oct. 11, 1946); Edmund Ezra Day to Governor Thomas E. Dewey, Mar. 1, 1948, Day Papers, Box 30, Division of Manuscripts and Archives, Cornell University. Colleges also found innovative ways to ease the housing shortage. Harvard, for example, ordered all freshmen whose parents lived in or near Cambridge to live at home. See Hylander, "Educational Features of the G.I. Bill," 170.

8. Arthur Hope, *Notre Dame: One Hundred Years* (South Bend, Ind.: Notre Dame University Press, 1948), 476; Michael Bezilla, *Penn State: An Illustrated History* (University Park: Pennsylvania State University Press, 1985), 207.

9. Hylander, "Educational Features of the G.I. Bill," 88; Olson, *GI Bill*, 67–68.

10. Olson, *GI Bill*, 68; Hylander, "Educational Features of the G.I. Bill," 221; Frydl, "G.I. Bill," 347.

11. Olson, *GI Bill*, 87–88.

12. Stoke, "The Veterans Educate the Nation"; "Education: Mark-up," *Time Magazine* (Oct. 20, 1947).

13. Milton MacKaye, "Crisis at the Colleges," *Saturday Evening Post* (Aug. 3, 1946).

14. Bezilla, *Penn State*, 206; "Veterans at College," *Life Magazine* (Apr. 21, 1947).

15. Lewis A. Coser, *Refugee Scholars in America: Their Impact and Their Experiences* (New Haven, Conn.: Yale University Press, 1984), 3–15.

16. Marcia Graham Synnott, *The Half-opened Door: Discrimination and Admissions at Harvard, Yale, and Princeton, 1900–1970* (Westport, Conn.: Greenwood, 1979), 200; Morton Keller and Phyllis Keller, *Making Harvard Modern: The Rise of America's University* (New York: Oxford University Press, 2001), 64–109.

17. Frydl, "G.I. Bill," 356; Olson, *GI Bill*, 72.

18. "The Veterans' Education Program," *School and Society* (Sept. 9, 1944); Argus Tresidder, "The Illiberal Arts," *Journal of Higher Education* (March 1946); "The Veterans and College," *Newsweek* (Nov. 10, 1947).

19. President's Commission on Veterans' Pensions, *Readjustment Benefits: Education and Training, and Employment and Unemployment*, Staff Report no. IX, Part B (Washington, D.C.: U.S. Government Printing Office, 1956), tables 6 and 7.

20. Walter Spearman and Jack R. Brown, "When the Veteran Goes to College," *South Atlantic Quarterly* (January 1946).

21. Olson, *GI Bill*, 87, 131.

22. "Counseling and Postwar Educational Opportunities," *American Council on Education* (July 7, 1945); Frydl, "G.I. Bill," 367.

23. Frydl, "G.I. Bill," 358–66.

24. Suzanne Mettler, *Soldiers to Citizens: The G.I. Bill and the Making of the Greatest Generation* (New York: Oxford University Press, 2005), 72; Hylander, "Educational Features of the G.I. Bill," 109.

25. "Academic Achievement of Veterans at Cornell University," *School and Society* (Feb. 8, 1947); Charles J. V. Murphy, "GIs at Harvard," *Life Magazine* (June 17, 1946); Edith Efron, "The Two Joes Meet: Joe College, Joe Veteran," *New York Times Magazine* (June 16, 1946).

26. Murphy, "GIs at Harvard."

27. "Class of '47," *Time Magazine* (June 16, 1947); Olson, *GI Bill*, 51.

28. Olson, *GI Bill*, 50–56.

29. Cover illustration, *Saturday Evening Post* (Oct. 5, 1946).

30. "Veterans at College," *Life Magazine* (Apr. 21, 1947). A GI Bill recipient at Cornell University exhibited good-natured optimism in an ad he took out in the "Wanted to Rent" section of the *Ithaca Journal*: "Young lady, two years old, wants furnished or unfurnished apartment or house. No crying at night, scribbling on walls, smashing windows. No pets. Two parents. Father is veteran. Mother is nervous wreck, but a house will remedy that." "On the Campus and Down the Hill," *Cornell Alumni News* (Nov. 15, 1945).

31. C. S. Forester, "Meet a Student Veteran," *Ladies Home Journal* (May 1945). See also Margery Ellen Wolf, "We Solved Our Housing Problem," *Reader's Digest* (April 1946).

32. John Norberg, *A Force for Change: The Class of 1950* (West Lafayette, Ind.: Purdue University Press, 1995), 228–29; John Rivoire, "The Pity of It All," *Cornell Daily Sun* (Jan. 18, 1947).

33. Norberg, *Force for Change*, 272–75. When checks were late, however, GIs did not hesitate to ask for immediate action.

34. Frydl, "G.I. Bill," 242; Olson, *GI Bill*, 63–64; "Bristow Adams Praises Veterans as Determined, Unafraid, World-wise," *Cornell Bulletin* (Jan. 18, 1946). Cornell, of course, was the "land-grant university" of New York State.

35. Governor Thomas E. Dewey to Edmund Ezra Day, Feb. 15, 1946, Day Papers, Box 41, Division of Manuscripts and Archives, Cornell University; "Colleges Must Take Veterans, Dewey Tells State Educators," *New York Times* (Mar. 8, 1946).

36. "Colleges Must Take Veterans"; Amy M. Gilbert, *ACUNY, the Associated Colleges of Upper New York: A Unique Response to an Emergency in Higher Education in the State of New York* (Ithaca, N.Y.: Cornell University Press, 1950), 27–43.

37. Olson, *GI Bill*, 70–71; Gilbert, *ACUNY*, 92–93; "Report on the Associated Colleges of Upper New York by New York State Education Department," July 1947, Day Papers, Box 10, Manuscripts and Archives, Cornell University; "Report on Evaluation Visit to ACUNY," Apr. 24–25 and June 12–13, 1947, Day Papers, Box 10, Manuscripts and Archives, Cornell University.

38. Benjamin Fine, "Education in Review: Associated Colleges, Started as an Emergency Unit, Is Now Hailed for Its High Standards," *New York Times* (Sept. 21, 1947).

39. Gilbert, *ACUNY*, 210–14, 241, 304–13, 322–52, 378–90, 405–10.

40. "Report on the Associated Colleges of Upper New York by New York State Education Department."

41. Bill Beeney, "What's Wrong at Sampson?" *Rochester Democrat and Chronicle* (May 10, 1948).

42. "Report on the Associated Colleges of Upper New York by New York State Education Department, July 1947; Gilbert, *ACUNY*, 278–79, 290–91."

43. Gilbert, *ACUNY*, 240–43, 437–43; Asa Knowles, "Proposals concerning Operation of the Associated Colleges of Upper New York subsequent to June 30, 1948," Mar. 6, 1948, Day Papers, Box 10, Manuscripts and Archives, Cornell University; "1,800 Vacancies at Associated Colleges," *New York Times* (Aug. 22, 1948).

44. Gilbert, *ACUNY*, 417.

45. Edward Humes, *Over Here: How the G.I. Bill Transformed the American Dream* (Orlando: Harcourt, 2006), 41–49, 60–72. Humes's book is based on a small number of interesting case studies of GI Bill beneficiaries, and we draw on several of them in this chapter and others.

46. Humes, *Over Here*, 6.

47. Norman Frederickson and William B. Schrader, *Adjustment to College* (Princeton, N.J.: Educational Testing Service, 1951).

48. Mettler, *Soldiers to Citizens*, 43–47, 206.

49. Ibid., 90, 94; Charles B. Nam, "Impact of the G.I. Bills on the Educational Level of the Male Population," *Social Forces* (October 1964).

50. "S.R.O."; Olson, *GI Bill*, 45; Michael J. Bennett, *When Dreams Came True: The GI Bill and the Making of Modern America* (Washington, D.C.: Brassey's, 1996), 19.

51. Robert Dallek, *Nixon and Kissinger: Partners in Power* (New York: HarperCollins, 2007), 33–44.

52. Mettler, *Soldiers to Citizens*, 107, 109.

53. Ibid., 121–30.

54. Ibid., 1–2, 112–33.

55. Ibid., 112–33; "Bristow Adams Praises Veterans as Determined, Unafraid, World-wise."

56. Mettler, *Soldiers to Citizens*, 131–35.

57. Keith W. Olson, "The G.I. Bill and Higher Education: Success and Surprise," *American Quarterly* (December 1973): 596–610. Olson is convinced, however, that the "Colleges in the early 1950s, after most of the veterans had left, resembled closely their prewar selves.... Important trends... in higher education since the close of World War II developed from the demands of the Defense Department and of a technological, consumer-oriented society, not from the influence of the G.I. Bill" (607, 610).

58. For a summary of concerns about the end of "Joe College activities" see Efron, "Two Joes Meet."

59. Olson, *GI Bill*, 608.

60. Daniel A. Clark, "The Two Joes Meet—Joe College, Joe Veteran: The G.I. Bill, College Education, and Postwar American Culture," *History of Education Quarterly* (Summer 1998): 165–89.

61. Donald H. Moyer, "The Veterans at Cornell," *Cornell Alumni News*, June 1, 1947.

62. *Higher Education for American Democracy: A Report of the President's Commission on Higher Education*, 5 vols. (New York: Harper & Brothers, 1948); Steven Brint and Jerome Karabel, *The Diverted Dream: Community Colleges and the Promise of Educational Opportunity, 1900–1985* (New York: Oxford University Press, 1989), 68–69; Lawrence A. Cremin, *American Education: The Metropolitan Experience, 1876–1980* (New York: Harper & Row, 1988), 251.

63. Cremin, *American Education*, 263.

64. Ibid., 253.

65. Olson, *GI Bill*, 70–72; Gilbert, *ACUNY*, 442.

66. Mettler, *Soldiers to Citizens*, 48–52, 57–58.

67. Hylander, "Educational Features of the G.I. Bill," 138, 158.

68. Jerome Karabel, *The Chosen: The Hidden History of Admission and Exclusion at Harvard, Yale, and Princeton* (Boston: Houghton Mifflin, 2005), 183–84.

69. Ibid., 158–60.

70. Brint and Karabel, *Diverted Dream*, 73–75.

71. Cremin, *American Education*, 252.

72. Robert C. Serow, "Policy as Symbol: Title II of the 1944 G.I. Bill," *Review of Higher Education* (Summer 2004): 481–99.

Chapter 5

1. Ira Katznelson, *When Affirmative Action Was White: An Untold History of Racial Inequality in Twentieth-century America* (New York: Norton, 2005), 117–18; Michael J. Bennett, *When Dreams Came True: The GI Bill and the Making of Modern America* (Washington: Brassey's, 1996), 26.

2. Systematic data are not available for Latinos, Native Americans, or Asian Americans.

3. Suzanne Mettler, *Soldiers to Citizens: The G.I. Bill and the Making of the Greatest Generation* (New York: Oxford University Press, 2005), 144.

4. Susan Ware, *Holding Their Own: American Women in the 1930s* (Boston: Twayne, 1982), 56–59.

5. Barbara Miller Solomon, *In the Company of Educated Women: A History of Women and Higher Education in America* (New Haven, Conn.: Yale University Press, 1985), 188; Susan M. Hartmann, *The Home Front and Beyond: American Women in the 1940s* (Boston: Twayne, 1982), 103–105.

6. "Syracuse Women Get New Course," *New York Times* (June 14, 1942).

7. Hartmann, *Home Front and Beyond*, 103–104. The military training programs included the Army Specialized Training Program (ASTP), Army Air Forces College Training Program (AAFTP), and Navy College Training Program. According to V. R. Cardozier, despite some tensions and "some harassment of women," relations between civilian students and military trainees "were generally pleasant, if not close." See V. R. Cardozier, *Colleges and Universities in World War II* (Westport, Conn.: Praeger, 1993), 106.

8. Hartmann, *Home Front and Beyond*, 103–104.

9. Helen Hosp, "Education in the New Age," *Journal of the American Association of University Women* (Winter 1946): 104.

10. Alice C. Lloyd, "Women in the Postwar College," *Journal of the American Association of University Women* (Spring 1946): 131–34; Milton MacKaye, "Crisis at the Colleges," *Saturday Evening Post* (Aug. 3, 1946); "Education: Lo, the Poor Co-ed," *Newsweek* (Apr. 29, 1946).

11. Members of the original Women's Army Auxiliary Corps (WAAC) were not enlisted in the military; hence, those who did not transfer after 1943 into the new Women's Army Corps (WAC, an official body within the U.S. Army) were not eligible for veterans' benefits after the war. Neither were the eleven hundred Women Air Force Service Pilots, who, along with the WAACs, had to wait until 1977 before they were granted military status. However, since 215,000 men of the Merchant Marine were also declared ineligible for veterans' benefits, it may be unfair to ascribe a sexist motive to denials of benefits to some women.

12. Mettler, *Soldiers to Citizens*, 145–46, 152.

13. Elaine Tyler May, *Homeward Bound: American Families in the Cold War Era* (New York: Basic Books, 1988), 20, 80.

14. Edward Humes, *Over Here: How the G.I. Bill Transformed the American Dream* (Orlando: Harcourt, 2006), 108–12, 127–34.

15. Lizabeth Cohen, *A Consumers' Republic: The Politics of Mass Consumption in Postwar America* (New York: Knopf, 2003), 138.

16. "Education Interests College G.I.s," *School and Society* (Feb. 10, 1945); Mettler, *Soldiers to Citizens*, 149–50.

17. Mettler, *Soldiers to Citizens*, 149.

18. Ibid., 144–50.

19. Ibid., 150–54.

20. "Gold Star Wives Start New Group," *New York Times* (Oct. 29, 1945); "War Widows Ask U.S. Aid," *New York Times* (Apr. 26, 1947).

21. *Hearings before the Committee on Veterans Affairs, Eightieth Congress, Second Session on H.R. 5301, a Bill to Extend the Educational and Training Benefits of the Servicemen's Readjustment Act of 1944, as Amended to Certain Widows and Children of Deceased Veterans*, May 20, 1948 (Washington, D.C.: U.S. Government Printing Office, 1948), 4, 5, 10, 12.

22. *Hearings before the Subcommittee on Education, Training, and Rehabilitation of the Committee on Veterans Affairs, House of Representatives, Eightieth Congress, First Session on H.R. 2106, H.R. 2172, Bills Providing Educational and Loan Benefits for Widows and Children of Certain Deceased World War II Veterans*, April 26 and 28 and June 6, 1947 (Washington, D.C.: U.S. Government Printing Office, 1947), 6–7.

23. Ibid., 20, 32–33.

24. Ibid., 18.

25. Kathleen Frydl, "The G.I. Bill" (PhD diss., University of Chicago, 2000), 403.

26. Benjamin Fine, "Young Women Ready for College Enrollment Find It Increasingly Difficult to Enter," *New York Times* (Jan. 12, 1947).

27. "Sarah Lawrence to Admit Fifty Men," *New York Herald Tribune* (Apr. 23, 1946); Jessica Winum, "Vassar's Vets," *Vassar Alumnae/i Quarterly* (Fall 2000).

28. Mettler, *Soldiers to Citizens*, 157; Hartmann, *Home Front and Beyond*, 106.

29. Herbert Williams to Faculty and Administrative Staff, May 31, 1946, Edmund Ezra Day Papers, Box 1, Division of Manuscripts and Archives, Cornell University; "Doors Closing for Women Students," *Journal of the American Association of University Women* (Spring 1946).

30. Lucille Allen to Arthur Adams, Nov. 24, 1947, Edmund Ezra Day Papers, Box 16, Division of Manuscripts and Archives, Cornell University.

31. "Doors Closing for Women Students," *Journal of the American Association of University Women* (June 1946).

32. Hartmann, *Home Front and Beyond*, 107.

33. Mettler, *Soldiers to Citizens*, 157.

34. Fred Hechinger, "Sway of Male Deplored in Colleges for Women," *Washington Post* (Sept. 7, 1947); Hartmann, *Home Front and Beyond*, 111.

35. Hartmann, *Home Front and Beyond*, 109–44; Mettler, *Soldiers to Citizens*, 235.

36. Hartmann, *Home Front and Beyond*, 116.

37. Katznelson, *When Affirmative Action Was White*, 118–20.

38. Frydl, "G.I. Bill," 304; Humes, *Over Here*, 221.

39. Katznelson, *When Affirmative Action Was White*, 129.

40. Mettler, *Soldiers to Citizens*, 56.

41. Humes, *Over Here*, 215–54.

42. Bennett, *When Dreams Came True*, 261.

43. Ibid., 261–62.

44. David Onkst, "Black World War II Veterans and the G.I. Bill in Georgia, Alabama, and Mississippi, 1944–1947," (MA thesis, University of Georgia, 1990), 82. For an indictment of the GI Bill as the most effective tool in postwar America in widening an already huge racial gap in education and employment, see Katznelson, *When Affirmative Action Was White*, 113–41.

45. Onkst, "Black World War II Veterans," 19–21.

46. Frydl, "G.I. Bill," 318, 325–28, 330.

47. Ibid., 303, 312.

48. Ibid., 316, 318, 332; Hilary Herbold, "Never a Level Playing Field: Blacks and the G.I. Bill," *Journal of Blacks in Higher Education* (Winter 1994–1995): 106.

49. Frydl, "G.I. Bill," 317.

50. Katznelson, *When Affirmative Action Was White*, 125–27.

51. Ibid., 130; Herbold, "Never a Level Playing Field," 107.

52. Keith W. Olson, *The GI Bill, the Veterans, and the Colleges* (Lexington: University Press of Kentucky, 1974), 74; Katznelson, *When Affirmative Action Was White*, 132–33; David Onkst, "First a Negro ... Incidentally a Veteran: Black World War II Veterans and the G.I. Bill of Rights in the Deep South, 1944–1948," *Journal of Social History* (Spring 1998): 517–44.

53. Katznelson, *When Affirmative Action Was White*, 132.

54. Onkst, "First a Negro," 517–44.

55. Herbold, "Never a Level Playing Field," 108, 134; Charles G. Bolté and Louis Harris, *Our Negro Veterans* (New York: Public Affairs Committee, 1947), 20, 28.

56. Bennett, *When Dreams Came True*, 260; Mettler, *Soldiers to Citizens*, 74–75.

57. "Campus Folkways," *Newsweek* (June 6, 1949); John Norberg, *A Force for Change: The Class of 1950* (West Lafayette, Ind.: Purdue University Press, 1995), 258–59.

58. James A. Atkins, "Negro Educational Institutions and the Veterans' Educational Facilities Program," *Journal of Negro Education* (Spring 1948): 141–53; Mettler, *Soldiers to Citizens*, 75.

59. Mettler, *Soldiers to Citizens*, 136–43.

60. Richard Kluger, *Simple Justice: The History of* Brown v. Board of Education *and Black America's Struggle for Equality* (New York: Random House, 1975), 260–66, 275–78, 282; Bennett, *When Dreams Came True*, 269–71.

61. Mettler, *Soldiers to Citizens*, 31.

62. Daniel Inouye, with Lawrence Elliott, *Journey to Washington* (Englewood Cliffs, N.J.: Prentice-Hall, 1967), especially 202–56.

63. Mettler, *Soldiers to Citizens*, 1, 31, 46.

64. Jerome Karabel, *The Chosen: The Hidden History of Admission and Exclusion at Harvard, Yale, and Princeton* (New York: Houghton Mifflin, 2005), 74–75, 86–109, 196.

65. Ibid., 597; Edmund Ezra Day to Newton Burnett, July 31, 1945, Day Papers, Box 33, Division of Manuscripts and Archives, Cornell University. To "materially reduce the proportion of Jewish students" in the summer session, Cornell rejected recent graduates from high schools (most of them in New York City) and matriculants from New York University and Hunter College. See Howard Anderson to President Day, July 6, 1945, Day Papers, Box 33. Anderson, the director of Cornell's School of Education, estimated the number of Jews currently enrolled by examining given names and surnames. In the appendix to his letter he listed all of the students he classified as Jewish and acknowledged that some of them "may be the children of foreign born but non-Jewish parents."

66. Mettler, *Soldiers to Citizens*, 208.

67. Brad Gooch, *City Poet: The Life and Times of Frank O'Hara* (New York: Knopf, 1993), 3–156; Bennett, *When Dreams Came True*, 252–53.

68. Karabel, *Chosen*, 597.

69. *Higher Education for American Democracy* (New York: Harper Brothers, 1948), vol. 3, 6; vol. 1, 36.

70. Olson, *GI Bill*, 69–71; Benjamin Ginsburg, *The Fatal Embrace: Jews and the State* (Chicago: University of Chicago Press, 1993), 98–100.

71. Edward N. Saveth, "Fair Educational Practices Legislation," *Annals of the American Academy of Political and Social Science* (1951): 41–46.

72. Karabel, *Chosen*, 181–83, 195–98. Karabel insists, however, that Harvard circa 1953 was "not so very different" from the Harvard of 1933.

73. Ibid., 210–13.

74. Saveth, "Fair Educational Practices Legislation," 41–46.

Chapter 6

1. President's Commission on Veterans' Pensions, *Readjustment Benefits: Education and Training, and Employment and Unemployment: A Report on Veterans' Benefits in the United States*, Staff Report no. IX, Part B (Washington, D.C.: U.S. Government Printing Office, 1956), 30. These figures are based on a survey of seven million men who were in the army on June 30, 1944. The results were originally published in *Higher Education* 1(7) (Apr. 2, 1945): 218–19.

2. The loan program included a much larger and more consequential home-loan guarantee benefit we discuss in the next chapter.

3. *Readjustment Benefits*, Part B, 140, 164; President's Commission on Veterans' Pensions, *Readjustment Benefits: General Survey and Appraisal: A Report on Veterans' Benefits in the United States*, Staff Report no. IX, Part A (Washington, D.C.: U.S. Government Printing Office, 1956), 50.

4. Ibid., 31, 43, 49.

5. Suzanne Mettler, *Soldiers to Citizens: The G.I. Bill and the Making of the Greatest Generation* (New York: Oxford University Press, 2005), 68, 79. The college and subcollege aggregate responses are not quite comparable, as the latter are restricted to "nonblack" males. Two categories of subcollege training elicited a less favorable response: Only 46 percent of those participating in correspondence courses and 33 percent of on-the-farm trainees regarded the GI Bill as a turning point in their lives (79).

6. Arnold Shaw, *Belafonte: An Unauthorized Biography* (New York: Chilton, 1960), 1–44.

7. Henry F. Pringle, "Are We Making a Bum out of G. I. Joe?" *Ladies Home Journal* (September 1946), 48.

8. *Readjustment Benefits*, Part B, 125.

9. Ibid., 152, 180.

10. Ibid., 125, 178.

11. Ibid., 158–64.

12. Ibid., 185.

13. Ibid., 186–87.

14. Ibid., 190.

15. Ibid., 199.

16. Arthur Gordon, "Keep Your Money, Uncle Sam," *Reader's Digest* (May 1949), 49–50.

17. Ibid., 50–51.

18. Ibid., 52.

19. Ibid., 51.

20. *Readjustment Benefits*, Part B, 113–14.

21. It was, of course, less than the nearly 50 percent these figures suggest at first glance. As a number of workers left the workforce during the decade, the number of new workers was greater than 12 million. Some subcollege trainees may not have entered the workforce after completing or leaving their training, while others pursued work in areas for which they had not been trained. The latter were part of the workforce, but they complicate our effort to assess the contribution of GI Bill subcollege training to the postwar economy. On the size of the American workforce during these years see U.S. Bureau of the Census, *Historical Statistics of the United States, Colonial Times to 1970* (Washington, D.C.: U.S. Government Printing Office, 1975), 127.

22. *Report on Education and Training under the Servicemen's Readjustment Act, as Amended, from the Administrator of Veterans' Affairs*, House Committee Print no. 210, 81st Congress, 2d sess. (Washington, D.C.: U.S. Government Printing Office, 1950), 35.

23. *Readjustment Benefits*, Part B, 34.

24. *Report on Education and Training*, 46.

25. *Readjustment Benefits*, Part B, 37–38.

26. *Report on Education and Training*, 54.

27. Albert Q. Maisel, "What's Wrong with Veterans' Schools?" *Collier's* (May 1948).

28. Ibid.

29. Ibid.

30. Ibid.

31. *New York Times* (June 30, 2007). We wish to thank Barbara Nessim, a graduate of the School of Visual Arts, for calling our attention to the school.

32. *Report on Education and Training*, 114–61.

33. *Readjustment Benefits*, Part B, 41.

34. *Report on Education and Training*, 131.

35. *Hearings before the House Select Committee to Investigate Educational and Training Programs under the GI Bill*, U.S. House of Representatives, 81st Congress, 2d sess. (Washington, D.C.: U.S. Government Printing Office, 1951), 508–42.

36. Ibid., 519.

37. *Report on Education and Training*, 73.

38. "Excerpt from the Report of the Council of Economic Advisers to the President, January 1947," Subcommittee on Employment and Manpower of the Committee on Labor and Public Welfare, U.S. Senate, *History of Employment and Manpower Policy in the United States: Twenty Years under the Employment Act of 1946* (Washington, D.C.: U.S. Government Printing Office, 1966), 45.

39. *Report on Education and Training*, Table A-6, 88–91; *Historical Statistics*, 140–45.

40. Ibid.

41. Ibid.

42. *Readjustment Benefits*, Part B, 43, 31.

43. Ibid.

44. *Report on Education and Training*, Table A-7, 91–95; *Historical Statistics*, 140–45.

45. *Historical Statistics*, 139.

46. *Readjustment Benefits*, Part B, 49, 51–52.

47. *Report on Education and Training*, Table A-8, 96.

48. *Readjustment Benefits*, Part B, 49–50.

49. Ibid., 53–54.

50. Ibid., 54.

51. Ibid., 119.

52. Ibid., 117.

53. Ibid., 117–18.

54. *Readjustment Benefits*, Part A, 72. Mettler identifies the source for the commission's statement as a VA study. Mettler, *Soldiers to Citizens*, 209.

55. Kathleen Frydl, "The G.I. Bill" (PhD diss., University of Chicago, 2000), 331.

56. Charles G. Bolté and Louis Harris, *Our Negro Veterans* (New York: Public Affairs Committee, 1947). The most extensive recent discussion is David Onkst, "Black World War II Veterans and the G.I. Bill in Georgia, Alabama, and Mississippi, 1944–1947" (MA thesis, University of Georgia, 1990).

57. Mettler, *Soldiers to Citizens*, 80.

58. *Readjustment Benefits*, Part B, 273.

59. David Onkst reports that in October 1946 the USES filled 6,500 jobs in three southern states. Of these, whites were placed in 86 percent of the skilled and semi-skilled positions, while blacks were placed in 92 percent of the unskilled jobs. Onkst also argues that black veterans tended to avoid the USES. Onkst, "Black World War II Veterans," 25–28. For a general history of the USES see Leonard P. Adams, *The Public Employment Service in Transition, 1933–1968: Evolution of a Placement Service into a Manpower Agency* (Ithaca: New York State School of Industrial and Labor Relations, Cornell University, 1969).

60. *Readjustment Benefits*, Part B, 268–302. Another employment benefit that carried over from the aftermath of World War I was veterans' preference in civil service appointments, which consists of a five-point addition to the civil service exam scores of able-bodied veterans and a ten-point addition for veterans with disabilities.

61. Ibid., 247–55. For discussions of these issues in the contemporary periodical press see, for example, J. Donald Kingsley, "Veterans, Unions, and Jobs," *New Republic* (Oct. 25, 1944): 513–14 and (Nov. 13, 1944): 621–23; Aaron Levenstein, "Superseniority—Postwar Pitfall," *Antioch Review* (Winter 1944/1945): 531–43; Walter J. Couper, "The Reemployment Rights of Veterans," *American Academy of Political and Social Sciences* (March 1945): 112–21; Boris Shishkin, "Organized Labor and the Veteran" *American Academy of Political and Social Sciences* (March 1945): 146–57; "Veterans' Job Showdown Near," *Business Week* (May 19, 1945), 100; "An Old Riddle Crops Up Again—How to Find Jobs for Veterans," *Newsweek* (May 21, 1945), 76–78; Jack Schuyler, "Veterans and Union Rules," *American Mercury* (December 1945), 666–71.

62. *Readjustment Benefits*, Part C, 60.

63. Ibid., 14.

64. Ibid., 99.

65. Ibid., 60. The precise totals are obscured by the incorporation of veterans of the Korean conflict in the VA tabulation. A subsequent table based on sample data (see p. 90) indicates that there were 3,782,000 World War II veterans who did not serve during the Korean conflict and who used VA mortgages before the end of 1955. To these should be added some among the 843,000 Korean conflict veterans who were

also veterans of World War II (about 20 percent of the total who served in Korea). Only 268,000 Korean conflict veterans had purchased homes with VA mortgages by the end of 1955, but it is likely that a significant of them were older veterans who had served in both wars.

Chapter 7

1. U.S. Bureau of the Census, *Historical Statistics of the United States, Colonial Times to 1970* (Washington, D.C.: U.S. Government Printing Office, 1975), 639–40.

2. President's Commission on Veterans' Pensions, *Veterans' Loan Guaranty and Direct Loan Benefits: A Report on Veterans' Benefits in the United States,* Staff Report no. IX, Part C (Washington, D.C.: U.S. Government Printing Office, 1956), 1.

3. See, for example, Sidney Margolius, "The Boom in Homes," *Collier's* (July 7, 1945), 20, 48; Frank Gervasi, "No Place to Live," *Collier's* (Feb. 16, 1946), 20–21, 78–81.

4. *Veterans' Loan Guaranty,* 2.

5. President's Commission on Veterans' Pensions, *Readjustment Benefits: A Report on Veterans' Benefits in the United States,* Staff Report no. IX, Part A (Washington, D.C.: U.S. Government Printing Office, 1956), 49.

6. *Veterans' Loan Guaranty,* 10–11.

7. Ibid., 60.

8. *Readjustment Benefits,* 49.

9. There were some four hundred thousand secondary loans, about one-sixth of all of the home loans guaranteed by the VA before this program was largely shut down in 1951. *Veterans' Loan Guaranty,* 62.

10. Ibid., 14–16.

11. Ibid., 60.

12. Ibid., 60, 90.

13. Ibid.; *Readjustment Benefits,* 50.

14. *Veterans' Loan Guaranty,* 80.

15. American Legion archive, Indianapolis, Indiana.

16. "Legion's Bill for Veterans in Congress," *National Legionnaire* 10(1) (January 1944).

17. Kenneth T. Jackson, *Crabgrass Frontier: The Suburbanization of the United States* (New York: Oxford University Press, 1985), 203.

18. The HOLC was conceived as an emergency measure, and its mortgage activities were terminated in 1936. The agency itself was liquidated in 1951. See Carey Winston, "Home Owners' Loan Corporation," in *The Story of Housing,* ed. Gertrude Sipperly Fish, 188–94 (New York: Macmillan, 1979), and Jackson, *Crabgrass Frontier,* 195–203, for brief but informative surveys of the history of the HOLC.

19. Curtis W. Tuck, "The Secondary Mortgage Market," in Fish, ed., *Story of Housing,* 405–408.

20. *Investigation of Veterans' Loan Guaranty Program: Hearings before the House Select Committee to Investigate Educational, Training, and Loan Guaranty Programs under the GI Bill.* House of Representatives, 82d Cong., 1st sess. (Washington, D.C.: U.S. Government Printing Office, 1952), 107–109.

21. Ibid., 175.

22. *Historical Statistics,* 646. These tabulations are based on data from the *U.S. Census of Housing* and from interim housing surveys by the Bureau of the Census.

23. Ibid., 262–63.

24. Some of the FHA loans turned up by this survey may have been supplemented by VA-backed secondary loans, and some of those listed under "other financing" may have utilized another form of government guarantee. However, refinements of

this sort, if we were able to make them, would not significantly shift the proportions reported here.

25. *Veterans' Loan Guarantee*, 13.

26. The VA does not permit access to its records of individual loan guarantees or direct loans and does not provide data disaggregated below the county level. Unfortunately, the county is an often misleading proxy for the distinction between urban and suburban location. This is obviously the case in many smaller urban areas, where the city and all of its suburbs are contained within one county, but it pertains as well, in different degrees, in larger metropolitan areas. Philadelphia County, for example, includes a number of suburbs, as well as the City of Philadelphia, while some of the localities in surrounding counties in Pennsylvania, New Jersey, and Delaware are urban or rural and are not suburban by any reasonable definition. It is important to bear in mind the limitations and potential pitfalls in using counties around major cities as even a rough proxy for suburban location.

27. Edward Humes, *Over Here: How the G.I. Bill Transformed the American Dream* (Orlando: Harcourt, 2006), 73–106.

28. U.S. Bureau of the Census, *U.S. Census of Population: 1960*. Vol. 1, *Characteristics of the Population*, Part 1, *United States Summary* (Washington, D.C.: U.S. Government Printing Office, 1964), 1–106.

29. The distinction between the wholly new suburb and the "invaded village" is nicely made in a sociological study written during the height of the postwar suburban boom: William M. Dobriner, *Class in Suburbia* (Englewood Cliffs, N.J.: Prentice-Hall, 1963).

30. Joel Garreau, *Edge City: Life on the New Frontier* (New York: Doubleday, 1991). For a still more complicated view of the "suburban periphery," intended as a correction to Garreau, see Robert Lang, *Edgeless Cities: Exploring the Elusive Metropolis* (Washington, D.C.: Brookings Institution Press, 2003).

31. Jackson, *Crabgrass Frontier*. We shall long be grateful to Jackson for this delightful, gently subversive characterization of the American suburb.

32. Sam Bass Warner Jr., *Streetcar Suburbs: The Process of Growth in Boston, 1870–1900* (Cambridge, Mass.: Harvard University Press, 1962).

33. Jackson, *Crabgrass Frontier*, 233. The paragraph in the main text draws heavily on Jackson's description of the Levitts and Levittown on pp. 234–38.

34. *Life* (Apr. 19, 1948), 12–13.

35. Ed Moore, Bill Kubota, and Bill Ferehawk, *Lustron: The House America's Been Waiting For*, video recording coproduced by WOSU–TV, Ohio State University, and KDN Videoworks.

36. Michael J. Bennett, *When Dreams Came True: The GI Bill and the Making of Modern America* (Washington, D.C.: Brassey's, 1996), 302.

37. Humes, *Over Here*, 90.

38. *Veterans' Loan Guarantee*, 102.

39. Ibid.

40. Ibid., 76. Even after 1946, more than 40 percent of veterans who used VA-backed mortgage loans purchased homes that were not new, and most of these purchases were probably not in suburbs. Ibid., 62. Among Mettler's survey respondents, 31 percent who had obtained VA-backed mortgage loans had purchased houses in small cities and towns, while 29 percent had used their loans to purchase houses in suburbs. Suzanne Mettler, *Soldiers to Citizens: The G.I. Bill and the Making of the Greatest Generation* (New York: Oxford University Press, 2005), 103.

41. We should also consider here the likelihood that the FHA would have expanded sufficiently to accommodate many and perhaps all of the veterans of World War II who needed government-guaranteed mortgage loans, had there been no Title III in the GI Bill.

42. Jackson, *Crabgrass Frontier*, 191; Owen D. Gutfreund, *Twentieth-century Sprawl: Highways and the Reshaping of the American Landscape* (New York: Oxford University Press, 2004), 58–59.

43. Jackson, *Crabgrass Frontier*, 248–51; Gutfreund, *Twentieth-century Sprawl*; Mark I. Gelfand, *A Nation of Cities: The Federal Government and Urban America* (New York: Oxford University Press, 1975), 222–34.

44. This is the argument, as well, of Warner, *Streetcar Suburbs*, which focuses on an earlier phase of American suburbanization. For good histories of still earlier phases, see Henry C. Binford, *The First Suburbs: Residential Communities on the Boston Periphery, 1815–1860* (Chicago: University of Chicago Press, 1985), and Michael H. Ebner, *Chicago's North Shore: A Suburban History* (Chicago: University of Chicago Press, 1985).

45. One difference worth noting is that a number of VA loans were issued without requiring a down payment, even after termination of the secondary loan provision.

46. June A. Willenz, *Women Veterans: America's Forgotten Heroines* (New York: Continuum, 1983), 195–96.

47. Ibid., 176.

48. David Onkst, "Black World War Veterans and the G.I. Bill in Georgia, Alabama, and Mississippi, 1944–1947" (MA thesis, University of Georgia, 1990), 31. On the *Ebony* survey see Lizabeth Cohen, *A Consumer's Republic: The Politics of Mass Consumption in Postwar America* (New York: Knopf, 2003), 171. See also Kathleen Frydl, "The G.I. Bill" (PhD diss., University of Chicago, 2000), 224, 295; Ira Katznelson, *When Affirmative Action Was White: An Untold History of Racial Inequality in Twentieth-century America* (New York: Norton, 2005), 128, 139–40.

49. Cohen, *Consumer's Republic*, 171.

50. Jackson, *Crabgrass Frontier*, 202. This discussion draws heavily on Jackson's; see 195–203.

51. For an excellent and a poignant study of how this assumption played out in a major American city, see Thomas J. Sugrue, *The Origins of the Urban Crisis: Race and Inequality in Postwar Detroit* (Princeton, N.J.: Princeton University Press, 1996).

52. Gelfand, *Nation of Cities*, 220, 222.

53. Jackson, *Crabgrass Frontier*, 208; David M. P. Freund, "Marketing the Free Market: State Intervention and the Politics of Prosperity in Metropolitan America," in *The New Suburban History*, ed. Kevin M. Kruse and Thomas J. Sugrue, 16 (Chicago: University of Chicago Press, 2006).

54. *Veterans' Loan Guarantee*, 91, 64.

55. Jackson, *Crabgrass Frontier*, 241.

Epilogue

1. U.S. Bureau of the Census, *Historical Statistics of the United States, Colonial Times to 1970* (Washington, D.C.: Government Printing Office, 1975), 1140, 1145; President's Commission on Veterans' Pensions, *Readjustment Benefits: General Survey and Appraisal*, Staff Report no. IX, Part A (Washington, D.C.: U.S. Government Printing Office, 1956), 162. According to this tabulation more than 840,000 of the 4.3 million civilian veterans of Korea returning by mid-decade had also served in World War II.

2. Quoted in President's Commission on Veterans' Pensions, *The Historical Development of Veterans' Benefits in the United States*, Staff Report no. I (Washington, D.C.: U.S. Government Printing Office, 1956), 60.

3. Ibid., 61–62. For a more complete discussion of the enactment and terms of the Korean GI Bill see *Readjustment Benefits*, Part A, 148–59.

4. For details about the 1966 act and for tabulations of educational benefits in relation to changing tuitions and college living costs see *Final Report on Educational*

Assistance to Veterans: A Comparative Study of Three G.I. Bills (Washington, D.C.: U.S. Government Printing Office, 1973).

5. Ibid., 19.

6. Montgomery was also the first congressman to insist the Pledge of Allegiance be made a regular part of the morning business operations of the House of Representatives.

7. Dan Ephron, "A Learning Disability," *Newsweek* (Nov. 26, 2007), 40–41.

8. Mary Beth Marklein, "College-bound GIs Get Extra Help: Big Philanthropists Kick in to Fill Gaps in Financial Aid," *USA Today* (Nov. 19, 2007).

9. Ephron, "Learning Disability," 41.

10. Anna Quindlen, "Because It's Right," *Newsweek* (Mar. 31, 2008).

11. "Bush Signs Emergency War Funding Measure: It Also Expands Veterans' Benefits under the GI Bill and Extends Unemployment Aid," *Los Angeles Times* (July 1, 2008).

Index

Page numbers in *italic* type refer to illustrations.